Charles Ethan Porter

African-American Master of Still Life

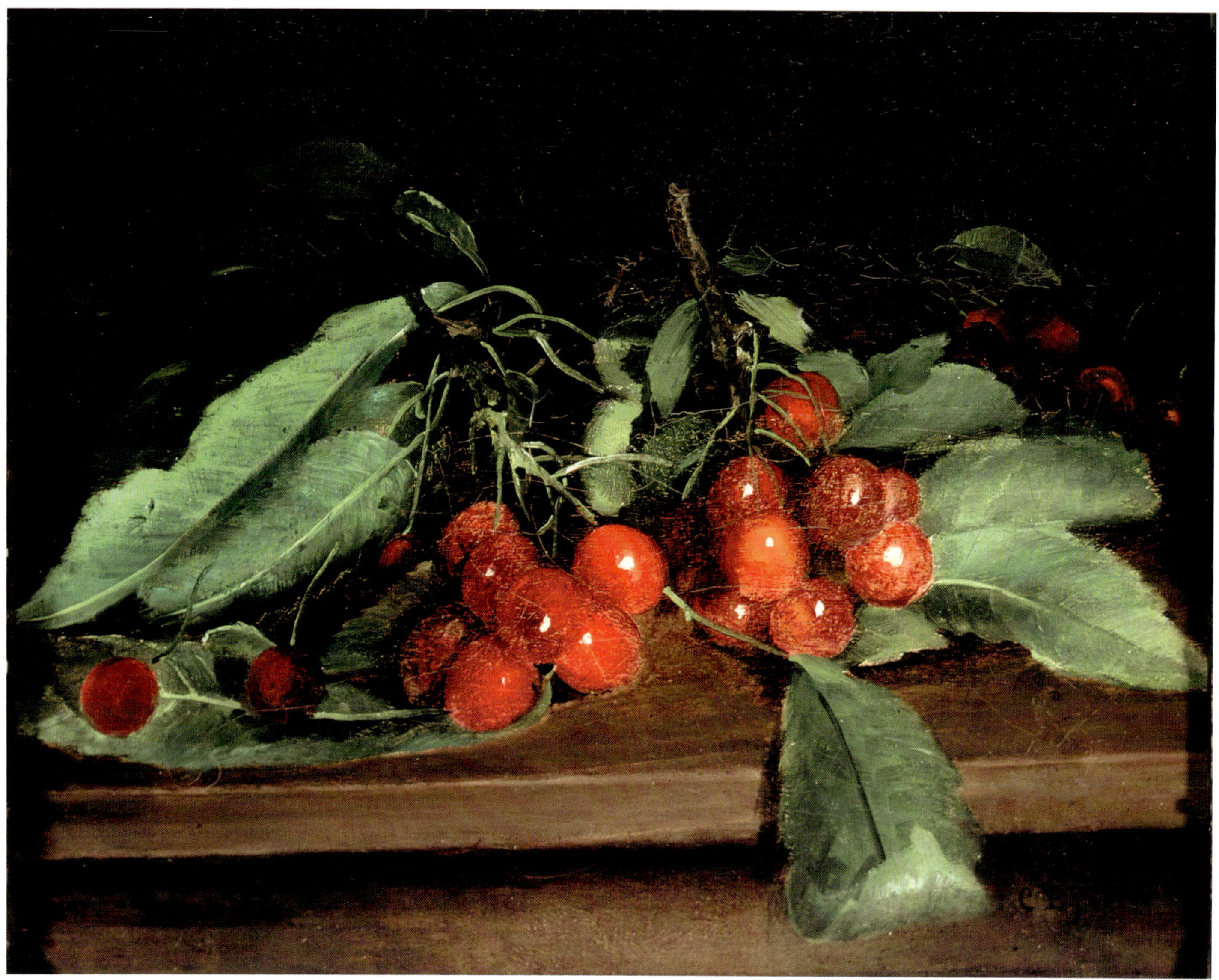

Cherries, c. 1885
Oil on canvas
10½" x 13"
Signed lower right
The Harmon and Harriet Kelley Foundation for the Arts

Charles Ethan Porter

African-American Master of Still Life

New Britain Museum of American Art
NEW BRITAIN, CONNECTICUT

Distributed by University Press of New England
HANOVER AND LONDON

The New Britain Museum of American Art
56 Lexington Street
New Britain, Connecticut 06052-1414
Telephone (860) 229-0257; Fax (860) 229-3445
www.nbmaa.org

Distributed by University Press of New England
One Court Street
Lebanon, New Hampshire 03766
www.upne.com

Library of Congress Control Number: 2007943359
Printed in the United States of America
ISBN-10: 0-9724497-6-0
ISBN-13: 978-0-9724497-6-2

Photography by: James Kopp, New Britain Museum of American Art
Edited by: Pamela Barr, New York
Designed and Printed by: Capital Offset Co., Inc., New Hampshire

Front Cover: *Peonies in a Bowl*, c. 1885 (see pg. 86)
First Frontispiece: *Cherries*, c. 1885
Second Frontispiece: *Roses*, c. 1882
Back Cover: *Still Life with Fruit and Basket*, c. 1888 (see pg. 80)

Contents

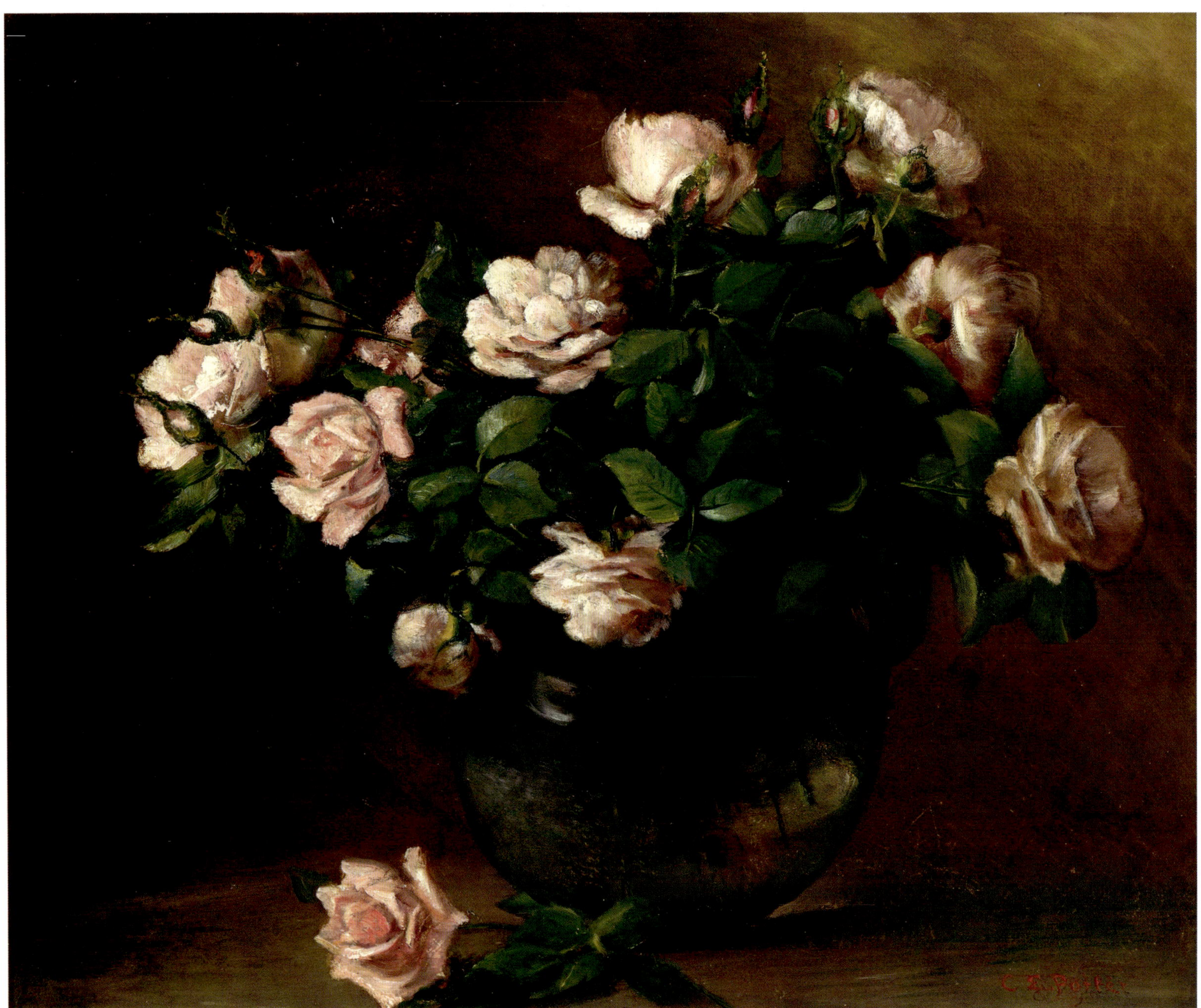

Roses, c. 1882
Oil on canvas
20" x 24"
Signed lower right
Collection of the New Britain Museum of American Art. General Purchase Fund.

INTRODUCTION *by Douglas Hyland, Director*

he first time I had the pleasure of seeing paintings by the eminent African-American artist Charles Ethan Porter was twenty-five years ago when I visited the well-known connoisseurs and collectors of American paintings, Dr. and Mrs. Frederick Baekeland, in their apartment. At that time I inquired about a beautifully romantic late nineteenth-century still-life painting by Charles Ethan Porter. Frederick Baekeland, who spent many years writing about the psychology of collecting as well as documenting little known and underappreciated American painters, told me that he had been searching for years to find out more about Porter, who was born in Hartford and lived most of his life in Connecticut. Dr. Baekeland had persevered, but despite his many efforts, very little had emerged in terms of biography, critical commentary or even the location of paintings. In subsequent years, it has been my pleasure to discover more and more about Porter. The well-known New York art dealer Michael Rosenfeld has specialized in uncovering the locations of works by Porter, acquiring them and subsequently placing them both in museum collections and in the hands of notable private collectors. Thomas Colville and Jeffrey Cooley, two notable art dealers living in Connecticut, have also managed to locate and sell extraordinary examples over the decades.

It has been gratifying to discover that various collectors, most of them African-Americans, have assembled collections of works by nineteenth and twentieth-century American artists such as Robert Scott Duncanson, Joshua Johnson, Henry O. Tanner, and Edward Bannister, among the nineteenth-century artists, and Romare Bearden, Jacob Lawrence and Jean-Michel Basquiat, among twentieth-century artists who have emerged at the forefront of African-American modernism. The Evans collection and the collection of Dr. Harmon and Harriet Kelley are just two significant examples. I worked with the Kelleys on a national tour of their collection in the 1990s, and the positive acclaim with which it was greeted at each museum where it was displayed is symptomatic of the rise and importance not only of these collections, but of the individual artists that have been purchased by the Kelleys.

Hildegard Cummings began her research on Porter over thirty years ago. She has painstakingly ferreted out every obscure document associated with Porter. From his birth in Hartford to his young adulthood in Rockville, his brief stay in New York, his subsequent sojourn in Paris and his lengthy period of activity in Hartford, it is astonishing how little has come to light in terms of primary documents. Mostly, the career and accomplishments of this artist are eloquently represented by the paintings which have been even more prized and eagerly sought after over the years.

In addition to Cummings, who has served with distinction as guest curator of this exhibition, I am thankful to Helen Krieble who founded the Connecticut Gallery, Marlborough. Her aim was to champion the nineteenth and early twentieth-century artists of Connecticut such as Porter who were not as celebrated as his contemporaries such as Winslow Homer, Thomas Eakins, and many other painters whose fame is now well established. Krieble organized the first major retrospective devoted to Charles Ethan Porter in 1987, displayed at the Old State House in downtown Hartford. The catalogue published in conjunction with this exhibition has proven to be the definitive work on Porter until the present.

The late Dorothy Archibald also helped rescue Porter from oblivion when she focused attention on his paintings displayed in a modest exhibition at the Town and County Club in Hartford. Archibald was an eccentric devotee of nineteenth and twentieth-century Connecticut artists.

Thus, except for the collaborative effort of Krieble and Cummings twenty years ago and the limited Town and County Club exhibition, recent scholarship devoted exclusively to Porter has been scant. The present exhibition, which will travel to the Studio Museum in Harlem (April 1st to July 15th, 2008) and to the North Carolina Central University Art Museum, Durham (August 3rd to October 7th, 2008), is the first ever devoted to Porter in an American art museum. I am most pleased that Thelma Golden and Lowery Sims at the Studio Museum and Kenneth Rodgers at the North Carolina Central University Art Museum are taking the exhibition.

Most of all, I am indebted to Hildegard Cummings who has believed in Charles Ethan Porter all these years and has devoted her considerable talents to the establishment of Porter among the first ranks of late nineteenth-century American artists.

On the staff at the Museum I wish to acknowledge the work of Paula Bender, Emily Blogoslawski, Shakeea Brister, Patrick Brown, Jackie Canevari, David D'Agostino, Donna Downes, Melanie Carr-Eveleth, Morgan Fippinger, Bernadine Franco, Judy Gaffney, Paul Grzyb, Zbigniew Grzyb, Marie Koller, James Kopp, Tom Lanson, Adrian Lavoie, Michael Lavoie, Patricia Levandoski, Linda Mare, Melissa Nardiello, Maura O'Shea, Linda Rousseau, Abigail Runyan, Andriy Shuter, Dina Silva, Susan Sterniak, Sue Sullivan, Michael Sundra, Claudia Thesing, Heather Whitehouse, Susan Williams and especially Daniel Fulco, who participated in this project for three years.

To ensure the broadest possible involvement, the Museum has enlisted a distinguished Steering Committee which has met several times and has provided both invaluable advice and support for the Charles Ethan Porter exhibition and all the activities scheduled in conjunction with the show. They include Dr. and Mrs. Frederick Baekeland, Marie Kirkley-Bey,

Danielle Burrell, Olga Callender, Robert Charles Hudson, Meckla Pinnix Clark, Hildegard Cummings, Theresa Hopkins-Staten, Harriet Kelley, Steven King, Jr., Beverly Jenkins, Richard LeGrier, Brenda Lopez, Donna Merritt, Loretta L. Pair, Eather Reynolds, Lew Robinson, Mike Scricco, Wanda Seldon, Rosemarie Tate, Martha Trask, and Eric Turner.

The following lenders have enabled the Museum to exhibit the very best examples of Porter's work: Dr. and Mrs. Frederick Baekeland, Khephra Burns and Susan L. Taylor, Kathryn and Kenneth Chenault, Logan and Penelope Delany, Kathleen del Rossi, Alphonse Fletcher Jr., Edgar B. French, Charlynn and Warren Goins, Mr. and Mrs. Wilbert R. Hasbrouck, Drs. Jeffrey and Sivan Hines, Dr. and Mrs. George Hollenberg, Harmon and Harriet Kelley, David Kimball of the Stagecoach Gallery, Mr. and Mrs. Conrad Kronholm, Mr. and Mrs. S. Lamont McEvitt, Juan Rodriguez, Dr. and Mrs. Stephen M. Rouse, The Schonberger Family, Ernest C. Wignall, Collection of Wilberding, Hobart, and other private collectors. The following museums and galleries have also generously lent outstanding Porters: Peg Alston/Peg Alston Fine Arts; Florence Griswold Museum, Old Lyme, Connecticut; Mattatuck Museum of Art and History, Waterbury, Connecticut; Michael Rosenfeld Gallery, LLC, New York City; San Antonio Museum of Art, Texas; and the Wadsworth Atheneum Museum of Art, Hartford, Connecticut. I applaud their participation.

I appreciate the financial support of the Connecticut Humanities Council; the David T. Langrock Foundation; Delta Sigma Theta Sorority, Inc.; Hartford Alumni Chapter of The Links, Inc. and the National Council of Negro Women, Hartford Section. Additionally, I thank the Greater Hartford Arts Council, the Connecticut Commission on Culture & Tourism, the Community Foundation of Greater New Britain, the American Savings Foundation, and our individual and corporate contributors whose annual donations help us meet our operating expenses.

I would like also to thank Mr. and Mrs. Joseph Krumholtz who have donated an exemplary Porter, *Still Life with Fruit and Basket*, which the Museum has in its permanent collection. With our General Purchase Fund we were able to purchase *Roses* in 2004. Having two major Porters, a still life and a flower painting on display on a regular basis, provides our visitors with an opportunity to enjoy outstanding examples by Porter. I am delighted that the University Press of New England will act as the national distributor for this catalogue.

Finally, this exhibition would not have been possible without a generous grant from the Henry Luce Foundation. As always, Ellen Holtzman has been enormously helpful. The late Henry R. Luce III (1925–2005) was a major force behind countless exhibitions and scholarly catalogues through the Luce Foundation. Additionally, he supported numerous museum expansions, among them the 2006 addition to the New Britain Museum of American Art. It could be argued persuasively that he was the single most effective patron of American art of the late twentieth century and the New Britain Museum would like to recognize his many contributions by dedicating this catalogue to Henry R. Luce III.

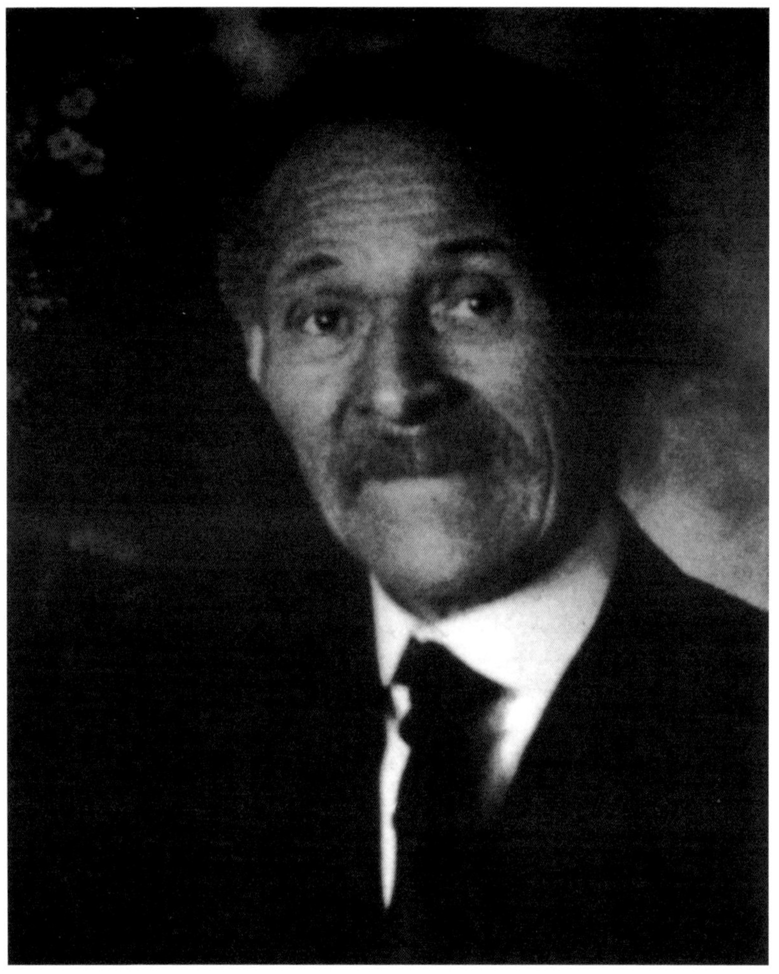

Charles Ethan Porter, c. 1911
Photo courtesy of the Vernon Historical Society

CHARLES ETHAN PORTER *African-American Master of Still Life*

by Hildegard Cummings

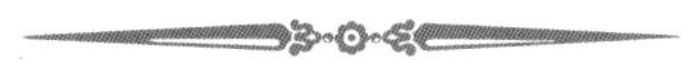

"The colored people—my people"

—Charles Ethan Porter to Samuel Clemens (Mark Twain), Paris, April 4, 1883

The artist Charles Ethan Porter (1847/49–1923) lived, as we all do, in several worlds at once—personal, professional, and public—over which we have limited control. Yet Porter's life was more profoundly constricted than that of most Americans. As one of very few African-American artists between the Civil War and World War I, he was an outcast in the professional and public spheres in which he chose to work. His accomplished still-life and landscape paintings, embracing artistic traditions he had no choice but to accept, were little appreciated in his lifetime and remain largely unknown.

Because of what W. E. B. DuBois termed the "twoness" of being both an American and a Negro, assessing Porter's art involves sensitivity to the prevailing attitudes of his era. His family merits special attention. While dear to Victorian America generally, family was a lifeline for an African American striving to live and work in a world that denigrated him. Porter's family was his succor, his support, and his model for how to face unjust and injurious conditions. His family members are alluded to in the pages that follow because their values and activities are deemed critical to an understanding of the Porter son and brother who became an artist.

Porter did not live long enough to think of himself as African-American, the name coined in the 1980s, which embraces the notion of pan-Africanism expressed in the 1920s by Marcus Garvey (1887–1940). In Porter's day, his race paid little attention to the continent of Africa or to African ancestry. In New England, where he lived, most blacks had a mixed African-Indian-Euro-American heritage, often, like Porter, with American ancestors going back to the Revolutionary era. They stressed their Americanness and wanted to be accepted as citizens. Like most Americans, they regarded Africa, if they thought of it at all, as a mysterious and uncivilized place. Proposals were made from time to time to exile them to Africa or other parts of the world, but very few black Americans saw any foreign nation anywhere, populated by a black race though it might be, as their "proper home" (as some white proponents declared it to be), and most resisted all efforts to evict them from American soil. Even President Lincoln was forced to abandon his plan to resettle America's black population in Central America.

"Negro," a term meaning black, with no overt connection to Africa, was commonly heard in nineteenth-century America, but it appears to have been employed mostly in a somewhat formal vein, as in speeches, books, and newspapers. Informally, as we know, it was corrupted by whites into an ethnic slur. Porter consistently referred to himself and his race as "colored." In his lifetime, both black and white Americans generally referred to Americans of African descent as "colored." Thus the telling of Porter's story will often follow that historic practice, even though today we regard Porter as African-American.

Porter grew up in a poor working-class family, yet he managed to obtain academic art training and have a long career, despite poverty, prejudice, and pronouncements that his race was incapable of making art. His story differs from that of more successful nineteenth-century African-American artists such as Henry Ossawa Tanner (1859–1937), who was the first member of his race to be elected to America's National Academy of Design. Tanner's father was a college-educated teacher and minister. Tanner's mentor and friend at the Pennsylvania Academy of the Fine Arts was Thomas Eakins, and Tanner had white patrons who helped finance his trip to France, where his religious paintings were awarded honors in the government-sponsored Salon exhibitions of the 1890s. Tanner settled in France because he believed that racial prejudice in America would overwhelm him.

Edmonia Lewis (1844–c. 1911), the first internationally known African-American sculptor, moved to Italy in 1867 to escape the terrible prejudice to which she had been subjected, including a charge of attempted murder and a vicious beating by vigilantes while she was a student at Oberlin College. Lewis, the daughter of a black father and a Chippewa Indian mother, carved white marble into Neoclassical images of abolitionist heroes and biblical figures, as well as subjects that addressed the alienation of blacks and Indians in American society. She insisted on being photographed with her pieces so that people would know she was the sculptor. She claimed that her real and most fitting name was "Wild Fire" and that her childhood had been a "wandering life, fishing, swimming and making moccasins."[1] The mystique she created for herself made her studio in Rome a tourist attraction.

Edward Mitchell Bannister (1826–1901), a mostly self-taught painter of quiet, spiritual landscapes, won first prize at the Centennial Exposition of 1876—to the surprise and dismay of authorities there—which made him the first black artist to win recognition in America. Raised in New Brunswick, Canada, with mentors who introduced him to art, music, and literature, he was an abolitionist and a barber in Boston when he married a woman who owned beauty parlors patronized by the city's black and white elite. Her business success enabled him to pursue a career in art. After moving to Providence, Rhode Island, in 1870, Bannister became known for his poetic French Barbizon style of landscape painting. He attracted wealthy white patrons, helped organize the Providence Art Club, and assisted in the development of the Rhode Island School of Design.

The white art establishment ignored Porter, but some colored people knew who he was and thought he should have been included, along with Tanner, Lewis, and Bannister, in the World's Columbian Exposition in

Chicago in 1893. I. Garland Penn named the four in *The Reason Why the Colored American Is Not in the World's Columbian Exposition*, a pamphlet with a foreword by Frederick Douglass, published in an edition of twenty thousand and distributed at the entrance to the fair by Ida Wells Burnett, an African-American publisher, journalist, and crusader who battled racial injustice.

While Porter's paintings demonstrate that he could indeed create fine art, there is much about the artist and his career that has yet to be learned. He lived when America kept people of color behind a veil, as DuBois said, rendering them invisible or meanly stereotyping them. The veil over Porter is thick, especially during the years he spent in New York City and in France. No personal papers—except a few letters that reveal little—have been discovered. A researcher must rely on secondary sources and will at times resort to guesswork, hoping that words such as "perhaps" and "possibly" will make it clear that speculation is involved.

In Porter's case, even accepted facts can complicate issues. His birth date, for instance, will probably never be known. In Paris in 1881 Porter filed a form that listed his birth year as 1847. Some months later he received surprising news from his mother, who had applied for a Civil War Dependent Parents pension because her soldier son Joseph, killed in 1864, had contributed significantly to the family income. A sticking point in her petition was documentation of Joseph's birth date, often a problem before birth certificates were required. The U.S. government finally accepted the affidavit of a Hartford doctor, who testified that, according

to a memorandum in his books, he attended Mary Porter at the birth of a male child, presumed to be the soldier, on April 19, 1848.

If, however, Joseph was born in 1848, rather than 1846 as previously believed, then Charles, who was a year younger, must have been born in 1849. Mary Porter signed affidavits attesting to that fact, but the family must have remained uncertain. Porter's gravestone reads 1849, while his death certificate and obituary say that he died at age seventy-six, which points to 1847. To add to the confusion, Charles and Joseph are listed in one of the pension affidavits as having the same April 19 birthday, a coincidence certainly possible but uncommon. Can this information be trusted when other sworn statements in the affidavits are conflicting or problematic?

Nevertheless, because of the quality and character of his art, every effort to pierce holes in the thick veil over Porter is worthwhile, whether it relates to a birth date or something more significant. Fragmentary though it is, his story contributes to the larger African-American story that is still in the making. It involves, among other things, family values, the American dream, the effects of suppression and prejudice, and the power of hope.

Porter's history also offers a glimpse into an aspect of America's nineteenth-century art world that has yet to be fully explored: the experience and significance of talented professionals who for one reason or another were excluded from the art establishment and thereby from critical and financial success. Was some part of Porter's ultimately disappointing career of his own making, because he painted fruit and flowers when the American art world's regard for still life was particularly low, when even housewives were painting roses and pansies on dinner plates and folding screens? Was Porter restricted to the so-called lesser art of still life by a dominant society that regarded him as uppity when he painted landscapes?

Despite successes that were spotty at best, Porter was able to support himself for some thirty years by painting and teaching. In later years, a dismaying deterioration appeared in his art for reasons yet unknown. Until that time, however, especially from the late 1870s to the mid-1890s, he created oil paintings, watercolors, and drawings that have earned him a place in the annals of American art.

Youth, 1847/49–65

"Charly received great credit for his drawing lessons and is called the best drawer in Tolland County."[2] These words written by his mother, Mary, in July 1864 may be the earliest intimation that Porter—a black man from the village of Rockville, Connecticut, about a dozen miles east of Hartford—might become an artist.

Mary was writing to her son Joseph, who was at Petersburg, Virginia, serving as a private in the Twenty-ninth Connecticut Regiment (Colored). Joseph had not been in the army long, as the governor of Connecticut had not called for volunteers for this regiment until nearly a year after the Emancipation Proclamation had authorized men of color to serve in the armed forces of the United States. The "Negro soldier bill" was a thorny issue in Connecticut. Newspapers reported in detail how fiercely Democrats in the state legislature opposed this latest evidence of Lincoln's "Black Republicanism." The Senate finally passed the bill, as had the House, strictly along party lines, but not before irate legislators decried it as "vile" and "the most disgraceful bill ever presented here."[3] "The Negro," declared one senator, horrified at the thought of arming black men, "is both ferocious and cowardly" and "will spread lust and rapine."[4]

Near a recruitment ad for the regiment in the *Hartford Daily Courant* for December 2, 1863, was another, urging attendance at the Pearl Street African Methodist Episcopal Church that evening "to consider the indispensable necessity of every colored man's volunteering."[5] A week later in Rockville, Joseph, Charles's older brother by one year, barely or possibly not yet the minimum age of eighteen, left home to enlist.

Joseph knew that his action would impose new burdens on his parents, since his wages at a Rockville textile mill were critical to the family's welfare. His father could not work at times because of illness and injury. His mother hired out to do laundry and housecleaning, and there were several small children at home. The three hundred dollar enlistment bounty must have been a tempting incentive, for the Porters were struggling. Rockville's Methodist Episcopal church had taken up a collection for them the previous April.[6] Joseph's decision, however, may have had little to do with money. Most northern blacks sensed that the Civil War had been about slavery all along and believed, along with Frederick Douglass, that their lives would improve if they helped the Union win. Once a black man is in the U.S. military, Douglass said in 1863, "there is no power on earth or under the earth which can deny that he has earned the right of citizenship in the United States."[7]

Joseph's letters to his mother exhibit both homesickness and courage. Once he enclosed a poem he had composed, which include these words: "Justice truth and rite must triumph/though it Cost my life and friends. . . . Bold will I face the raving cannon."[8] Near Kell House, Virginia, on October 27, 1864, a musket ball crashed into his head and ended his life in a skirmish that routed the enemy at the cost of heavy casualties to his regiment. His heartbroken mother found comfort only in knowing that he had become a Christian before leaving home. He was buried in Rockville in December, a few days before the colored soldiers of Connecticut's Twenty-ninth were welcomed back to Hartford with a citywide celebration.

Mary and her husband worried about yet another soldier son. William, his father's namesake, was twenty-two, newly married, and living in Guilford, when on August 1, 1863, impatient with Connecticut's delay in creating a black regiment, he joined the Fourteenth Rhode Island Heavy Artillery (Colored).[9] By January 1864 he was on garrison duty at Fort Esperanza on Matagorda Island, Texas. From May 1864, first at Fort Parapet above New Orleans and later at Fort Jackson below the city, William's battalion had the arduous job of rebuilding damaged fortifications and preventing contraband from reaching Confederate lines. The U.S. government's early policy of using black soldiers almost exclusively for menial labor was not only unjust but made no sense after Negro regiments had demonstrated their mettle in battle. The practice often continued, however, even after a War Department directive of June 1864 banned it, since assigning colored soldiers to excessive fatigue duty usually stemmed from the racism of the white officers in charge.

William always assured his family that he was fine, but it was not true. In March 1864 his entire company had been placed under arrest for refusing to accept less pay than white soldiers. This discrepancy lowered morale and promoted unrest in all the Negro regiments and imposed hardship on the soldiers' wives and children, who were less likely than whites to get financial help. The lower rate of pay was regarded as an insult as great as the mandate that only white men could be the commissioned officers of colored regiments. Congress finally passed legislation granting equal (and retroactive) pay to Negro soldiers on June 15, 1864. Most had not been compensated for months.

That summer William became seriously ill but did not tell his parents. He had been healthy, his commanding officer later wrote, "until he was taken down with the malarious fever, which was so prevalent at the Post last summer, since which time he has never gained his strength, and seems to be still failing."[10] Sergeant William H. Porter received a disability discharge on January 25, 1865. He had been near death for several months, could not work for two years after his discharge, and suffered debilitating intestinal ailments for the rest of his life.

If grief for two military sons were not enough, there was more for the Porter family to cope with in the 1860s. "Tell Charles," Joseph wrote

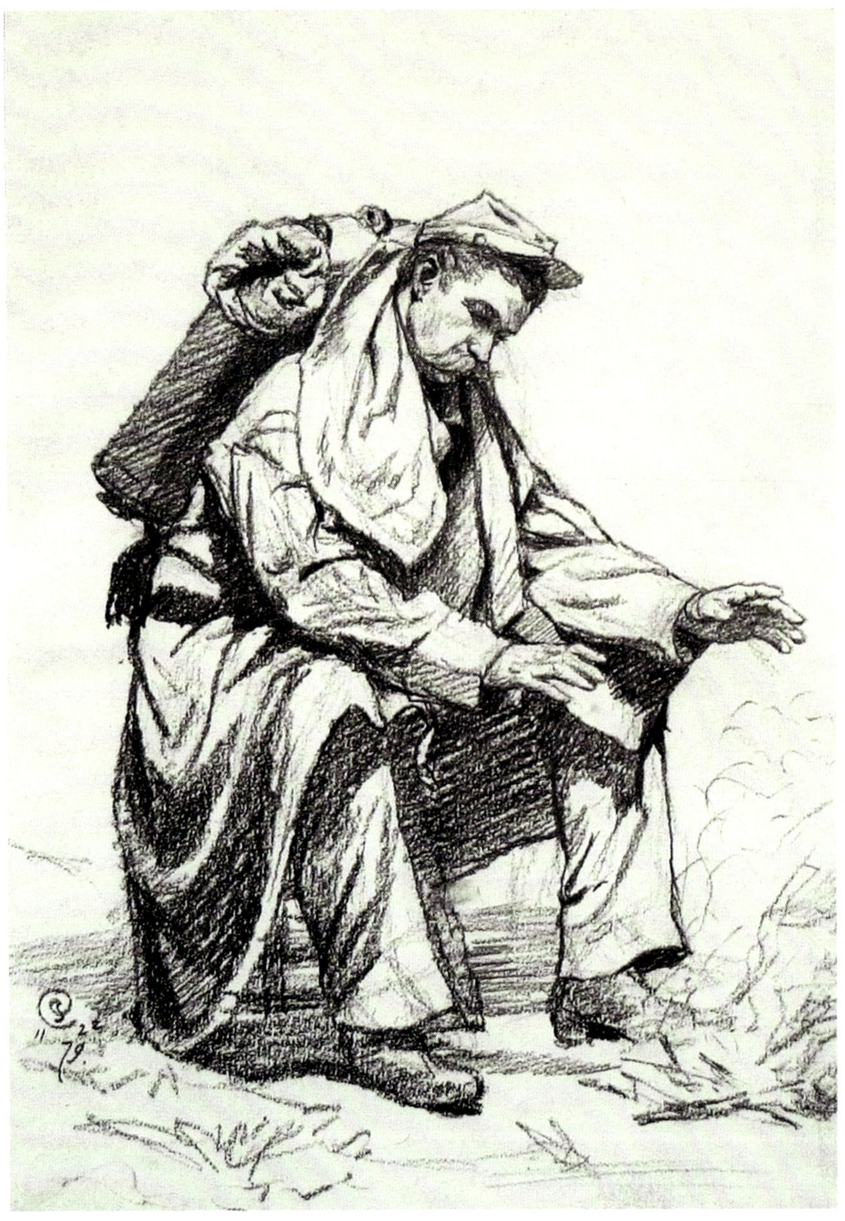

Catalogue 14
Civil War Soldier, 1872
Pencil on paper
8¼" x 6" (sight)
Monogrammed and dated lower left
Collection of Charlynn and
Warren Goins

from Virginia in September 1864, "I have seen the dead body[s] of soldiers laying above the ground in great number."[11] Joseph must have known that his artistic brother would be interested in such an image. Both young men had already witnessed death of a different kind. Beloved brothers and sisters had fallen ill and died, one by one, in rapid succession: Edwin in 1858 at age twenty-three; Ada in 1860 at only ten months. Three deaths had occurred in 1862: George, ten, in April; Dwight, five, in July; and Ida, nine months, in October. And still to come in 1867 and 1868: Frederick, three; and Arthur, thirteen.

Virtually every American family suffered losses during the Civil War, which ravaged an entire generation of young men, while diseases that are treatable today killed many little brothers and sisters at home. One wonders how his personal bereavements affected Porter, a sensitive adolescent who was yearning to be an artist.

It is not known why William and Mary Porter left Hartford, where they were living when Charles was born and where there was a small black community. One consequence of their move across the Connecticut River to East Hartford by 1850 and a few years later to nearby Rockville, where they were the only black family, is that their children received a public school education that, for Charles, included high school. Hartford schools were segregated until 1868, and Hartford's high school, like others in New England cities, charged tuition and had entrance examinations that usually required knowledge of Latin and Greek.

In the public high school of the Vernon Center School District, which included Rockville, Porter undertook a course of study that emphasized English composition and elocution and included algebra, geometry, "Mental and Natural Philosophy," and possibly chemistry and logic. A glowing evaluation of this "upper school" by its School Committee was recorded in the *Hartford Daily Courant* in April 1862, at the end of a winter term, when students exhibited their learning in a public "exhibition": "For accuracy of scholarship, promptness in recitation, it equaled, if not excelled any examination we ever attended."[12] Charles enjoyed school and said that his talent for picture making made him popular there.[13]

He was the Porters' sixth child and their first to attend high school, graduating in 1865. At the time, two younger siblings, James and Arthur, were working in a local textile mill, at ages thirteen and ten. Poor families often tried to give at least one son some higher education so that he might attain a better life and ultimately benefit them all.

The religious education of the Porter children was also affected by the family's move to a place where they were the only persons of color. In Hartford, where blacks and mulattos totaled about 5 percent of the population in 1850, two churches served them: Pearl Street's African Methodist Episcopal Zion Society and the Talcott Street Congregational Church. The Porters probably had worshiped at the former, because they joined the Methodist Episcopal Church in Rockville. Their children attended religion classes there that led Joseph to become an evangelical Christian before he went to war.

Mary wanted that same spiritual awakening for all her children and wrote Joseph in May 1864 that Charles was doing well in school but "the best of all is that he commenced seeking the Saviour about 2 weeks ago . . . [He] does not think that he has yet obtained real evidence of his acceptance with God but says that he does not mean to give up but intends to seek until he knows his sins are forgiven and that he is truly connected to God." She implored Joseph to pray until "all our family are brought into the fold of the precious redeemer. O what a joyful transporting thought."[14] Porter's parents were devoted Methodists all their lives, and Charles himself maintained membership in Methodist churches for most of his. Family members also became active in the African Methodist Episcopal Church in Meriden.

While the education of his children was undoubtedly important to William Henry Porter Sr., who, unlike his wife, appears not to have been literate, he must have chosen to settle in the small white community of Rockville because he thought he could make a living there that best met the needs of his large family. Born a free man in rural Belchertown, Massachusetts, near Amherst, he had likely done outdoor work since childhood. The various jobs he is known to have had in Rockville ranged from day laborer, farm laborer, and teamster to butcher and, briefly, night watchman for a railroad.

Although light-skinned, William and Mary Porter and their children always presented themselves as colored. William Porter's ancestry is unknown, but since census takers sometimes saw him as white and sometimes black, he must have been of mixed heritage. Growing up in Belchertown, with few colored residents around, he must have come to terms with what it meant to be an anomaly in a community. At some point he moved south to Vernon, where he married Mary Dolphin of Ellington, Connecticut, in 1838 and stayed at least until his two eldest children were born before moving to Hartford.

Mary had black, white, and Indian heritage, the latter probably through her mother's line and certainly by way of her father, Ethan, and his father, Edward (Ned) Dolphin, of Hartford. In the 1840s an elderly Indian by the name of Ned Dolphin often fished for pickerel in Rockville, using live bait that he skittered across the water from a boat in the Indian manner. He was said to be able to sound a "warhoop" that made the woods ring. He may have been Mary's paternal grandfather. Her maternal grandfather, Jabez Pottage, a native of Windham, Connecticut, had fought in the Revolutionary War. He lived next door to her family in Ellington.

In March 1857 William Porter bought a small tract of land in Rockville near the crest of Fox Hill, an elevation that offers a bird's-eye view of the town and, on a clear day, of much of the Connecticut River Valley. Its terrain and its proximity to textile mills made it an undesirable home site, but Porter intended to build on it anyway. He paid thirty-five dollars toward the seventy-five dollar price in March 1857, another seventeen dollars in July 1858, and eighteen dollars in October 1858. Then, probably because of the family's troubles in the 1860s, the final five-dollar payment to secure the title was not made until July 1871.[15] Years later, Judge Dwight Loomis,

a U.S. Congressman from Rockville, would state in an affidavit that he was "particularly well acquainted" with the Porters from 1860 to 1870 and that they were then "extremely poor and destitute of the comforts of life."[16] Later, in the 1880s, Loomis bought some of Charles' paintings. He may have recognized Porter's talent much earlier and perhaps even given financial assistance, but there is no evidence of such patronage.

Two weddings in the 1860s, however, must have lightened the lives of the Porters. The two eldest daughters married energetic, ambitious men who expanded the close-knit family circle beyond Rockville and drew its members into the activities and concerns of the black middle class. Mary Porter, named for her mother, married Henry Vanness in 1865, a Massachusetts native who had come to Rockville the year before as a railroad freight handler and worked his way up to conductor, a position then held, it was believed, by no other black in the nation. Vanness was honored by his associates and his community for the exemplary manner in which he performed his duties for forty-three years. He knew his passengers, it was said, as well as Mark Twain knew his river men and pilots. Stories about Conductor Vanness, sometimes with a photograph, appeared in Hartford newspapers. He was active in organizations devoted to issues affecting his race. He and Mary became her parents' next-door neighbors on Fox Hill.

In 1860 Cynthia Jane Porter, a year older than Mary, had married Richard Alonzo Jeffrey of Meriden, a town southwest of Hartford. The Porters and the Jeffreys began at once to criss-cross the thirty-five miles or so between Rockville and Meriden. Alonzo, as he was known, was a man of black, white, and Indian heritage, whose forebears were early leaders in the struggle for equal rights in Connecticut. In 1828 the Middletown A.M.E. Zion Church had been formed in his father's home. The Jeffreys were related to the Bemans, a Connecticut family equally tireless in the fight for abolition, suffrage, and temperance. Cesar Beman of Colchester had been a slave who gained freedom by joining the colonial forces in the Revolutionary War. His grandson, the Reverend Amos G. Beman, minister of the Temple Street Church in New Haven, had conducted Hartford's first black school in the 1830s, been a delegate to a statewide Anti-Slavery Society Convention in New Haven in 1838, and a conductor on the Underground Railroad. He was Alonzo Jeffrey's uncle.

Both Alonzo and his brother George owned barbershops, invaluable conduits for disseminating information to colored communities before and after the Civil War. The Jeffrey brothers carried on the fight for civil rights and temperance and were especially active, along with members of the Porter family, in the 1870s and 1880s.

Well before the onset of the Civil War, the Porter, Vanness, Beman, and Jeffrey families—and thousands of other black families like them—were determined to be accepted as citizens of the United States, with the attendant rights and privileges that offer Americans the opportunity to make good lives for themselves and their children. With the Union victory in 1865, hope soared that the long hard struggle for equal opportunity might finally be coming to an end. That spirit of optimism must have inspired young Charles to believe that he could become a professional artist. He would shortly take the first step on that journey—precarious for all aspiring artists but much more so for him.

Training, 1868–74

In 1868 Porter packed some belongings and left Rockville to study painting in Wilbraham, Massachusetts, a town outside Springfield. The school he chose, about twenty miles north of Rockville, was at the time too far away for him to live at home, but otherwise he probably found it a comfortable fit. Commonly called the Academy at Wilbraham, its proper name was Wesleyan Academy, signaling its affiliation with the Methodist Church. (Established in 1804, it is today the Wilbraham and Monson Academy.) A member or members of Rockville's Methodist Church may have recommended the school to Porter or even helped him attend. He could have chosen to study privately with an artist, but there were none in Rockville and only a handful in Hartford and Springfield.

At Wesleyan Academy, Porter may have met others of his race. The academy had enrolled people of color since before the Civil War, and the Alumni Memorial Chapel had been a stop on the Underground Railroad. Although most students came from the northeastern United States, some were from Cuba, China, and Thailand. If the relative diversity of the student body was new to Porter, the academy's strict rules were not, for he had grown up with them. No liquor, tobacco, card-playing, or profanity headed a long list of restrictions, which included even no buying and

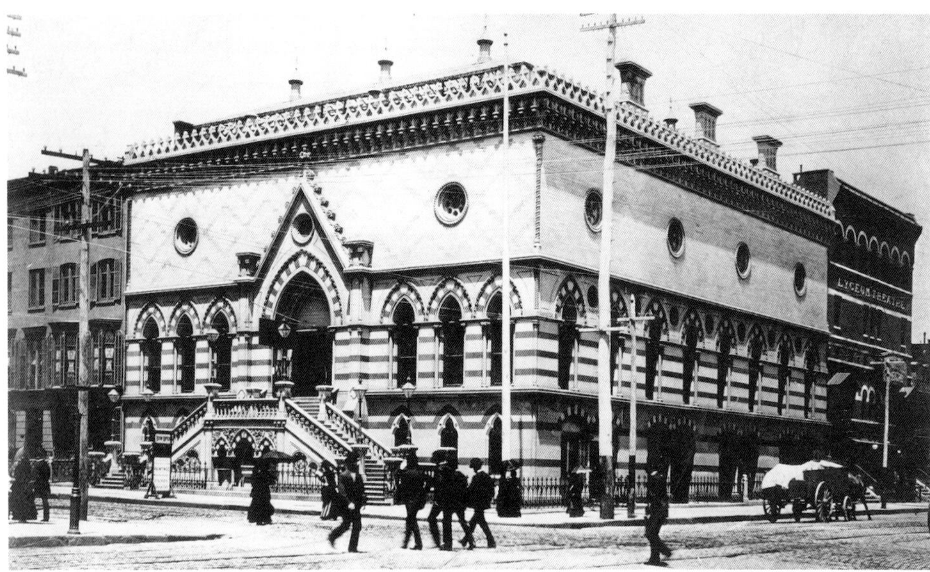

Figure 01–**National Academy of Design Building, between 23ʳᵈ and 4ᵗʰ.**
Photo courtesy of the National Academy of Design, NYC.

using of confectionary and pastry.[17] Wesleyan Academy was a boarding school designed to be preparatory for college, but most students, like Porter, were classified as general and thus could take courses part time or one term at a time, whenever they could manage it. Students on the general roster usually lived in the town rather than in the dormitories.

Porter is listed in the school catalogue for the academic years 1868–69 and 1869–70,[18] but he was there earlier, at least for the spring term of 1868, because the *Tolland County Journal* for July 25, 1868, announced his return from "the academy at Wilbraham, where he has been diligently pursuing the study of painting."[19] "Specimens" of his work, the article noted, were at Mr. Shelton's bookstore in Rockville: "He has certainly the makings of an artist in him. We think it becomes our citizens to encourage him all they can."

Oil painting was one of several offerings in Wesleyan's Fine Arts Department, costing, like "Water Colors, from nature," ten dollars per term and meeting for two hours daily.[20] Courses in pastel, crayon, ink

drawing, drawing from the object, and drawing from copies ranged from six to eight dollars. The art teachers were Ada E. Philbrook in 1868–69 and Rosa P. Merrill in 1869–70. It is not known if Porter took courses other than painting. Despite his listing in the Wesleyan Academy roster for 1869–70, Porter returned for the fall term, which began in late August, only briefly or not at all, for a few weeks later he was admitted to a prestigious school where hundreds of the nation's would-be artists wanted to study and where many of the leading American artists had.

The Venetian palazzo that stood on the corner of Twenty-third Street and Fourth Avenue (now Park Avenue South) in New York City was probably unlike any building Porter had seen (figure 01). Completed four years earlier, it was the home of the National Academy of Design, an institution established in 1825 that conferred membership on outstanding professional artists. Its art school was for students of exceptional ability, who had to submit examples of their work to a panel of senior Academicians. Applicants needed, among other things, to prove that they could draw convincingly "from the round," as in "a fair shaded crayon drawing from a cast of a hand, foot, head or other part of a statue of the human figure."[21] Porter must have submitted such a drawing in September 1869 in order to be admitted to the Academy, as he was, for the term that began in October. He may have been the first of his race to study at this school; the notation "color'd" follows his name on the register.[22] He studied there through spring 1873.

Porter's greatest hurdle must have been money. The Academy school was free, but living expenses had to be met. In the 1860s his parents were in no position to help, though his brother-in-law Alonzo Jeffrey, the barbershop owner, may have been. There is no evidence that any of Rockville's mill owners, businessmen, or influential citizens such as Dwight Loomis contributed to the cost of Porter's art education. In neighboring South Manchester, the Cheney family owned a silk mill and other entrepreneurial enterprises, which it governed with a beneficent paternalism. The Cheneys supported the arts, and several family members were artists, most notably Seth Wells Cheney (1810–1856), an Associate of the National Academy. (Election to membership was first to Associate Academician, then later, for a select few, to Academician.) But if the family aided Porter financially in the late 1860s, it has been forgotten.

The artist Henry Bryant (1812–1881) befriended Porter at some point. Primarily a portraitist, Bryant was an East Hartford native who lived in New York in the 1840s and was an Associate of the Academy. About 1850 Bryant returned to East Hartford for good. The two could have met when young Porter was being called the best drawer in Tolland County, for news of all kinds spread rapidly in the small towns east of the Connecticut River. Bryant might have urged Porter to aspire to the National Academy and offered advice about living in New York, but it is doubtful he could have provided financial aid. In 1869 he was busy developing the Celestial Indicator, a two-in-one device that is essentially a planetarium inside an armillary sphere, which can display the principal celestial circles, including the orbital motion of the planets. Bryant received a patent for his invention in 1872.

Porter himself reportedly said that he supported himself by giving art lessons while he was at school in New York.[23] The Academy school operated weekdays from eight in the morning until nine-thirty at night and Saturdays until two, so there was little time for anything else. Porter's determination was such, however, that he may have found a way to fit teaching into his schedule.

Porter's course of study at the National Academy is fairly well documented. In the centuries–old tradition of art academies of the Western world, students began at the Antique School, which required detailed drawings of casts of antique Greek and Roman sculptures. All students were required to work at the Antique School for at least the first ten weeks of each academic year. In 1871–72 and again in 1872–73 Porter also gained entry into the Life School, where he drew from the live model and attended lectures on anatomy and perspective. In 1872–73 his good standing at the Life School got him into the Painting Class, a new offering and the ultimate level, where students worked from still-life objects and from the live model. Admission to the various levels was based solely on merit, and many students did not progress far. While the Antique School could have as many as two hundred pupils, the Life School had far fewer (seventy-one in 1873) and the Painting Class fewer still (twenty-five in 1873).[24] Thus the record reveals that Porter's studies at the National Academy went well.

He had, moreover, matriculated when the Academy was revising and expanding its education programs. In January 1870 Lemuel Wilmarth

(1835–1918) was hired as the first full-time instructor, responsible for teaching both the Antique and Life Schools. Like its European counterparts, the Academy had not previously had a faculty but expected Academicians to visit classes from time to time to evaluate students' progress and offer guidance. Now, however, students could expect to develop an ongoing relationship with a master artist. Wilmarth had been the first American to study in Paris with Jean-Leon Gérôme (1824–1904) and, like the Frenchman, is known for a meticulously detailed, highly finished academic style. He often painted still lifes, which became Porter's specialty.

Beginning in 1871 Porter's art was exhibited occasionally. A work called *Autumn Leaves* was shown in a special summer exhibition at the National Academy.[25] The following May, an exhibit by Academy students of about 150 drawings from antique casts merited a brief mention in the *New York Times*. Porter was one of eight students whose drawings were said to be among the best.[26]

Porter submitted three works to the Tolland County Agricultural Fair in his hometown in November. While the group won a premium totaling one dollar, a single drawing by an amateur was awarded fifty cents. When the *Tolland County Journal* announced the awards, an editorial was at the bottom of the same page. "Improvement of natural gifts is commendable in any one," the untitled essay begins. "In this fast age, it is pleasing to see a young person striving against adverse circumstances to rise about the average." Porter is not named, but there is no doubt that the piece is about him and that readers of the newspaper would have known it:

In our town there is a young man who came among us years ago, attended the public schools, and there displayed more than ordinary talent in drawing. He seemed to feel that there was much beyond him to be reached, and struggled upward with but little encouragement from home or outside friends. After some years he was heard of in New York City, at the Academy of Design, paying his own way by teaching, and showing most commendable industry in perfecting what has proved to be remarkable skill in drawing and painting.

The piece goes on to describe Porter's three entries in the fair, probably studies done at the Academy:

First was a full-length female figure, on a dark background, so finely executed that it was mistaken at first for a marble statue. The second was a head, life size, of the mythical hero Paris, son of Prium [*sic*], standing out from its dark surroundings with startling clearness. The third was a collection of autumn leaves in watercolors, deserving much praise.

The editorial ends with a rebuke to the art jurors:

Among the various reports from different committees in the last *Journal*, no mention is made or notice taken of these pictures, while it would seem as if they should have occupied a most conspicuous place among the "Arts & Fine Arts." Aside from premiums offered by this society, our townsman needs the encouragement of more than a passing notice, while in this way a true appreciation is shown of talent, which is real genius.[27]

Before ending his studies at the National Academy in June 1873, Porter exhibited *Fruit* at the sixth annual exhibition of the American Society of Painters in Water Color, held at the Academy in late winter.[28] The society's exhibitions were always large (354 American and 223 English watercolors in 1873), so it is not surprising that published reviews took no notice of Porter's entry. The catalogue for the exhibition, however, provides the first firm address for Porter in New York: "YMCA, 23rd St. & 4th Ave." (The address in the Academy's second summer catalogue of 1871 was the YMCA Mail Desk, which may or may not indicate residency.) The location of this Young Men's Christian Association, just across the street from the National Academy of Design, could not have been better. Until the twentieth century, most city residents tried to live within walking distance of their places of business. Colored persons, however, could seldom live where they liked.

In March 1869, a few months before Porter began his art studies in the city, a long article in the *New York Times* chronicled the condition of New York's colored population, which it estimated at about twelve thousand. This number is the same as the 1860 census figure, but at least three thousand more blacks had streamed into the city from the South in the early years of the Civil War. Black families had fled the city in droves, however, during the Draft Riots of 1863—when for five days armed working-class mobs, angry at the thought of going to war to benefit a

race they saw as inferior and seeking their jobs, terrorized and brutally attacked colored people, including children in an orphanage. Memories of these terrible riots were still strong in 1869, yet even white people who had been appalled by them were not ready to mingle with or accept the city's colored population.

The *Times* article listed the few neighborhoods, all of them undesirable, in which colored people could live. Porter might have sought a YMCA for advice about housing in 1869, as the Y's mission was to help young men with housing, employment, and social and spiritual needs, but how much help the organization could have given someone who was subject to racism is problematic. The Y was itself segregating blacks at the time. "Colored YMCAs" had come into being after the Civil War. The first one in New York had been organized independently in 1866 on Wooster Street, in a neighborhood where a black population of about 4,500 lived in squalid tenements amid crime-ridden saloons and houses of prostitution. Touted as the only free reading room and place of social resort of a healthful moral character for colored young men in the city, it was by 1870 an auxiliary of the New York YMCA, had grown to more than one hundred members, and was in larger quarters above the Freedman's Bank on Bleecker Street near Macdougal. It closed, however, in 1872, apparently for lack of financial support. Situated in one of the most troubled neighborhoods in the city and with no residential facilities, it was never a place likely to comfort an educated young man from a Connecticut village.

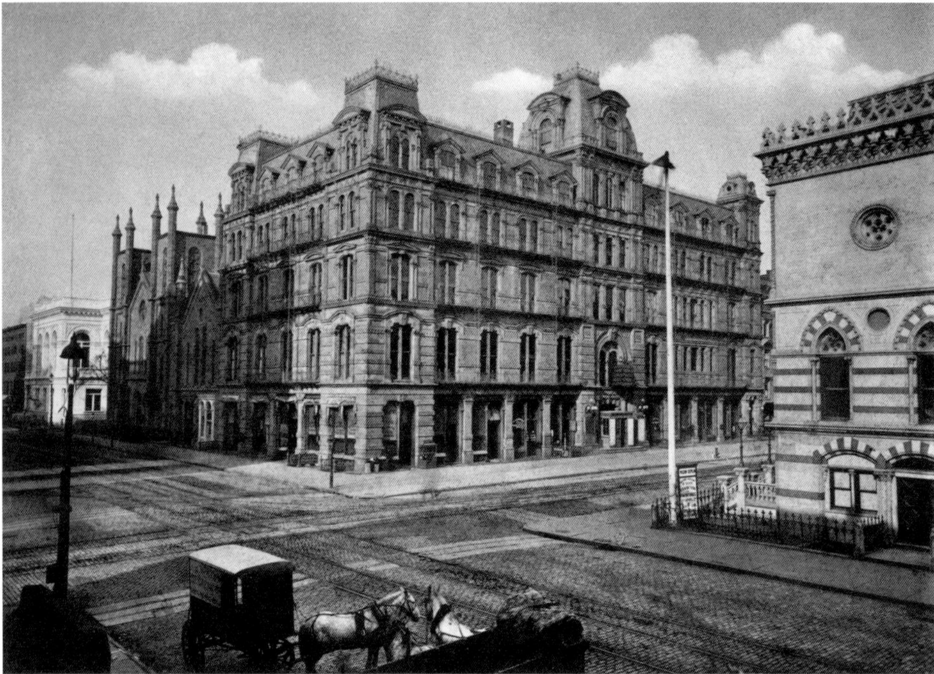

Figure 02–**YMCA "Association Building," between 23rd and 4th.**
Photo courtesy of the Kautz Family YMCA Archives at the University of Minnesota Libraries Archives.

One can only guess at Porter's experiences in New York. "I met, in every direction," reads the *New York Times* exposé, "the most startling evidences of the powerful effects of prejudice. Of all the difficulties with which they have to contend, that of prejudice against them for their color's sake throws all others into the shade, and would seem under present circumstances to be almost insuperable."[29]

The *Times* article lists many examples of racism. No colored man, no matter how talented, is ever employed as an artisan or apprentice. A colored applicant for the most menial job is hired only when no white person is available and then is paid less, expected to work harder, and endure jeers without a murmur. Landlords refuse to rent to colored people or charge huge sums for rooms in crowded, rundown tenements. Respectable hotels and restaurants almost invariably refuse service and generally overcharge when they do not. Theaters either deny entry or relegate blacks to the rows under the eaves, and proprietors of ice-cream, oyster, and dining saloons, and owners of liquor stores, even of a second or third rate class, refuse to furnish them with refreshments. The *Times* reporter was disgusted that a group of Christian ministers barred fellow colored ministers from attending a religious convention.

In 1873 Porter was undoubtedly the only colored resident at the Twenty-third Street YMCA, the first Y to have residential space. The five-story structure, completed in late 1869, was the concept of the association's Irish secretary Robert Ross McBurney and would become the model for YMCAs throughout urban America (figure 02). Designed in the French Renaissance style by James Renwick Jr., the architect of Grace Episcopal Church and Saint Patrick's Cathedral, the building featured rooms radiating from a large central lobby, so that members' comings and goings could be observed. Carved woodwork, grand fireplaces, and posh furnishings prompted *Harper's Weekly* to enthuse in 1870 that the interior "was fairly entitled to be designated the handsomest club-house in the city."[30]

More important to association leaders was that the amenities promoted "muscular Christianity," the innovative four-fold YMCA program that regarded physical culture as a necessary component of religious, social, and mental health. The building had an auditorium, organ, lecture hall, classrooms, well-stocked library, social parlors, games rooms, well-equipped gymnasium, bowling alley, and baths. Rent from ground-floor stores and upper-story offices financed the mortgage, while residential rental spaces paid the working expenses of the main organization, which was headquartered in the building.

Because of its location opposite the National Academy of Design, the Twenty-third Street YMCA was home to some of the most famous artists of the day, including John La Farge, William Hart, Alexander Helwig Wyant, Sanford Robinson Gifford, Horace Wolcott Robbins, and Joseph Oriel Eaton. Richard Morris Hunt's famous Tenth Street Studio Building had been the model, but the YMCA had nearly twice the number of studios—forty in all on its top two floors—conveniently reached by elevator. A gallery accommodated large pictures.[31] A public reception on December 17, shortly after the building was dedicated, enabled several thousand visitors to see the studios. In this place, surrounded by art professionals who took a keen interest in one another's work, who exchanged ideas and discussed artistic issues on a daily basis, and who relaxed and celebrated with one another and with interesting clients and friends, Porter had a taste of the future he imagined possible.

Even if Porter lived only briefly at the "Association Building," as this YMCA became known, he might have been drawing or painting across the street at the National Academy of Design on the last Wednesday in March 1872, when a lively celebration was taking place outside. He may even have abandoned his easel to join in. A military and civic parade with a large contingent of marchers, black and white, was marking the two-year anniversary of the ratification of the fifteenth amendment to the U. S. Constitution, which assured voting rights regardless of race. The parade, headlined by the *Times* as a "Mass Meeting of Colored Men," wound its way through New York streets, around statues of Washington and Lincoln, and ended with a flourish at the Association Building, where a commemorative concert took place that evening.[32]

In June 1873 Porter was in Rockville, seeking students, but he probably returned to New York in the fall. From then until the following summer, he most likely studied with the artist Joseph Oriel Eaton (1829–1875), who taught students in his Association studio.[33] A well-known portrait, genre, and landscape painter from Ohio, Eaton was admired for his careful craftsmanship. He had been elected an Associate of the National Academy of Design in 1866 and exhibited frequently at its annual spring exhibitions. He was also active in the Society of Painters in Water Color and the Artist's Fund Society, and he showed with the Brooklyn Art Association, especially in the last years of his life, when he was a successful painter of children's portraits.

Eaton had come to New York and to the Twenty-third Street YMCA in 1869 following a trip to Europe. His studio became a meeting place not only for his artist friends and for students such as William Merritt Chase, who would soon become a star of American art, and Archibald Willard, who painted *The Spirit of '76* (Abbott Hall, Marblehead, Massachusetts), but also for the well-known writers Bret Harte and Sarah Orne Jewett. Eaton tried to find buyers for the work of young artists and gave them practical advice. When Chase was suddenly without funds for art lessons because of his father's financial losses, Eaton urged him to paint more of the flower and fruit pieces with which he had had some success. Eaton may have given Porter a similar suggestion and may even have allowed him to share his studio. Many artists, even those who lived in their studios in the Association Building, sublet or shared their space.[34] Since Eaton went home to Yonkers every evening, Porter could have slept in his studio with little inconvenience to his mentor.

Eaton's sudden death from pneumonia was a blow. "He was a true friend to poor, struggling men in his profession, a number of whom are deeply indebted to him." So reads one obituary, and others say much the same: "His genial nature made him hosts of warm friends, and more than one struggling artist will miss his beneficence."[35] Newspapers noted that many artists attended Eaton's funeral; Porter was probably among them.

New York City, 1875–77

American artists had begun to seek summer places in the countryside, where they could escape the city and paint the landscape. Porter's summer retreat was always his parents' home in Rockville. In June 1874, when he returned, only two children were there: Frank, age five, a brother born about the time that Charles first left for New York; and Ella, sixteen, a daughter of his brother Edwin, who had died just after she was born. William Jr. had returned to Rockville from Guilford and was working as a brakeman on the railroad. William Sr., it appears, was building the house he had long dreamed of, for the property on Fox Hill was now mortgaged. The Porters moved there between 1875 and 1879.

The artist, who planned to return to New York in the fall for further study, presumably with Eaton, worked that summer on at least two paintings. One was a still life, described in the *Tolland County Journal* as a "very pretty and natural sketch in oil," which was displayed in a Rockville store window in September, price \$35. The *Journal* noted its exterior setting and its remarkable depiction of an insect: "The painting represents a heap of red, luscious apples, in a shady nook of a heavy stone wall. In front is a bumble bee, so natural that one can almost hear him buz[z], intent on extracting the sweets of a clover blossom."[36]

There is no way to know what the newspaper meant by "sketch." At the time the word could mean anything from a work that was simply small to one that looked sketchy or unfinished to a finished oil done *en plein air* or in the studio from fieldwork. Porter certainly could have piled apples in front of a stone wall and painted the scene outdoors. Portraying the bee, however, would have been another matter and must have required him to study a specimen.

We learn that Porter was already portraying apples and insects realistically, but in this painting the irregular shapes, tones, and textures of a "heavy stone wall," along with a bee gathering nectar from a flower, might distract one's eye from the apples. Known Porter still lifes from the late 1870s always project clarity and simplicity. The focal groups of fruits or flowers are richly colored, strongly lit, and silhouetted against plain dark backgrounds.

Another painting that Porter completed that summer was a landscape of Lake Snipsic, the large lake that borders the towns of Rockville, Ellington, and Tolland. At the end of July, the *Tolland County Journal* announced that Porter's view of this beloved Rockville icon—whose Indian name of Mishenipset (big pool) had been corrupted locally to Shenipsit, Snipsic, and even Snip—was coming along well. This is the earliest reference to Porter's efforts to paint imagery that the art world of the late nineteenth century considered finer, more difficult, and more important than still life:

> Water below, dark pine grove on the south, the many-colored meadows on the other side, gradually rising to the Tolland hills, the comfortable and cosy farm-houses, backed by the rich green foliage of the woods towards the north, combine to make the view one of rare beauty and richness.[37]

When *Snipsic from Russian Rock* was displayed in a store window in October, it was "much admired and praised by all," according to the *Tolland County Journal*, which had no doubt that it was Porter's "greatest and best effort" and thus approved the high price tag, $175.[38] Porter himself must have been proud of this painting, as a beginning professional generally asked for much less money at that time.

This picture is unknown, but it appears that Porter later simplified his landscape compositions as well as his still lifes. The description of the Snipsic painting recalls the bucolic views that William Hart (1823–1894) and his brother James MacDougal Hart (1828–1901) had been painting near Farmington, a village just west of the Connecticut River and Hartford. Painstakingly composed and realistically rendered in their city studios from sketches and studies done outdoors, works by the Harts and fellow late Hudson River School painters depicted "humanized" scenes of water, woods, meadows, and homesteads rather than the awesome mountain and cataract panoramas of their forerunners. Their peaceful visions of a prewar, pre-industrial America seemed to comfort viewers in the aftermath of the Civil War. William Hart had a studio in the Association Building in New York, where Porter could have observed his creative process. Porter probably followed Hart's example by creating this landscape in his own studio, with the option of revisiting the nearby site if he felt the need.

Porter opened a studio in the Exchange Building in downtown Rockville, where he taught at least one student good enough to exhibit at the Tolland County Agricultural Fair in October. "Willie Frink," the Fine Arts Committee reported, "exhibited three sketches in oil, and his teacher, C. E. Porter, some very fine paintings of fruit and flowers."[39] The article reveals that Porter was already attracted to the subject matter that would become his bread and butter.

Porter did not go back to New York in the fall as planned. Some townspeople realized that he could not afford to. In November, a musical benefit was held for him in the hall of the First Congregational Church. Some 150 tickets were sold, and Porter contributed a painting for a lottery, which was won by one of the town's wealthiest citizens. The painting was of Snipsic Lake, but the newspaper report did not say whether it was the picture that Rockville had admired in October.[40]

Porter returned to New York a few weeks later. He remained in the city through most of 1877, yet almost nothing is known about him at a time when one would expect a new professional artist to be exhibiting as often as he could. Only two Porter works are listed in extant exhibition catalogues for these years: *Moss Study* was shown at the Society of American Painters in Water Color in February 1875, and a painting called *Fruit* was in the annual spring exhibition of the National Academy of Design in 1876. Porter did not exhibit at the Watercolor Society again and showed only three more times—in 1885, 1886, and 1889—at the National Academy.

A city directory published in May 1876 lists Porter's home address as 35 Union Square, as does a business directory for 1876–77.[41] Porter's stay in the square, though apparently limited, must have been exhilarating. At the juncture of Fourth Avenue and Broadway, Union Square was the city's gathering place. It had opened in 1839 as an upscale residential area with a private central park, along English models. The site of patriotic rallies in support of the Union during the Civil War, Union Square later became the place to stage a protest, hold a mass meeting, organize a parade, or otherwise make one's point in public. In 1871 the park had been razed and refurbished in accord with a design by Calvert Vaux and Frederick Law Olmsted that eliminated all fencing in order to emphasize the square's role as a public space. By then, labor union rallies and Socialist protests were common there. By then, too, Union Square had become one of the city's busiest cultural and retail centers. The Academy of Music, established in 1854, had Tammany Hall as a next-door neighbor by 1870. A lavish Tiffany & Co. building was soon nearby, joining luxury department stores such as A. T. Stewart's famous "Cast Iron Palace," banks, theaters, concert halls, restaurants, and at least one art gallery. Wholesale and manufacturing establishments, which would take over by 1890, were beginning to move in.

Porter's home and studio at 35 Union Square was between Sixteenth and Seventeenth Streets on the west side of the square. A small mixed-use building, it had for several years housed a few artists, including the celebrated illustrator Edwin Austin Abbey (1852–1911), whose stay may have overlapped Porter's residency by a few weeks or months. Other artists lived nearby. Interesting for Porter, surely, was that Morston Constantine Ream (1840–1898), a specialist in fruit and dessert still lifes, was working at 39 Union Square. Formerly a daguerreotypist and photographer's apprentice, Ream had turned to painting only some half dozen years earlier but had already gained attention for work shown at the National Academy of Design and the Brooklyn Art Association. He would exhibit at the Pennsylvania Academy of the Fine Arts in 1876. His brother was Carducius Plantagenet Ream (1837–1917), a well-known fruit painter whose still lifes were widely distributed by Louis Prang's famous chromolithograph firm. Porter already may have known the brothers' work, but, in any case, he could have seen Morston's paintings at Moore's Art Rooms in Union Square and possibly at the artist's studio. The two might even have been friendly, for Morston moved into 35 Union Square when Porter moved out.

Whatever his personal circumstances, Porter must have been disturbed by the upheavals in the New York art world of the 1870s. What he witnessed and experienced undoubtedly had an impact on his decision in late 1877 to leave New York and establish a studio in Hartford, Connecticut.

Just weeks after Porter finished his studies at the Academy, the United States experienced an economic downturn that became known as the Panic of 1873. The bankruptcy on September 18 of the Philadelphia banking firm Jay Cooke and Company set off a devastating domino effect. There was a run on banks; the New York Stock Exchange closed for ten days; 28,000 businesses failed by 1875; unemployment reached 14 percent by 1876; and 89 of the country's 364 railroads, the leading postwar industry, went bankrupt. Jay Cooke was an art collector, but it is unlikely that he and his fellow entrepreneurs bought much art in these years. The depression did not lift until spring 1879.

In the art world, other developments had longer lasting consequences. Before the Civil War, American artists were heralded at home and could get top dollar. Afterward, major American collectors, more cosmopolitan after postwar trips to Europe, preferred contemporary French art and Old Masters. Sales of American art weakened and would remain weak until the 1890s. There were also more young artists in New York City than before, without enough exhibition space or patrons for them all. The demand for European art spurred expansion of the commercial art market, but influential dealers like S. P. Avery began to stock more European than American art.

Young American artists, who had begun flocking overseas in the early 1870s to study, especially at the academies at Munich and Paris, may have unwittingly added to their drop in sales by their obvious enthusiasm for the contemporary art they saw abroad. They were eager to be equally progressive and bluntly decried as old-fashioned and insular the established American artists who had been their mentors.

The manner of selling art in New York was also changing. For years American artists had relied on studio receptions and open studio days— often in lavishly decorated "show" studios—to exhibit and market their work. A personal meeting with the artist and some haggling over price were part of the process. In the late 1860s, however, there were signs that the buying public was losing its enthusiasm for acquiring art this way. The most successful receptions were the exhibition openings at the National Academy of Design, where one could look without feeling the pressure to buy. More places to purchase art were becoming available, including galleries; supply, framing, and gift shops; and luxury department stores like A. T. Stewart's, where prices were set and the artist was not hovering about. Such venues were especially appealing to people who worried about their ability to judge art; those who were more confident looked for bargains at auctions and dealers' sales, which also increased in number.

The period also saw a sharp rise in the quantity and quality of art criticism, which appeared not only in newspapers and general magazines such as *Scribner's* but also in new periodicals devoted to art. As criticism became more professional, many people grew less sure of their critical acumen, a situation compounded by the broad range of art styles and subjects that appeared in the decades after the Civil War. Landscapes had become prevalent, along with genre scenes that were fairly new to the American art scene. Most viewers were more familiar with portraits, which totaled nearly half the paintings in the Academy exhibitions until shortly before the Civil War. For many, confronting unfamiliar art in an impersonal space became more comfortable than seeing it for the first time in an artist's studio.

Artists, however, wanted to maintain a bond with potential patrons and began mounting temporary exhibitions at the leading gentlemen's clubs, whose members were a mix of notable business, artistic, and literary figures. The monthly exhibitions held at the Union League, Century Association, and similar clubs were safe havens for local artists, because the exhibits received publicity but were not open to the public and therefore not reviewed. Club members and their wives liked them because the art that was for sale had been juried by artist members of the club.

Many if not most of the artists who exhibited were themselves club members or aspired to be. Oliver Lay (1845–1890), a portrait and genre painter who had a studio apartment in the Association Building, all but bolted down to the Century Club to sink into an easy chair and light a cigar when he heard he was made a member. He relished the clubby feeling and knew that his career would get a leg up as well. The American Impressionist John Henry Twachtman (1853–1902) thought maintaining his membership in the Players Club so important that he endured the humiliation of peddling a painting from place to place one long day in an effort to raise the membership fee.

As the art market grew ever more structured and impersonal, the art dealer emerged as a powerful figure. As Kenneth John Myers has noted, "By the end of the 1870s even the most stalwart local artists realized that they needed professional help with the marketing of their work."[42] He points to Jervis McEntee, who wrote in his diary in 1878, "The more I think of it, the more I am convinced of the necessity of business management of the sale of our pictures."[43] One hurdle, then as now, is that a dealer could agree to promote an artist's work or reject it out of hand. There are instances, as well, of dealers dictating the look and range of an artist's imagery.

These changes in the American art world of the 1870s threatened the preeminence of the National Academy of Design and its art school. In 1875 the school was in such financial trouble that Lemuel Wilmarth, the chief instructor, was not rehired, and classes were cancelled for an indefinite period. Discussions between Wilmarth and the disenfranchised students resulted in the formation that year of the Art Students League, the first independent art school in the nation, funded entirely by membership fees and organized on democratic principles. Wilmarth was president and instructor, but in fall 1877 the National Academy reopened, and he returned to his former post, leaving the new school in a precarious state. Many former Academy students opted to stay at the League nevertheless. In a matter of months the League restructured itself and hired a faculty. William Merritt Chase, once Porter's fellow student, now back from studies in Munich that admirers had funded, was named chief instructor. The League ended the year 1878 on a high note and has been an important institution in New York ever since. (A colored student was not enrolled until April 1887.)[44]

Troubles at the National Academy of Design were not confined to its art school. Former students who had studied abroad began to see the Academy as too conservative, and others in the art world agreed. "Church and Bierstadt and their fellow artists have done all for American art that they will do," wrote the influential critic Clarence Cook as early as 1868 about the growing gap between the artistic generations.[45] Debates arose about whether truth in art comes from the careful drawing, meticulous detail, and smooth finish associated with the older generation or from the evocation of emotion, beauty, and poetry that characterized the work of the younger artists, who were becoming known as the "new men."

The Academy's fiftieth anniversary exhibition, in 1875, shook the art world because of the large number of young European-trained artists it included. No reviewer could ignore them or the questions their strong showing raised about the overall value of foreign training, the relative merits of French and German study, and the implications of both issues for the development of American art. Margaret C. Conrads has concluded from her study of the Academy's exhibitions in the 1870s that the crux of the matter for critics and artists was "how American art could absorb the best of European aesthetics and technique while retaining its originality and independence."[46]

After a second strong showing in 1876, the "new men" were hailed as the saviors of American art. Clarence Cook exclaimed: "There is so much

independence and feeling shown as to justify the hope that the tide has turned and that we shall soon be no more bound in the flats and shallows of the last ten years."[47] The precision of Porter's draftsmanship, born of his inherent talent and honed by the Academy's conservative curriculum, must have become a handicap when the artists being extolled were slighting realism in favor of art that aimed primarily at an emotional response.

A group of the "new men," who had been meeting privately for about three years to air their grievances, defected from the Academy on June 1, 1877, to form the Society of American Artists. Most were young artists who had recently trained abroad, but the designation "new" now included every artist who spurned imitation, factual truth, and realism and tried instead to communicate feeling, beauty, and poetry. The Society of American Artists began holding annual spring exhibitions in 1878 that rivaled those of the Academy for more than twenty years. Students at the League immediately aligned themselves with the Society. It was not a formal bond, but the connection was close. For years the faculty of the League was drawn almost exclusively from the membership of the Society of American Artists.

Porter's attraction to still life probably added to his problems. Although of greater interest in America in the 1860s than previously, still life was considered one of the least important subjects.[48] Prominent artists such as William Merritt Chase, John LaFarge, and J. Alden Weir painted a number of still lifes, but they made their reputations with other subjects. Exhibitions at the National Academy included very few still lifes. In 1870 only 34 of 477 entries were still lifes; in 1875, 41 of 533.[49] Not surprisingly then, few still-life paintings were mentioned in the reviews and then not always in complimentary terms. A reviewer of the 1878 Watercolor Society exhibition was jubilant that "mere prettiness, flower-pieces and the like have had their day."[50] A critic of the 1880 exhibition found it "positively pleasurable to note the comparative fewness of the still-life pictures, particularly of fruits and flowers and things that generally look better in vases and dishes on the table than they do in frames on the walls."[51]

When a still-life painting did get a nod, the artist was almost always a woman. Perhaps the occasional brief mention was meant to satisfy the growing number of women who were studying art with the goal of artistic and professional parity with men. Indeed, women artists did often prefer to paint still life in this period, and flower painting also became a hobby or a moneymaking venture for housewives and female amateurs. "The female mind seems to run naturally to the painting of flowers and fruits," the *New York Times* declared in 1870.[52] Yet Porter's association with still life, despite its low status in the period, should not have doomed his bid for professional success, for several contemporaries who had that specialty, male and female, acquired solid reputations.

Every American artist was affected by the revolution in the art world in the 1870s, but young Porter was more vulnerable than most. He was not one of the "new men"; he had not studied abroad; he was not painting "important" subject matter; he was not noticed by the new art periodicals; he was not welcome at gentlemen's clubs; and he appears to have been without a dealer. The color of his skin made him unacceptable to a majority of Americans and apparently to everyone who mattered in the art world: artists, critics, dealers, and collectors.

By the 1870s most of the gains of Reconstruction had been lost in the North as well as the South. As colored Southerners began to migrate north and west, a backlash by the dominant white society was underway. At the 1876 Centennial Exposition, where Edward Bannister won a painting prize before anyone knew he was colored, recognition of non-whites was limited to ethnological exhibits about cultures still in a primitive phase. Minstrel shows and cartoons relentlessly caricatured colored people and furthered prejudice. A number of Bible scholars and scientists were trying to prove the inferiority of African-Americans. When Porter moved to Hartford in 1878, it was said that he had previously confronted shameful obstacles. As racism grew ever more widespread as the century drew to its close, he would encounter more.

Hartford, 1878–81

In an article headlined "A New Painter, A Colored Man," the *Hartford Daily Times* for December 18, 1877, announced that Porter was considering a move to the city.[53] His oil paintings of apples and watercolors of butterflies struck the writer as extraordinary. The artist should have no trouble finding pupils, he said, if he comes to Hartford. Porter made the move. Although his presence cannot be documented until the following March, he probably arrived earlier.

In the late 1870s, the art world would have regarded an artist's transfer from New York to Hartford as a giant step backward. Art periodicals and the New York press covered Boston and Philadelphia and sometimes mentioned art in Chicago and Cincinnati but not Hartford. Yet as Porter was considering a return to the city of his birth, Harry French, an editor of the *Hartford Evening Post*, was preparing *Art and Artists in Connecticut*, the first book about the artists of a single state, which was warranted, his newspaper said, because Connecticut had more artists "of genuine ability" than any other, with "the most brilliant names" belonging to Hartford.[54] The claim for Hartford, at least, was an exaggeration. Frederic Edwin Church (1826–1900) was the city's star, a former resident whose glory days had been heady, and fellow local William Gedney Bunce (1840–1916) was abroad painting views of Venice that won him an international reputation, but other Hartford artists were generally unknown outside the city. Still, in the late 1870s, Hartford was not a bad place for an artist.

Porter intimated that the portraitist Henry Bryant, an older friend who had returned to Hartford from New York two decades earlier, had convinced him to settle in Connecticut's capital. Hartford's manufacturing and insurance companies had prospered during the Civil War. Despite economic depression elsewhere, the city was experiencing a postwar building boom that included a grand new capitol, under construction when Porter came to town. Leading citizens were interested in art and culture, and artists had begun coming to the city. In the 1860s the city's population had doubled, but Hartford never had more than nine or ten professional artists. Suddenly, in the mid-1870s, the number of artists tripled. Most lived and worked downtown, in the Charter Oak Insurance Building and other imposing new Main Street structures, where modern amenities such as elevators attracted buyers to the open studio receptions that were still popular in the city.

Daniel Wadsworth's paintings gallery on Main Street, now the Wadsworth Atheneum Museum of Art, and the personal collection of Mrs. Samuel L. Colt, widow of the famous firearms manufacturer, were notable. Three or four downtown art stores exhibited and sold art by nationally known and local artists. The cluster of artists' studios within two or three blocks of one another on Main Street constituted an art colony of sorts. Historic buildings such as Charles Bullfinch's Old State House, along with grand new buildings, Olmsted-inspired green space, and the broad Connecticut River made Hartford a pleasant place. Harriet Beecher Stowe and Mark Twain, who declared he had never seen a prettier city, had chosen to live there.

Hartford's aesthetic tastes were comfortingly conservative. No "new men" fresh from study in Europe and full of controversial progressive ideas were there. Traditional academic training was valued, and Porter stood out from the city's mostly self-taught artists because of his. He was also the only male to specialize in fruit and flower painting. Some Hartfordites remembered that he was not the first person of his race to pursue an art career in the city. Twenty-five years earlier, Augustus

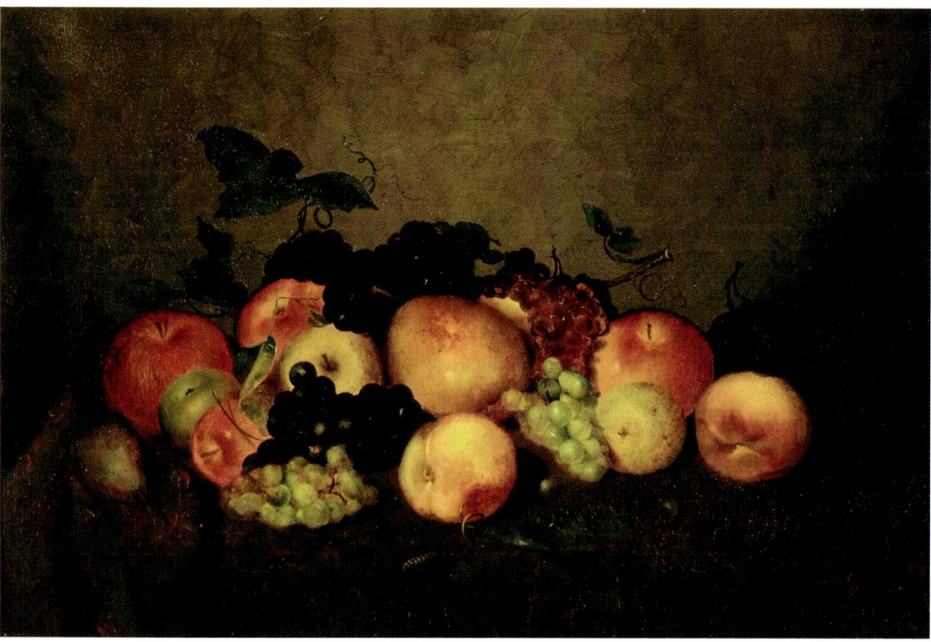

Catalogue 01
Fruit: Apples, Grapes, Peaches, and Pears, c. 1875
Oil on canvas, 17⅛" x 23½", Signed lower right
Connecticut Historical Society Museum and Library

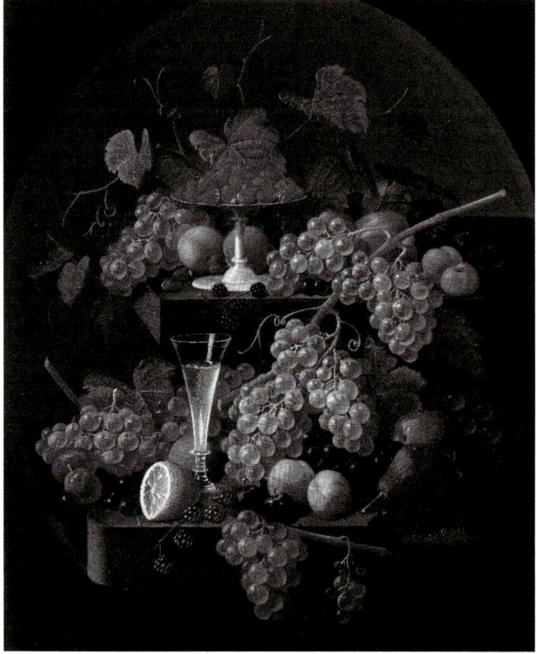

Figure 03–Severin Roesen
Fruit and Wine Glass,
c. 1860–65
Oil on canvas
29⅞" x 25⅛"
Collection of the
New Britain Museum
of American Art
Charles F. Smith Fund,
1964.53

Washington (1820/21–1875) had been a leading daguerreotypist. He immigrated to Liberia in 1853, convinced that American society would not treat his race fairly within his lifetime. Some ten years later Nelson A. Primus (1842–1916), a member of one of Hartford's premier black families, had painted in his hometown before moving to Boston to pursue a career as a portraitist.

Porter must have believed that Hartford was not a dead end for an artist. Bryant was content with the unconventional choice he had made— to leave a successful career in New York for a kind of hinterland. Porter's situation was different, and he would have learned that some artists who had done well in Hartford had in time moved on to New York. He may have been hoping to return himself—or perhaps he already planned to study in France. In any case, he needed to sell paintings, and, in the late 1870s, Hartford must have represented a better market than New York.

It is not known how Hartford artists responded to Porter. We know little about the city's artists and their relationships in the 1870s, though the proximity of their studios suggests interaction. Whether he was welcomed as a colleague or not, Hartford gave Porter what New York never could: his family lived nearby.

Porter brought to Hartford, or soon produced in the city, paintings that are known today. *Fruit: Apples, Grapes, Peaches, and Pears*, dated 1875 (catalogue 01), may be the work that represented him at the National Academy of Design exhibition that year. This diamond-shaped arrangement of fruits and a few leaves—so unlike (except for some tendrils) the extravaganzas

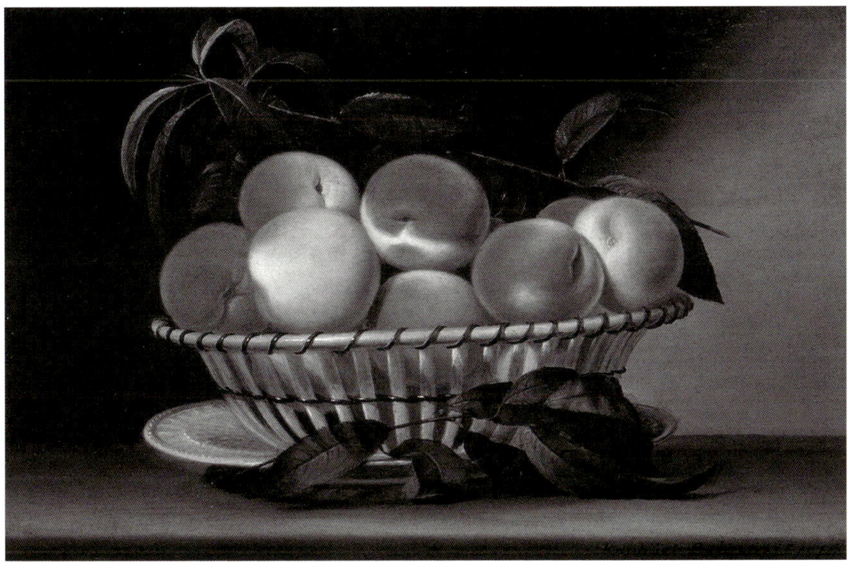

Figure 04–Raphael Peale (1774–1825)
Bowl of Peaches, 1816
Oil on wood panel
12⅝" x 19¼"
Collection of the New Britain Museum of American Art
Harriet Russell Stanley Fund, 1961.01

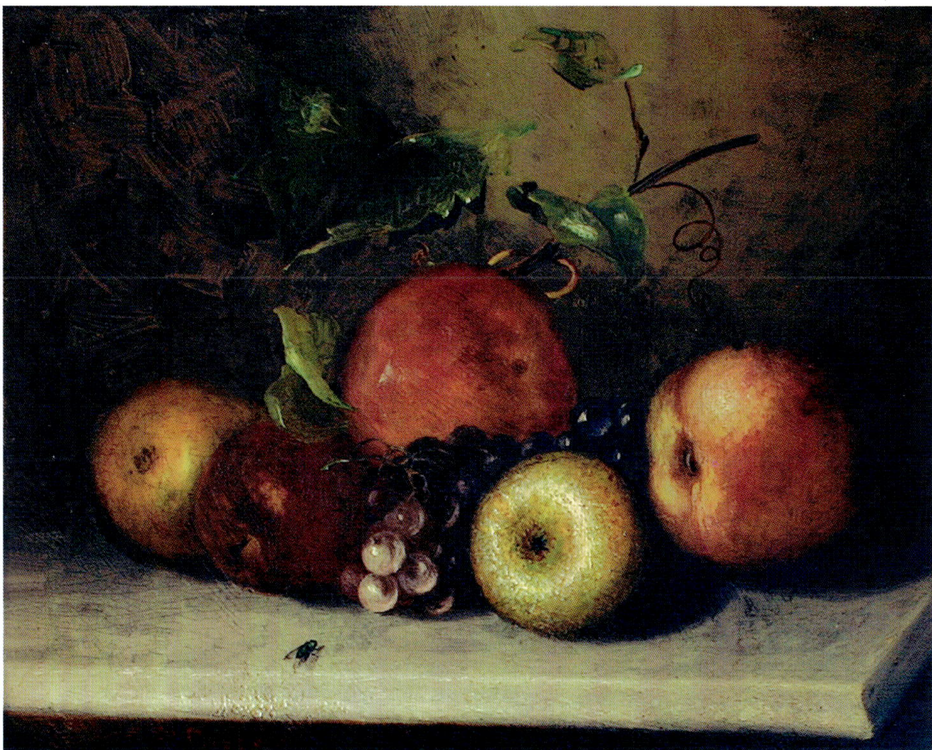

Catalogue 02
Apple with Fly, c. 1875
Oil on canvas
9½" x 11"
Signed lower left
Dr. and Mrs. Stephen M. Rouse

that Severin Roesen and his followers had offered Americans at mid-century (figure 03)—recalls the traditions of the Peale family, the first artists in America to paint still life. The Peales' small groupings of fruits and leaves on a tabletop were widely exhibited in the first half of the nineteenth century and became a formula for the genre.

Porter omitted the tableware that the Peales often included, but he rendered fruit realistically, as they did. The soft, almost overripe "feel" of the fruit in the 1875 painting, however, is distinct from the crispness that characterizes the work of the Peales (figure 04). Moreover, Porter's fruit is not

flooded with light but seems rather to glow from within, the colors deepened into jewel tones like those of an illuminated Tiffany lampshade. The painting appears to be an anomaly in Porter's work; it may represent an attempt to stir the heart in the manner of the "new men" in New York. It is, in any case, an attractive, even compelling, artwork because of the character and arrangement of its glowing orange, green, and deep purple hues.

Another early painting that stands apart is *Apple with Fly* (catalogue 02). Fruit and a fly on a white marble slab recall the imagery of the famed Düsseldorf artist Johann Wilhelm Preyer (1803–1889), who worked in the

Dutch Baroque tradition and had been well represented in New York's popular Düsseldorf Gallery. The gallery had closed by the time Porter arrived in the city in 1869, but in March 1873 he may have seen the Preyer still life at Goupil Gallery that the *New York Times* thought might be one of the most remarkable artworks of the day.[55] Certainly he would have noticed the marble-slab still lifes of Preyer's outstanding student Helen Searle (1830–1884) at National Academy exhibitions, as well as those of the brothers Ream—Carducius and Morston—at the Academy and the Brooklyn Art Association. Fruit pieces in the Preyer tradition often include a fly as a memento mori.

Neither *Fruit* nor *Apple with Fly*, however, are as polished in style or technique as a Preyer, Searle, or Ream. Different as his two paintings are from one another, Porter imbued them both, without in any way making them seem amateurish, with some of the elemental directness and intensity of folk art. That need not diminish them, and arguably it even adds to their charm.

In these early works, Porter was making choices that distinguish him from more popular contemporaries. The fruit paintings of Searle and Morston Ream are often chock-full of silver, porcelain, and glassware, or costly treats like those in Ream's "dessert" still lifes. Porter rarely painted such things, wanting perhaps to achieve richness and complexity by other means. He had, after all, been brought up to care more for spiritual than material matters. Possibly his reasons were mundane: he may not have had access to objects that could serve as models. Or perhaps he had

trouble learning how to achieve in paint the look of silver, porcelain, or crystal. (There is no glassware in Porter's early work.)

Porter's omission of the pretty tableware usually seen in still-life paintings of the era did not matter in Hartford. The realism of Porter's apples was remarkable enough:

> There is the faithful color; there are the golden or ruddy
> "specks" on the green skin; there, on other kinds, are the deep
> red cheeks of the fruit, that deepened in August noon . . . and
> there is the circular gleam, or line of shimmering light, on the
> turn of the shoulder, or top of the fruit, making it seem like
> looking at a real apple.[56]

Apples on the Ground (catalogue 03) shows apples spread apart so that all but one can be readily admired. At odds with their realism is a bed of straw, more artful than real, which is textured like lace and gleams like gold. Yet the realistic apples and the decorative straw are complementary. Several Porter apple pictures from the late 1870s include "gold lace" straw.

Porter achieved success with apple pictures and painted them for years, in arrangements of a few to more than a dozen apples and, in at least one instance, to a great number spilling out of an overturned basket. A Hartford reporter wrote in April 1878, "Porter's apples are certainly extraordinary productions."[57] At one time Porter felt that one of his apple paintings was his masterpiece; while some people in Hartford knew which one he meant, that information has been lost.

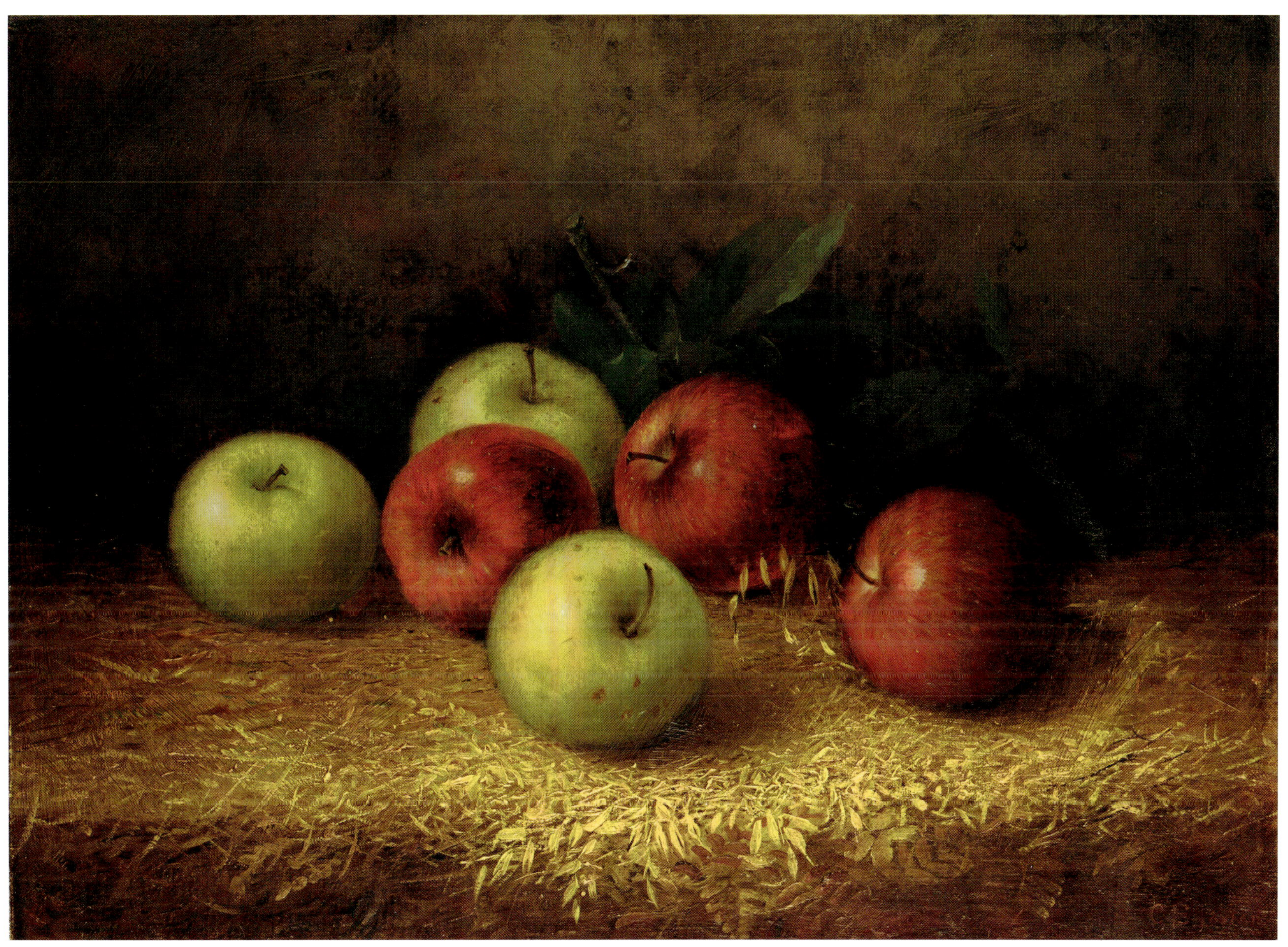

Catalogue 03
Apples on the Ground, c. 1878
Oil on canvas
17⅞" x 21⅞"
Signed lower right
Wadsworth Atheneum Museum of Art, Hartford, CT.
Gift of Dorothy Clark Archibald

Porter was also fond of outdoor settings, which rivaled the popularity of tabletop still lifes in the 1860s and 1870s. The convention derived from the British critic John Ruskin (1819–1900), who championed the English Pre-Raphaelite painters and directed readers of his *Modern Painters* (1845) to be similarly true to nature. Devoted American Ruskinians—so-called American Pre-Raphaelites—were most influential in fostering close nature studies in the early 1860s, but their influence lingered.

Porter's *Autumn Leaves,* shown at the National Academy in summer 1871, and *Moss Study,* at the Society of Painters in Water Color in 1875,

were typical Pre-Raphaelite subjects, and so is the *Study of a Dead Cockerel* (catalogue 04). Were this a titmouse or blue jay, we would expect to be looking at an iconic image by one of the Farrer brothers, Thomas (1839–1891) and Henry (1843–1903), or by the Hills—father John William (1812–1879) and son John Henry (1839–1922). Although Porter's subject is not a New England songbird but a young rooster, John Henry Hill's *Black-Capped Chickadee* in his *Sketches from Nature* (1867) could have served as a model (figure 05). The cockerel, however, with its coxcomb-crowned head turned to one side and a soft overall scruffiness, is more touching. Hill wrote, "Dead birds make excellent studies . . . do not waste time on stuffed specimens if you can get the real."[58] Porter's cockerel looks real.

The *Dead Cockerel* surfaced a few years ago as one of eight drawings, some inscribed with dates from the late 1870s; it is likely from that time as

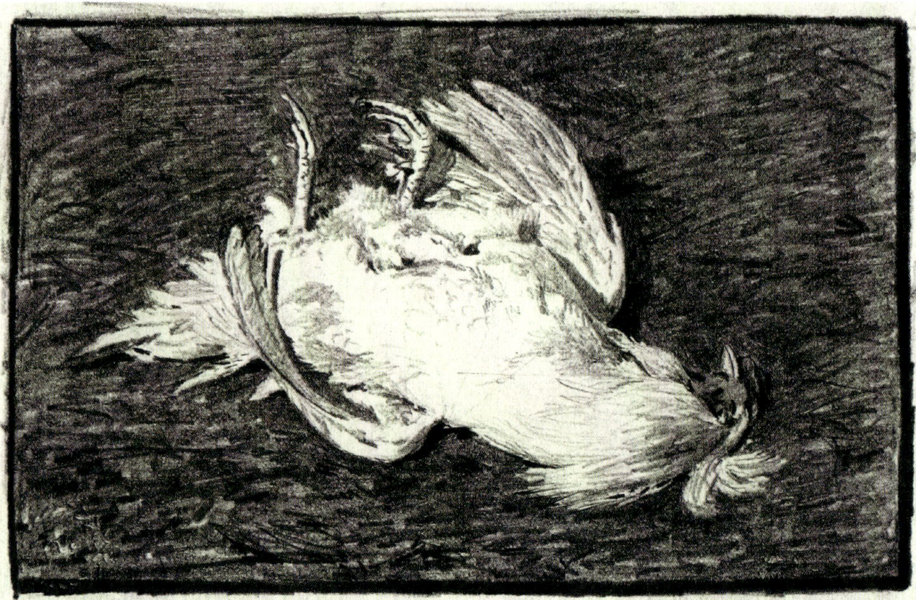

Catalogue 04
Study of a Dead Cockerel
Pencil on paper
4" x 6" (sight)
Collection of Charlynn and Warren Goins

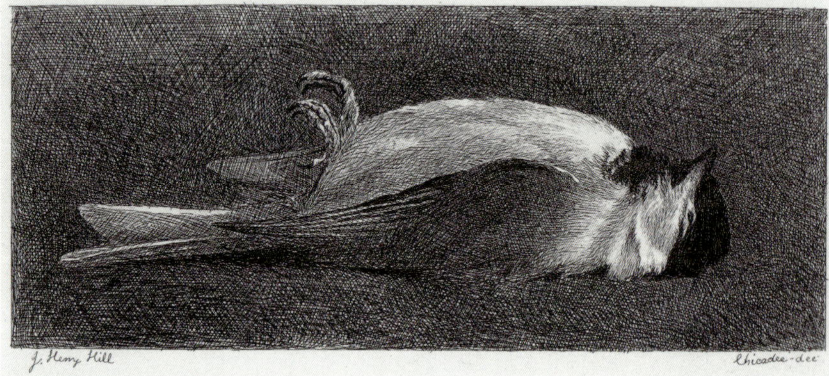

Figure 05–John Henry Hill, **Black-Capped Chickadee**, c. 1866 (etching)
New York Public Library Print Collection

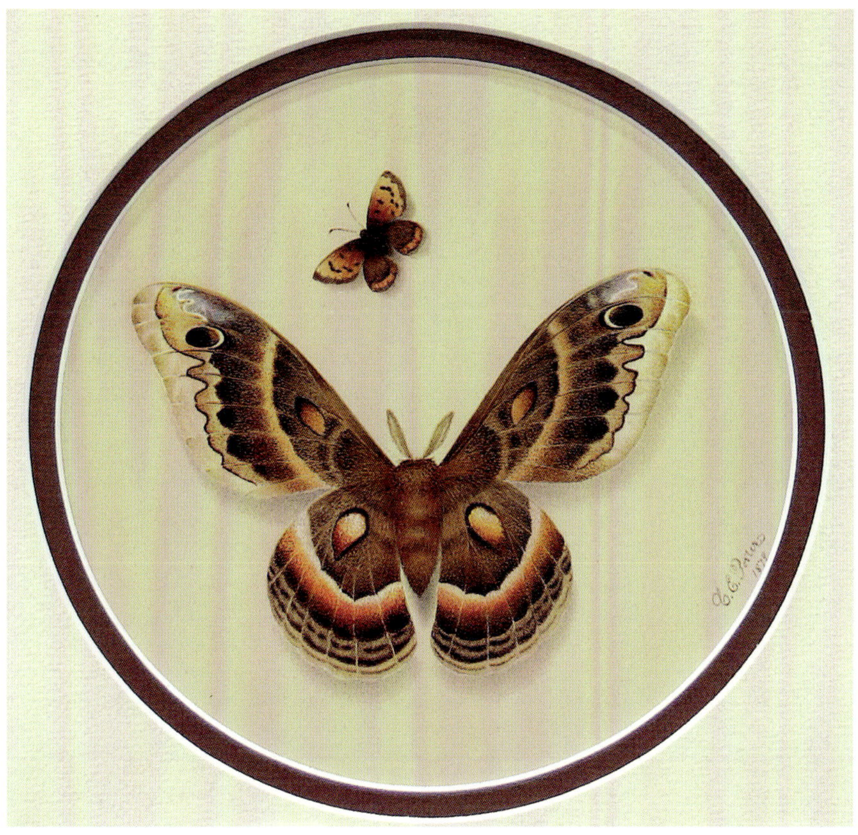

Catalogue 05
Moth, 1878
Watercolor and gouache on paper
8" round
Signed and dated lower right
Kathleen Del Rossi

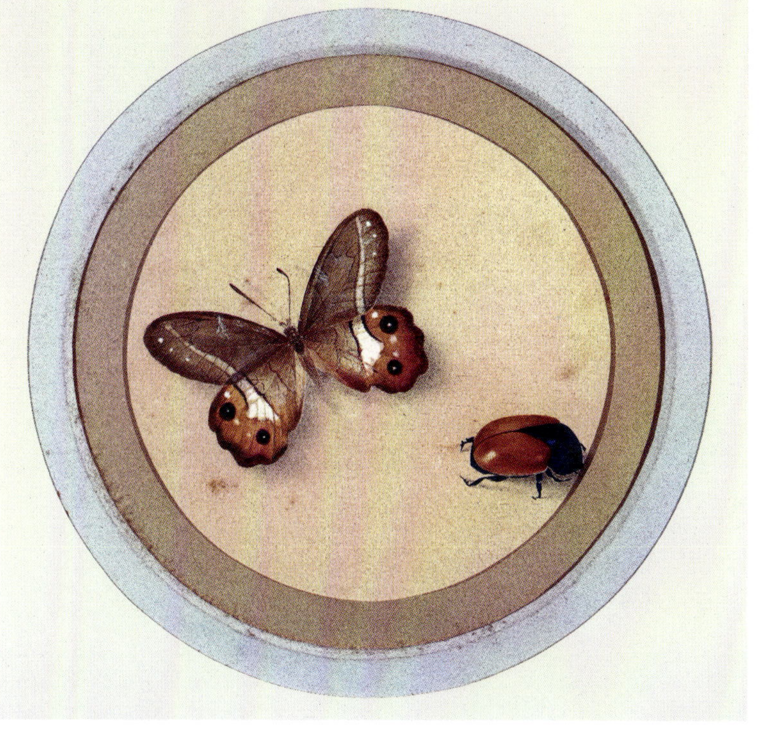

Catalogue 06
Butterfly and Beetle on a Plate, c. 1878
Watercolor and ink on paper
5" round
Monogrammed lower left
Private collection

well, for Porter exhibited other work then that relates to Pre-Raphaelite nature studies.

Hartford was dazzled by Porter's witty trompe l'oeil images of insects and found his watercolors of butterflies "amazing for the fineness of their execution—displaying, under the microscope, the individual feathers that make up the diamond-dust of the butterfly's wing; and these he painted without microscopic aid!"[59] His insects seemed alive. When A. D. Vorce & Co., the leading art emporium in town, exhibited a Porter watercolor of several kinds of butterflies in April 1878, the *Hartford Daily Times* believed their "varied hues and characteristic action could only have been taken from the life."[60] In an 1878 depiction of the giant Cecropia silk-moth (catalogue 05), a small companion flying in the distance helps give the illusion of life.

In another instance, a Porter butterfly shares space on a luncheon plate with a beetle (catalogue 06). Flies have alighted on still another plate (catalogue 07). The artist was surely asking Hartford to admire his skill,

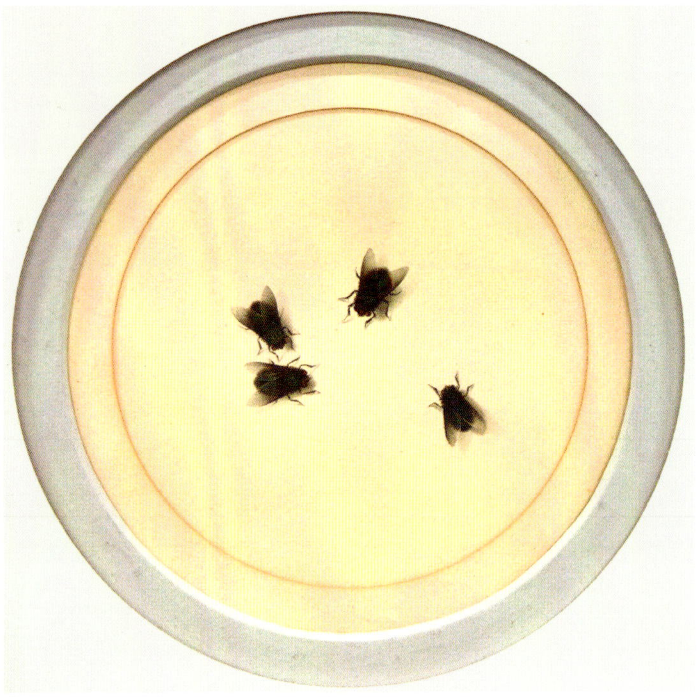

Catalogue 07
Flies on a Plate, c. 1878
Gouache/ink
4½" x 4½" round
Signed ?
Collection of Charlynn and Warren Goins

and it did: "Specimens of Mr. Porter's painted flies, at Vorce's, can be studied with increasing admiration by the aid of a magnifying glass. They are really microscopic studies; yet the artist in painting them used no aid but the eyes Nature gave him."[61] After 1879, however, nothing more is heard about Porter's insects. Since trompe l'oeil is hard on an artist's eyes, he may have had to stop. Such novelties can also quickly lose their appeal. Had he hoped to find employment as an illustrator of entomological studies? Porter had, at the very least, demonstrated that he could rival and in some ways best the other painters in Hartford. It was an important point for someone of his race to make.

Porter also painted bits of plant life reminiscent of a series by William Trost Richards from the early 1860s, when Richards was most intensely Pre-Raphaelite. The art critic Henry Tuckerman (1813–1871) had said of Richards' little paintings, "We seem not to be looking at a distant prospect but lying on the ground with herbage and blossoms directly under our eyes."[62] In June 1878 at Vorce's, where Richards showed one of the large gray sea views occupying him at the time, Porter offered "a heap of pansies, with brake and foliage, a true transcript from nature."[63] Perhaps it was *Pansies* (catalogue 08). If the flowers and plants in this colorful little work

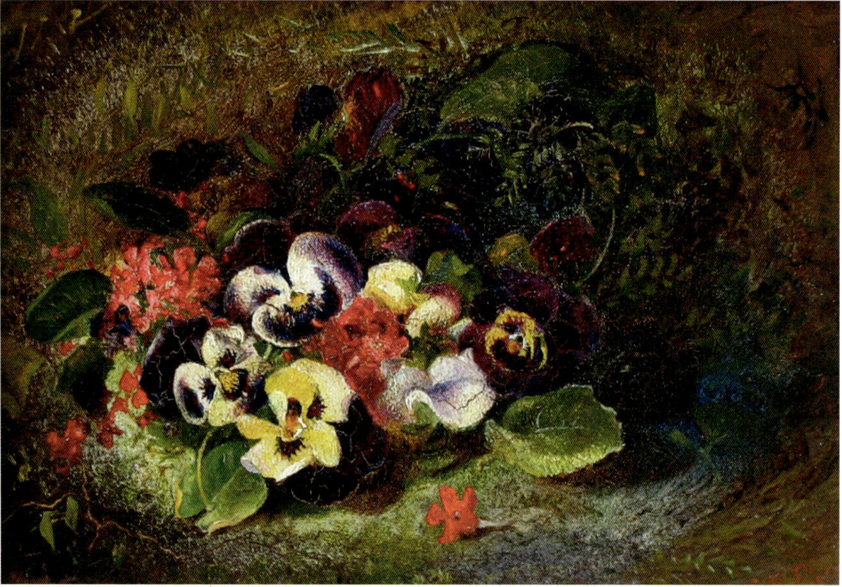

Catalogue 08
Pansies, 1870s
Oil on board
6" x 8"
Signed lower right
Mr. and Mrs. S. Lamont McEvitt

look more arranged than natural, *Forest Floor* (catalogue 09) depicts leaves and flowers directly under our eyes in a convincingly realistic manner.

In Hartford, Porter was first heard of not as an artist but as a participant in a religious revival unlike any the city had known. Meetings began on January 6 under the leadership of Dwight L. Moody and Ira D. Sankey and continued—after designated pinch hitters George Pentecost and George Stebbins came on board in February—until March 19. The newspapers were filled with reports of revival events. Moody was by all accounts the Billy Graham of his day. On a tour of Great Britain a few years earlier, Moody and Sankey had connected with throngs of people— more than 2.5 million in London alone—with their innovative mix of Moody's short but passionate evangelical sermons and rousing gospel hymns sung and usually composed by Sankey. After the British tour, the YMCA, in response to the ongoing financial depression in America, sent Moody and Sankey, as well as acolytes like Pentecost and Stebbins, on religious revival tours throughout the northeastern United States.

Hartford's roller-skating rink, where the daily revival meetings were held, regularly packed in 3,500, sometimes two or three times a day, and, even so, hundreds of people were turned away. Special prayer meetings in the city's churches and numerous "after meetings" were overcrowded as well. A person could spend the better part of every day in revival activities, and many people in Hartford apparently did so in winter 1878.

New to the city and presumably eager to establish himself as an artist, Porter nevertheless got caught up in the revival. He was an outstanding

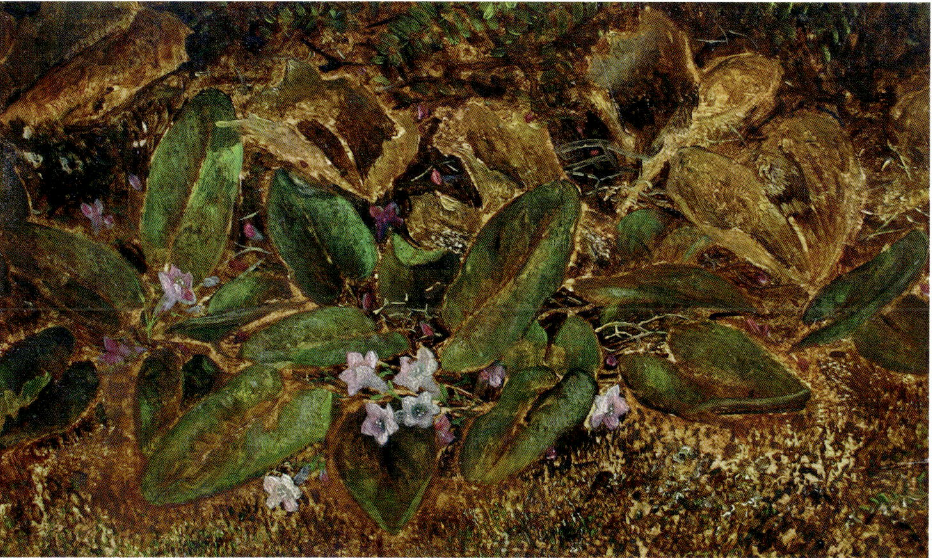

Catalogue 09
Forest Floor, c. 1878
Oil on board
5¼" x 8¼"
Signed ?
The Schonberger Family

member of the "rink choir" organized for the Hartford meetings. In early March his "high and clear alto" was called "phenomenal" and "heard above all the other voices—leading as it were, the songs."[64] What cannot be gleaned from the extensive coverage of the rink meetings—accounts that summarized Moody's sermons and often printed all the words of Sankey's hymns—is the extent to which the choir was interracial.

The director, Charles A. Jewell, a local man undoubtedly belonging to Hartford's influential Jewell family, led three rink choirs—male, female, and combined—which he appears to have programmed for particular purposes and occasions. Choirs sang before the principals made their entrance, they sang during the meetings, and they sometimes backed the solos. It seems unlikely that anyone could have dropped into a rink choir at will or during some free time. Porter's participation probably involved a commitment—one that most likely began before March.

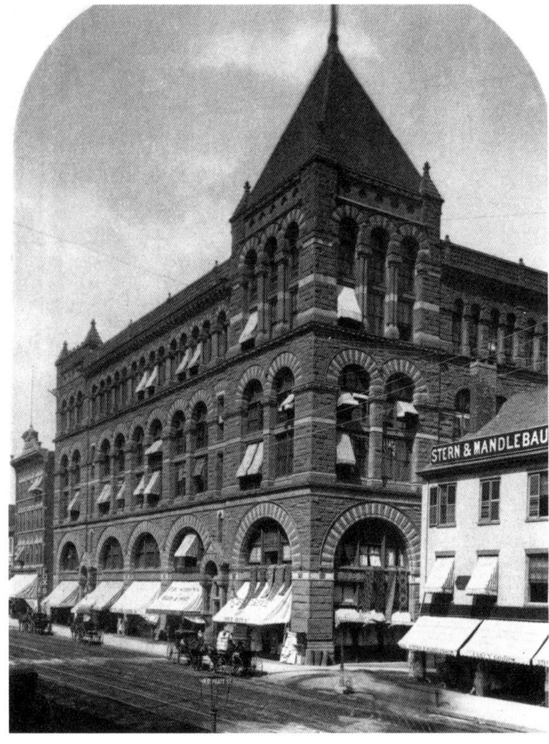

Figure 06–**Richardson Building, Main St., Hartford.**
Photo courtesy of the Connecticut Historical Society Museum and Library.

After the Hartford revival, the choirs made excursions to revivals in New Haven, Springfield, and Boston, where they sang thirty numbers and Moody had them repeat the chorus of "I Will Sing of My Redeemer" a half dozen times. The male choir was so caught up in the spirit of the revivals that it decided to form a permanent organization.

Before coming to Hartford, Moody and Sankey had held a series of YMCA-sponsored revivals in Brooklyn and Manhattan. In New York in 1876 they conducted seven services a day for some three months at P. T. Barnum's Hippodrome, where audiences often filled the hall to its six-thousand-person capacity. YMCA membership in New York City doubled as a result. Porter may have known of these meetings or attended some.

Obligated to leave Hartford in order to meet their commitments in other cities, Moody and Sankey seamlessly passed the torch to Pentecost and Stebbins. Shortly before departing, Moody was able to instigate the formation of a YMCA in the city, which he said should be right downtown: "I come down Main street every evening, and it seems to me a highway to perdition."[65] Porter, who was living in a Main Street building, probably was pleased to have a YMCA nearby and made good use of it in later years.

When the *Hartford Daily Times* for March 2, 1878, broke the news that the phenomenal voice in the rink choir belonged to an unknown colored man, reporters raced to learn about him, and two days later the *Hartford Daily Courant* was able to announce that the young singer was a remarkable painter with a studio in the Cheney Building (presently known after its architect, Henry Hobson Richardson [figure 06]): "One rarely witnesses such fidelity and masterly handling as is exhibited in the subjects which he has essayed."[66] The article was headlined "A Hartford Genius." A couple of weeks later a Porter fruit piece was on view in an elegant Main Street jewelry store; Vorce gallery exhibited a painting of fruit and watercolors of butterflies soon after. Porter had new work at Vorce's a few months later: "An excellent portrait from his easel is one of his latest works. In flower and fruit pieces, and insects and butterflies, he is unsurpassed."[67]

In September 1879, the *Hartford Daily Times* asked whether the city knew it had "an artist whose paintings, in minute accuracy of detail, and particularly in fidelity to nature in some of the most difficult points of color, are hardly surpassed by any painter in America."[68] He deserves fame, the article asserted, and were he in Paris or New York he would soon have it. Frederic Edwin Church, the *Times* reported, had recently visited Porter, bought paintings, and declared him to have "no superior as a colorist, in the United States."[69] Word spread that Porter was devoting the winter to landscapes because Church had urged him to. When Church visited again in April, he "expressed great pleasure with [Porter's] landscape effects, particularly the atmospheric."[70]

In autumn 1880 Porter went to the Adirondacks for six weeks of sketching and painting. In early December he declared that he would now paint landscapes exclusively, except for commissioned florals and fruit pictures. The announcement was greeted with guarded optimism:

> The same luxuriousness of imagination and glow of color which warm his still life are carried over into landscapes, and give them a rare attraction. This talent, when clarified and sobered, will, with good opportunities, in time produce pictures of special and high charm, while even his present accomplishments are decidedly noteworthy.[71]

That Porter was eager to paint landscapes is understandable. The European and American art worlds had long ranked subject matter in importance, and still life was relegated to the bottom of the hierarchy. Landscape painting was increasingly valued in nineteenth-century America, rising to a level that would rival and surpass portraiture and historical and mythological subjects, while still lifes, especially of flowers and fruit, were slipping ever lower. The prevailing view was that anyone could paint them; magazines and newspapers offered instruction. In spring 1880 a young artist swept into Hartford claiming he could teach flower painting in a few lessons. "As there are many young people, especially ladies, now giving attention to these arts, a visit to Mr. Stern's place will prove both entertaining and profitable," the *Hartford Daily Times* suggested.[72] Flower painting was also a favorite at Hartford's Society of Decorative Arts, a school formed in 1877 and newly located in the Cheney Building when Porter moved there.

The Hartford Society of Decorative Arts (which would become the Hartford Art School, now affiliated with the University of Hartford) aimed at providing good but inexpensive art training for women who needed or wanted to earn money from arts and crafts. Harriet Beecher Stowe, Mrs. Samuel Clemens, Elizabeth Colt, Mrs. Charles Dudley Warner, and the others on the advisory board aimed to create an art school that would train people to become either professional artists or skilled craftspeople. The *Courant* explained their approach:

> It has seemed to the society that before any really good artistic work could be produced by Hartford women, a thorough course of elemental drawing, from objects, nature and life was essential. Thorough instruction in the principles which underlie all good art work, under a teacher who will insure a free, spirited, and correct style of drawing, will develop and utilize the artistic talent which already exists among us.[73]

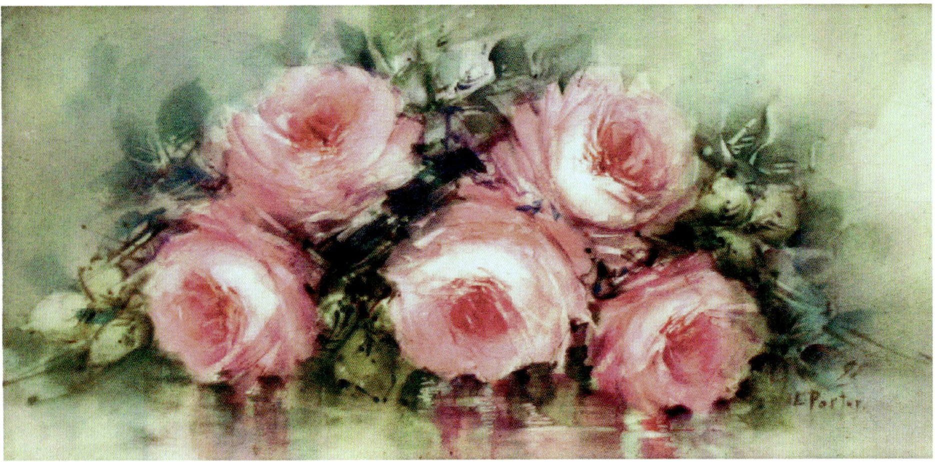

Catalogue 10
Roses
Ceramic panel
4½" x 9⅝"
Signed lower right
Collection of Charlynn and Warren Goins

A female student of William Morris Hunt was the first teacher, and the painter James Wells Champney (1843–1903) soon became the chief instructor, the first in a series of respected male professionals.

Porter was one of few professionals and the only man to participate in the society's inaugural exhibition, in April 1880—with a fruit piece said to have been commended by Church. A month later the society showed four of his florals and a string of fish. (He had not been able after all to limit his production to landscapes.) Porter may have perused the art periodicals that the society provided for students and perhaps even slipped into the drawing studio at times to refresh his skills. His friendly relationship with the society may account for a recent surprising discovery: a ceramic tile that Porter decorated with roses (catalogue 10). The society offered instruction in porcelain decoration, and Porter may have had access to the kiln, perhaps to experiment with a new medium or explore an income-generating opportunity.

Mindful of its original mission to help needy women, the Society of Decorative Arts held a five-day bazaar in June 1880 to benefit the Union for Home Work. The booth for the *Bazaar Budget*, a special newspaper with articles by Harriet Beecher Stowe, Mark Twain, and Charles Dudley Warner, displayed miniature fans autographed by such literary figures as Tennyson, Emerson, Celia Thaxter, and Louisa May Alcott, along with others decorated and signed by the artists Porter and William Gedney Bunce. Mark Twain was an auctioneer for these little treasures.

When Porter lived in Hartford, he was often able to see family members in Rockville and Meriden. His sister Cynthia's husband, Richard Alonzo Jeffrey, a barbershop owner in Meriden, was always involved in civil-rights and community issues. In 1877 and 1878 he presided over the Lincoln Club, an organization for colored men that he and his brother George founded in Meriden to honor the great emancipator. He was also High Priest of the Capitol Chapter of the Royal Arch Masons, #4, a colored lodge that often met in the Cheney Building, where Porter had his first Hartford studio. Jeffrey exhibited Porter's paintings in his barbershop. (His brother George and Porter's brother James probably did the same in their Meriden barbershops.) Jeffrey owned an ornamental horseshoe, made and gilded by a Meriden artisan, which Porter had decorated with a painting of trailing arbutus vines. When this odd piece was displayed in a Meriden store window in February 1879, it excited a good deal of favorable attention.

Jeffrey also had an impact in Porter's hometown of Rockville, when in 1878 he built an observation tower sixty feet high at the crest of Fox Hill, near the home of Porter's parents. The wooden structure rose from a concrete base twenty feet square to a ten-foot-square platform that offered a view of much of the Connecticut River Valley. On a good day Mount Tom and Mount Holyoke in Massachusetts could be seen with the naked eye. The fifteen-cent admission fee also bought the use of a telescope at the top. Ice cream and other refreshments were sold in the enclosed base. A popular attraction, the tower existed until February 1880, when a blizzard knocked it down. Ten years later Porter turned the surviving base into his studio.

Alonzo Jeffrey was close to his brother George, who succeeded him as president of the Lincoln Club in 1879. That year George was also an officer of Meriden's Greeley Club and participated in many of the YMCA's Lyceum debates, including one in which he encouraged a Negro exodus from the South. As vice president of the I. C. Lewis Division, Sons of Temperance (Alonzo was treasurer), George gave a speech entitled "Sacrifice" that was so well received in Meriden that he was asked to give it again in Brooklyn. He played Shakespeare's Othello in a Meriden production that featured a Desdemona from the Union Square Theater in New York. In 1879 he successfully sued one Hervey Rogers, who had accused him of stealing coal but considered it a far worse crime to have been "insulted by a man of Jeffrey's color."[74]

In 1878 the Jeffrey brothers expanded the membership of the Lincoln Club to colored persons who lived outside Meriden. It is not known whether Porter, who was about to arrive or had only just moved to Hartford, attended this once-a-year meeting on Lincoln's birthday. Nor it is known whether he had gone to Lincoln Club meetings in New York in the early 1870s, sometimes held at 37 Union Square, next door to the studio he occupied in 1875. He was, however, on hand for the 1879 gathering in Meriden, along with his brothers William and James, who were officers of the club, and with four leading figures in Hartford's black community: William B. Edwards, Lemuel Perry, Francis N. Allen, and Vincent E. Davis. Like other members of the Lincoln Club, these were middle-class men, an assessment that for nineteenth-century blacks is best defined, as Leslie Harris and others contend, by education and participation in moral reform and racial uplift activities rather than by occupation or wealth.[75]

In the black communities of Hartford and Meriden in the late 1870s, as in the New York of the 1860s that Harris writes about, cultural, political, and social markers were the most important factors in determining class position. Porter's brothers and his Lincoln Club companions from Hartford were leaders in their churches, Masonic lodges, and other community organizations but were trapped by a racist economic system in jobs as porters, messengers, janitors, and coachmen. The 1880 federal census for Hartford lists just seven colored professionals—three ministers, two music teachers, and two singers—in an African-American population of 1,280.[76] (Porter is recorded at his father's house in Rockville when this census was taken.)

Several white men attended the Lincoln Club meeting in 1879, including the governor of Massachusetts and federal, state, and local officials.

One was Vincent Colyer (1825–1888), a member of the Connecticut House of Representatives from Darien. Colyer was also an artist who had a studio in the Association Building when Porter lived there. Surely Porter knew the aspects of Colyer's history that had prompted the Lincoln Club to invite him. Colyer had abandoned his New York studio after the attack on Fort Sumter in April 1861 in order to minister to the troops, beginning with thousands of religious tracts and hymnals that he handed out. After Bull Run, he garnered supplies from the YMCA and went to Washington to help the wounded and dying who crowded the hospitals in and near the capital. He established a hospital for black troops and a school for children of former slaves. In 1863 he raised a regiment of Negro troops and was named its colonel. Colyer also helped blacks who had been displaced and mistreated during the war and became involved in legal efforts to get financial redress for people affected by the Draft Riots of 1863.

Porter also would have known about Colyer's art career, which may not have been familiar to others at the Lincoln Club. In 1869 Colyer had been appointed a special U.S. Indian Commissioner and traveled through the Southwest and Alaska visiting Indian tribes. In his official capacity, he established the reservation system that is still in use in the Southwest and promoted the establishment of schools for Indians. At the same time he was constantly making sketches and watercolors of the people and land-scapes, which he later translated into paintings in New York. He main-tained his Association studio until 1876 but had a home on Contentment Island off the coast of Darien, where his friend the famous landscape painter John Frederick Kensett had died in 1872 after a vain attempt to save Colyer's wife from drowning.

Whether or not Porter was at the next Lincoln Club banquet, in 1880, he would have heard about it. William, his eldest brother, gave the prin-cipal address, an eloquent plea for the importance of education that the *Meriden Daily Republican* thought "very creditable to him and his race." The newspaper described the speech in considerable detail: William's belief that the colored race had a special appreciation for the blessings of liberty; that education is vital if the race is to feel equal and be seen as equal; and that great obstacles against prejudice had already been over-come, despite numerous reasons to feel discouraged.

> Mr. Porter dwelt for some time on the opportunities every col-ored man, woman, and child in the land had to make themselves worthy of the blessings bestowed upon them by emancipation. This must be done by self-reliance, and giving our children as they grow up, the advantages of education, a priceless boon that insures the equality of man.[77]

"Mr. Porter," the newspaper added patronizingly, "was loudly cheered and he well deserved to be, for he delivered an interesting address, filled with beneficial thoughts, presented in an easy fluent way." As was often the case, the manner in which a colored person presented himself was more important to many whites than the message. For the Porter family and the other Lincoln Club members in that room, however, few messages could have been more meaningful.

It is safe to assume that Porter often saw his family in Rockville and Meriden while he lived in Hartford, and clearly he mingled with colored people in the city as well. He once lived across the street from Holdridge Primus, a man who managed to combine his "proper place" as a factotum with a successful business career. Both the mother and the aunt of the distinguished African-American author Ann Petry received Porter paintings in Hartford as wedding presents. Perhaps such friends were familiar with Porter drawings like the eight discovered a few years ago. In addition to the Pre-Raphaelite *Dead Cockerel* there are three surprisingly modern-looking images of white men, including *Under the E. R. Bridge*, 1877 (catalogue 11) and a pencil and ink wash portraying an art instructor, possibly Lemuel Wilmarth (catalogue 12). The other four images are of colored persons.

A soft-pencil drawing dated November 19, 1880, is an eloquent portrayal, in an academic style, of a standing male nude (catalogue 13). A charcoal and pencil drawing, dated 1879, shows a Civil War soldier warming his hands at a fire (catalogue 14, see page 15). A watercolor depicts a young man holding a book open to a map, possibly of Africa, because an inscription reads "Porter's 'Hesitation' in "Africa" (Va.)"— followed by "Don't see the point" (catalogue 15). The words are puzzling, since the big push for colonization to Africa had passed. The punctuation is equally mystifying.

The remaining image is *The Banjo Player*, dated 1880 (catalogue 16), a realistic, beautifully rendered pencil drawing of a seated man playing the musical instrument that African slaves introduced to America. It brings to mind Henry Ossawa Tanner's *The Banjo Lesson* (1893; Hampton University Museum, Hampton, Virginia). Art historian Judith Wilson regards Tanner's image of an old man instructing a boy as a psychic breakthrough anticipating the African-American community's "twin emphases in the twentieth century on racial pride and vernacular culture." She notes that only four years after *The Banjo Lesson*, W. E. B. DuBois began calling for his race to follow Negro ideals. Wilson sees Tanner's image as the first rejection of the longtime program of the A.M.E. church, which advocated the imitation of Anglo-Saxon culture.[78] Porter drew his banjo player thirteen years before Tanner painted his iconic work. That span of years saw countless caricatures of banjo players by white men who deprived their African-American subjects of the humanity, dignity, and self-esteem that Porter and Tanner saw so clearly and so tellingly recorded.

The *Hartford Daily Courant* for March 19, 1881, was the first to report Porter's intention to study abroad. He would sell at auction all the paintings in his studio: "Gems of landscape, fruit, flower, fish and figure pieces, nearly a hundred in number, all of which have been painted with the strictest regard to excellence of finish and truthfulness of composition." The artist planned to leave Hartford in May for two years, "during which time he will devote himself to study."[79] The auction was soon set for the evenings of April 28 and 29. All three Hartford papers lauded the

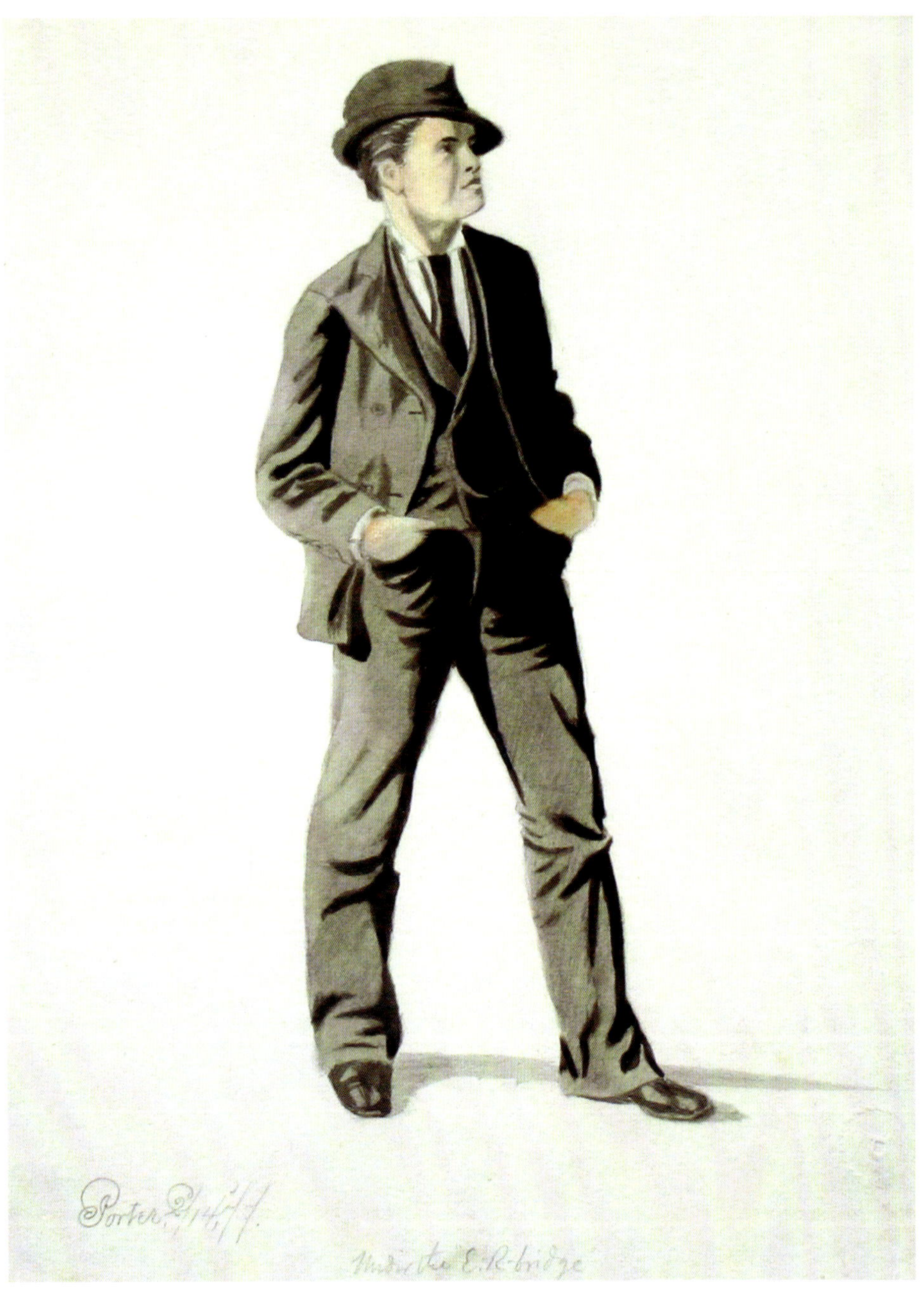

Catalogue 11
Under the E. R. Bridge, 1877
Watercolor on paper
9½" x 6½" (sight)
Signed and dated "Porter 2/14/77" lower left
Inscribed "Under the E. R. Bridge" lower center
Collection of Charlynn and Warren Goins

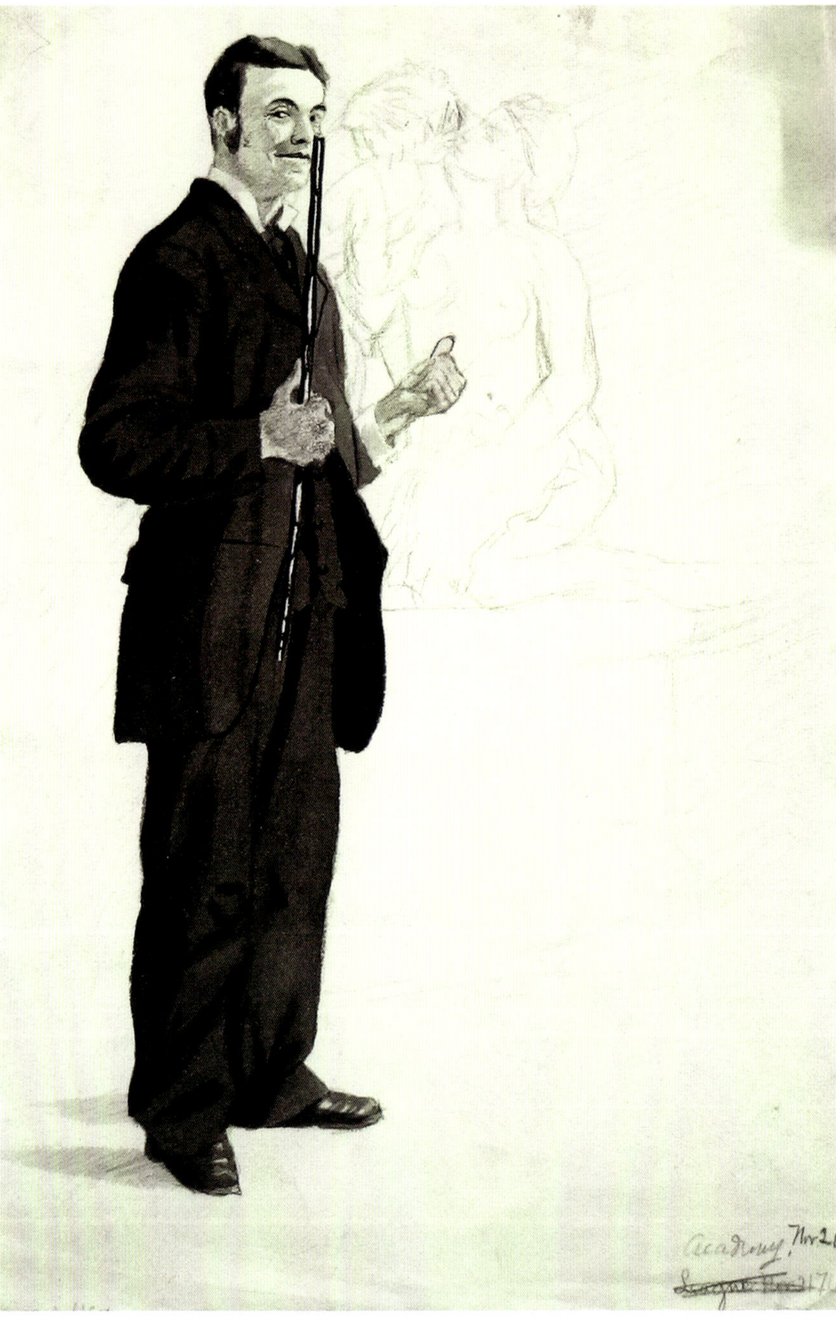

Catalogue 12
Art Instructor
Pencil/ink wash on paper
10" x 6" (sight)
Inscribed lower right "Academy Nov. 21, 76"
Collection of Charlynn and Warren Goins

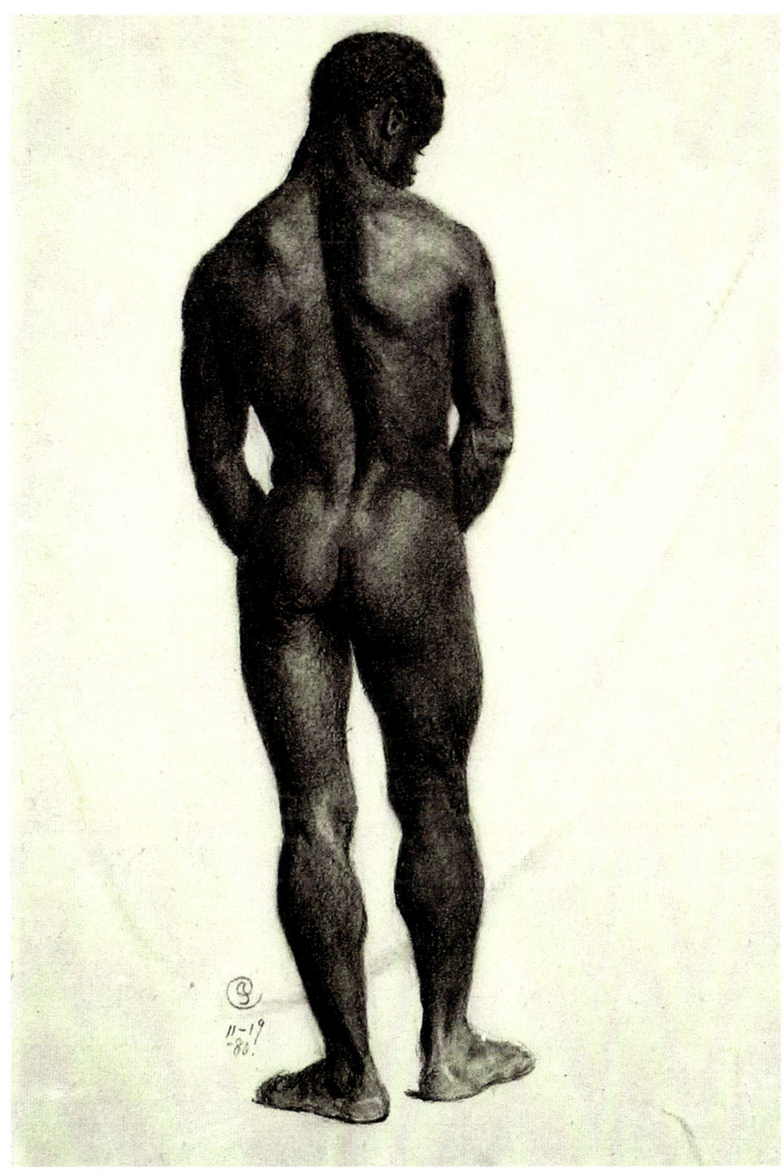

Catalogue 13
Standing Male Nude, 1880
Soft pencil on paper
8½" x 5½" (sight)
Monogrammed and dated
"11-19-1880" lower right
Collection of Charlynn and Warren Goins

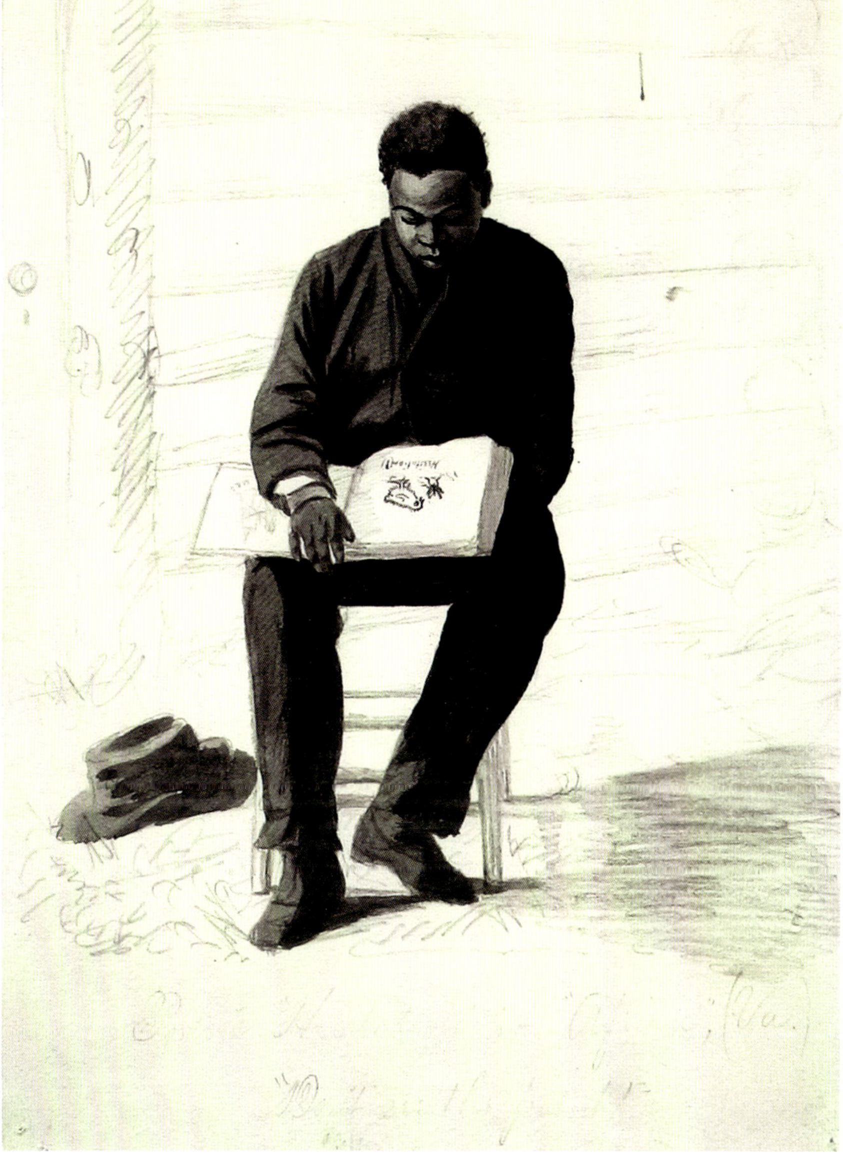

Catalogue 15
Boy and Book
Watercolor on paper
8¼" x 5½" (sight)
Inscribed lower center "Porter's 'Hesitation' in "Africa" (Va.)"
Collection of Charlynn and Warren Goins

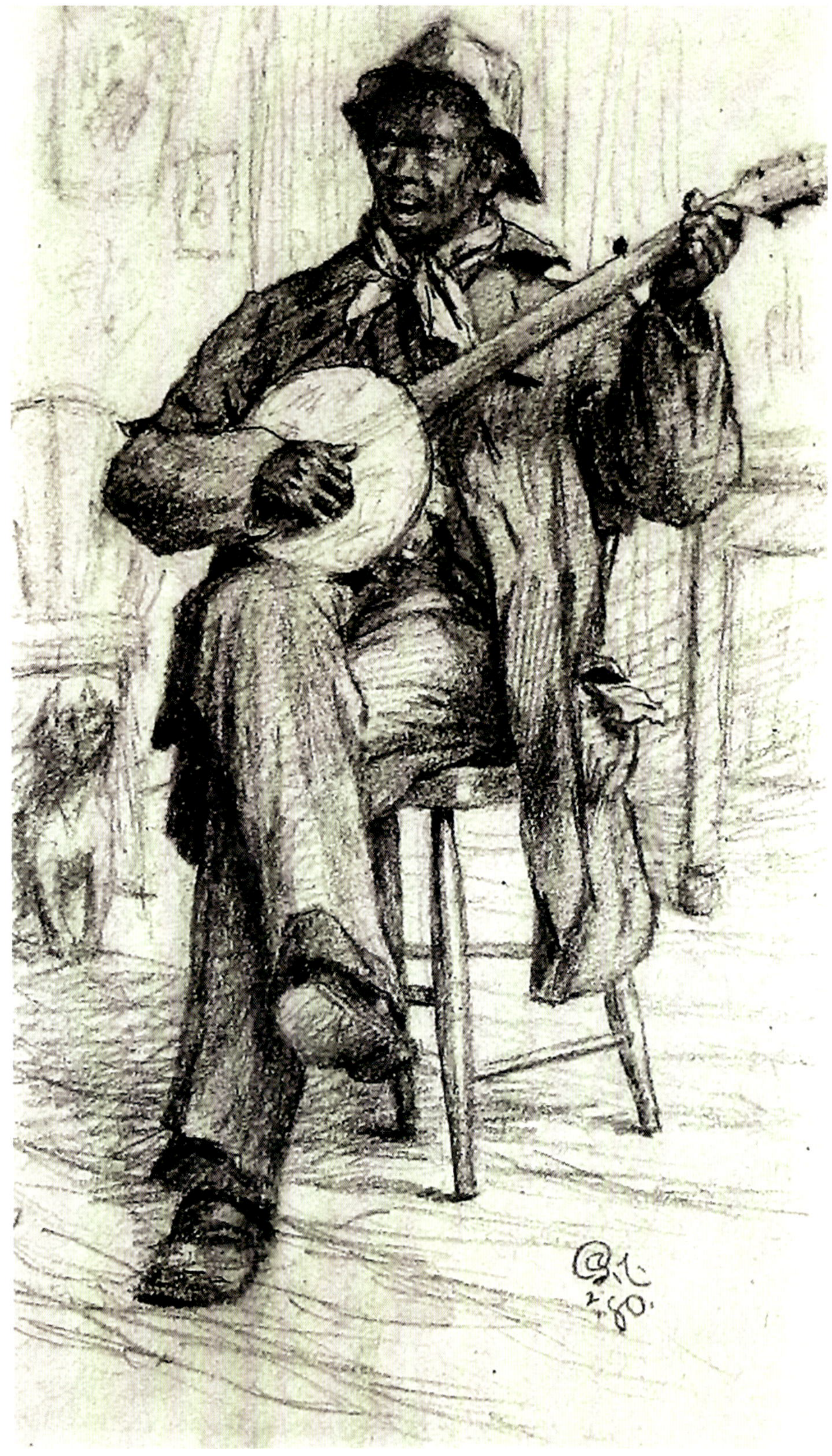

Catalogue 16
Banjo Player, 1880
Pencil on paper
7½" x 4" (sight)
Monogrammed and dated lower right
Collection of Charlynn and Warren Goins

minute accuracy of the work Porter had been doing for the past two or three years and regarded the auction as an opportunity to obtain some unusually fine paintings. "Many people daily visit Porter's studio in the Cheney Building to see his paintings," the *Hartford Daily Times* reported on April 26.[80]

Half the paintings sold on the first night of the sale, at prices ranging from $5 to $105 for a total of $1,062. These prices were low, but art generally sold below value at local auctions. That was the draw for buyers, while artists welcomed the ready money and the clearance of works on hand. Whether a second night did better or worse was unpredictable. Porter's sale totaled about $1,800. Framing costs and the services of the auctioneer reduced his share to $1,350, and after settling other bills Porter had about $1,000 for his two-year trip. He must have hoped to sell work while he was abroad and perhaps send paintings home to Hartford's art stores, as Hartford native Dwight Tryon (1849–1925) had done.

Porter did not go to Europe in May, as originally announced, but to Rockville for the summer. A notice in the *Hartford Daily Courant* for August 1, however, mentioned an excursion: "D. W. Tryon, the artist, has been sketching in the neighborhood of Rocky Hill for a couple of weeks, and C. E. Porter has been working with him."[81] Tryon, who grew up in East Hartford, had just returned from four years in Paris with the triumph of three pictures in the most recent spring Salon. His primary teacher had been Jacquesson de la Chevreuse (1839–1903), and he had also spent time in the village of Barbizon with Charles-François Daubigny (1817–1878) shortly before the esteemed artist's death. Porter had much to discuss with Tryon.

In early November the Hartford papers reported that Porter had left for Europe. The announcement was only a bit premature. Porter sailed out of New York on the steamship *Bothia* on November 19, bound for Liverpool. After a quick tour of London, he moved on to Paris. He already knew that an artist who had been his stalwart supporter in Hartford would not be there on his return: Henry Bryant lay dying when Porter began the journey that would transform his art.

France, 1882–83

Porter traveled to Paris in November 1881 with letters of introduction from leading citizens of Hartford, including Samuel L. Clemens (1835–1910), better known as Mark Twain. Porter may have approached the author, whom he could have met when Clemens was an auctioneer at a benefit event the artist participated in. Olivia Clemens could have suggested that her husband ease Porter's entry into a foreign country with such a letter, since she had been on the board of Hartford's Society of Decorative Arts, a group that had a particularly friendly relationship with Porter. Or perhaps it was Clemens' butler, George Griffin, a key figure in Hartford's black community, who secured the letter for his artist friend. In the letter Clemens asks Karl Gerhardt, a young man studying sculpture in Paris, to commend Porter to people the author had previously arranged for Gerhardt to meet. Porter was soon settled on the Left Bank, just down the street from Gerhardt, who kept an eye on him for a while.

"Mr. Porter reports good progress in his drawing," Gerhardt wrote Clemens as early as January 1, 1882.[82] Two months later Gerhardt noticed progress himself, adding that Porter put so much feeling into some of his heads that he ought to try portraits.[83] (He seemed unaware that a Porter portrait had been admired several years earlier in Hartford.) In April, Gerhardt wrote that he had told Porter, as instructed, that Clemens had been pleased to receive a letter from Porter but was too busy to answer it.[84] Then, in May 1883, after more than a year with no mention of Porter in the extant correspondence, Clemens had a question for Gerhardt. He had received a second letter from Porter, asking for help in getting orders for paintings, as his money was nearly gone. The author was uncertain how to respond, because, as he explained,

> A long time ago, Josephine [Gerhardt's wife] intimated in one of her letters that Porter had gone to the dogs or was on his way there. She gave no details, brought forward no facts. I meant to write her, then and there, and say that whenever one flings a flask of dynamite under a person's character, he should always go into the details of the matter, and state exactly why he felt justified in doing that thing. . . . Tell me all you have heard against him, keep back nothing whatever.

Clemens said he would consider helping Porter if he were worthy. His words reveal a patronizing attitude typical of the day:

> At the same time I must remember, and you must also remember, that on every sin which a colored man commits, the just white man must make a considerable discount, because of the colored man's antecedents. The heirs of slavery cannot with any sort of justice be required to be as clear and straight and upright as the heirs of ancient freedom. And besides, whenever a colored man commits an unright action, upon his head is the guilt of only about one tenth of it, and upon your heads and mine and the rest of the white race lies fairly and justly the other nine tenths of the guilt. So, when you have told me all there is to tell about Porter, I shall doubtless judge his case charitably enough.[85]

Unfortunately, we do not know what Gerhardt reported and what Clemens decided. Porter remained in France for another six or seven months, but he probably petitioned others in Hartford besides Clemens, so we cannot presume that the author came to his aid. What made Mrs. Gerhardt think Porter had gone wrong—had strayed from his strict Methodist upbringing and his determination to improve his art—probably will also never be known. An investigation of the Gerhardts by Clemens researcher Barbara Schmidt, however, suggests that the couple's relations with the author might have been at least partly self-serving. The two may not have wanted to commend Porter to anyone, least of all Mark Twain.

Schmidt's account of the Clemens-Gerhardt relationship begins February 21, 1881, when a young woman arrived at Clemens' home in Hartford and pleaded with the author to look at a sculpture by her husband, a draftsman and chief mechanic at the Pratt and Whitney Machine Tool Company.[86] Touched by her earnestness and air of sincerity, Clemens went to her house, where, to his astonishment, Mrs. Karl Gerhardt showed him a realistic lifesize statue of herself that was nude to the waist. Clemens wrote his friend and fellow author William Dean Howells about the experience:

> Well, sir, it was perfectly charming, this girl's innocence & purity —exhibiting her naked self, as it was, to a stranger & alone, & never once dreaming there was the slightest indelicacy about the matter. And there wasn't; but it will be many a long day before I run across another woman who can do the like & show no trace of self-consciousness.[87]

Whether Harriet Josephine ("Hattie") Gerhardt was truly ingenuous or supremely savvy is a question, but she got the result she must have been dreaming of: Clemens and his wife, Olivia, decided to finance Karl Gerhardt's education in Paris.

It was not an impulsive move. Clemens asked painter James Wells Champney (1843–1903), chief instructor at Hartford's Society of Decorative Arts, and John Quincy Adams Ward (1830–1910), the prominent sculptor of portrait busts and monuments, to assess Gerhardt's work. He decided on an initial sum of three thousand dollars that was meant to cover five years of living expenses while Karl studied at the École des Beaux-Arts, the prestigious national art school. Backed by recommendations from Clemens' important artist friends, the sculptors Ward, Augustus St. Gaudens

(1848–1907), and Olin Warner (1844–1896), Gerhardt arrived in Paris in March 1881, passed the École's entrance examinations on the first try, and was studying at the school by August. He soon asked for and got additional money from Clemens to pay for live models and private instructors, and the author even agreed to fund drawing lessons for Hattie, or Mrs. Joe, as he fondly called her. In 1883, after only two years abroad, the Gerhardts were running out of money, but when Howells looked in on their living quarters, shared with infant Olivia and her wet nurse, he reported that "virtuous poverty spoke from every appointment," and Clemens offered further funding.[88] Clemens also knew by then that a work by Gerhardt had been accepted at the 1883 Paris Salon: a small medallion portraying Mark Twain.

Letters flew back and forth between Clemens and the Gerhardts. Many were from Mrs. Joe, who seemed desperate to stay in the author's good graces: "I wonder & wish so very often if you do love us just a little bit— even aside from the talent and do you know I do not like to have you fond of anyone else but me and truly, I often get quite jealous thinking that perhaps you do a great deal."[89]

If Mrs. Gerhardt was worried that Porter might draw some of the author's attention (and money) away from her husband, she need not have been. Clemens seemed bewitched by the couple and told the Gerhardts in August 1883 that they were "the only investment we have made in the three years that has really paid."[90] In 1885 Clemens may have used his influence to gain Gerhardt a commission for a Nathan Hale statue for the new Connecticut Capitol in Hartford. The first edition of *The Adventures of Huckleberry Finn*, published that year, had as its frontispiece a photograph of a bust of Mark Twain sculpted by Gerhardt. Several major commissions soon followed.

Despite growing disillusionment ("The principal feature of Gerhardt's character is thanklessness," Clemens wrote in his notebook in April 1885), he persuaded the family of the dying Ulysses Grant to have the young sculptor cast the only death mask.[91] When Gerhardt refused to give the mask to the Grants on the grounds that it was his personal property, Clemens was appalled but yielded to pressure from both factions to intervene when a lawsuit seemed imminent. In the end he forgave Gerhardt all personal debts owed to himself—about $17,000, or more than $300,000 today—in order to get the stubborn sculptor to relinquish the mask, an important piece in itself but invaluable to all sculptors hoping one day to make a bust or statue of the general. Clemens may never have known that Gerhardt had surreptitiously made a second mask.

Schmidt's research skills have enabled her to uncover the Clemens-Gerhardt story, but Porter knew so little of the relationship between the author and the Gerhardts that in his April 4, 1883, letter to Clemens, in which he sought help ("It is certainly very embarrassing for me even to write you such a letter as this"), he added that "Mr. and Mrs. Gerhardt are doing nicely. By the way they have a little one so he tells me."[92]

In recent years a rumor has circulated that Clemens financed—in total or in large part—Porter's stay in France. Surely that assumption is misguided.

Contact between Clemens and Porter was formal and infrequent. Porter diffidently called the Clemenses his friends in his first letter to them, in 1882 ("for so I presume to call you for the interest you have shown in my welfare is sufficient evidence that you are my friends"), but by his own account the letter was never answered.[93] It is not known whether his only other letter to the author, written more than a year later, brought him the modest help he asked for: "Something in the nature of an order would be just the thing."[94] In this letter Porter told the author how he stood financially. The Hartford auction had left him with just under a thousand dollars, not enough for him to stay abroad for at least two years, as he had hoped. If Clemens had arranged to support Porter financially, he would have known what Porter's assets were. His financial dealings with Karl Gerhardt were carefully considered and documented; patron and protégé were regularly in touch. Even if Clemens occasionally sent Porter money or got him an order for a painting, evidence is likely to have survived. The Clemenses did own a Porter peony painting (location unknown), which may be seen in a photograph of their dining room in the 1890s (figure 07). The painting is one of Porter's larger works and appears to date from the Paris years or soon afterward. Perhaps Clemens got a good report from Gerhardt and purchased it. It would appear, nevertheless, that any financial help Porter received from the author was minimal at best.

Little is known about Porter's years in France. His few extant letters are vague. "I'm getting along nicely with my study," he wrote his parents

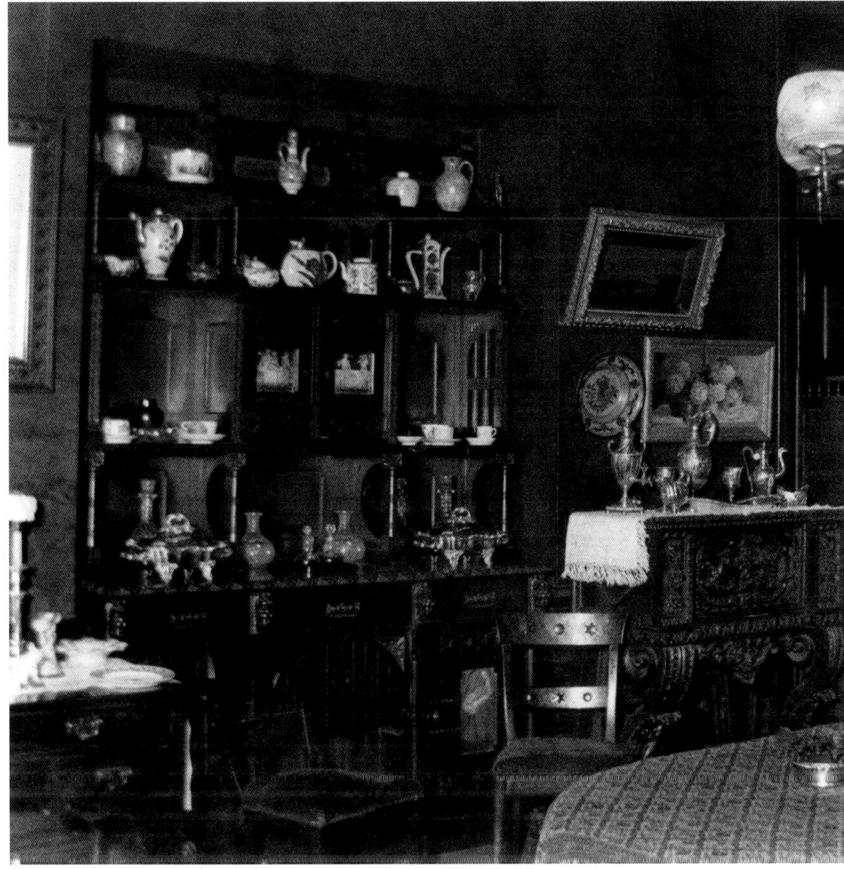

Figure 07–**Mark Twain House Dining Room, 1890s**
Photo courtesy of the Mark Twain House & Museum

on December 11, 1881, just days after arriving in the French capital.[95] On February 29, 1882, he wrote to Clemens that he was "in one of the best schools."[96] In his only other letter to the author, dated April 4, 1883, he wrote he had "spent seven months in the country" and "am at present in one of the popular schools."[97]

In December 1884, nearly a year after Porter returned to Connecticut, the *Hartford Daily Courant* offered additional information, much of it incorrect, about his training in France:

Entering at once the well-known Julien [*sic*] school, he enjoyed the immediate instruction and criticism of Gerome, Boulanger, Robert Fleury, Lefebvre, and Bouguereau. Then the high recommendation of Lefebvre admitted Mr. Porter to the École des Beaux-Arts, in which the most severe technical training is insisted upon. The summer months, meantime, were devoted to equally hard work in the study of landscape painting with some of the greatest masters of that branch of the art.[98]

Porter never attended the École des Beaux-Arts. In December 1881, just after arriving in Paris, he registered to take courses at another national school, the École Nationale Supérieure des Arts Décoratifs, popularly known as the Petit École. The artists that the *Hartford Courant* names as Porter's teachers were not affiliated with the Petit École. Though less prestigious than the École des Beaux-Arts, the Petit École was one of the best art schools in the city. Founded in the eighteenth century to train workers in drawing and mathematics, it had developed by the nineteenth century into the place to learn ornamental design. Its courses in anatomy, perspective, and drawing were meant to train sculptors but were equally valuable to easel painters who wanted to strengthen their skills before attempting the *concours des places*, held in March and October, required for entry to the École des Beaux-Arts. Many young men studied at the Petit École for months before attempting the difficult examination. A Porter watercolor of pitchers and an Arabian teapot, inscribed as done in Paris, might have been an assignment at the design school (catalogue 17).

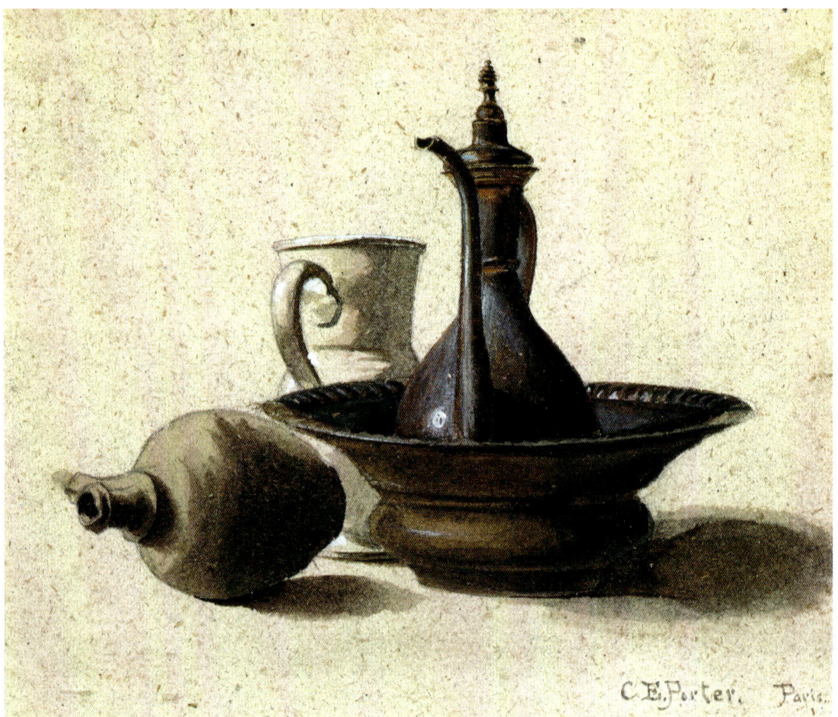

Catalogue 17
Still Life of Various Pitchers, 1882/83
Watercolor on paper
7½" x 8½"
Signed and inscribed "Paris" lower right
Courtesy of Juan Rodriguez

It is unlikely that Porter studied with Jean-Léon Gérôme (1824–1904), a prominent realist painter and sculptor who favored Orientalist subjects. Gérôme presided over an atelier at the École des Beaux-Arts, where men who were not yet admitted to the school sometimes worked, but Porter is not listed in the records. He may have been particularly interested in Gérôme, who had taught Lemuel Wilmarth, his professor at the National Academy of Design, and he certainly would have had numerous opportunities in Paris to study Gérôme's meticulous imagery, but unless he managed to get private lessons, Porter did not receive Gérôme's instruction or criticism.

Porter may, however, have had contact with two and possibly all four of the other artists listed by the newspaper, as they were instructors at the Académie Julian. When Porter wrote Clemens in April 1883 that he was in one of the popular schools, he could have been referring to the Académie Julian. Even though he had spent seven months in the countryside, as he told Clemens, and may have summered there again, Porter could have worked at one or more of the Académie's ateliers during his two-year stay in France. Students often came and went at the Académie, which had no entrance examinations and charged only a modest fee. The *Courant* article may have been mistaken in saying that Porter entered the Académie Julian immediately after his arrival in Paris. Porter may have decided against the Petit École after registering, however, or perhaps he attended classes at both schools concurrently. The specific reference to Jules Lefebvre suggests that Porter did study at the Académie Julian.

In the 1880s William Bouguereau (1825–1905) and Tony Robert-Fleury (1837–1912) were associated with one of the Académie's men's ateliers, and Jules Lefebvre (1836–1911) and Gustave Boulanger (1824–1888) with another. Each pair took turns, month-by-month, critiquing students' work. The heads that Porter was drawing, which Gerhardt mentioned to Clemens, are more likely to have been done at a school like the Académie

Julian than at the Petit École. An attraction of the Académie was that its training, based on drawing from casts and live models, was like that at the École des Beaux-Arts. Moreover, Rodolphe Julian and the well-known artists he hired as professors prepared interested students for the École's *concours* and helped the most talented exhibit at the annual spring Salon, a mark of honor that, for Americans especially, went a long way toward professional success back home.

Porter must have been keenly disappointed that he never had a work in the Salon. "I am very anxious to get something in the Salon before my return," he wrote Clemens on April 4, 1883. At his "popular" school, he added, "I am not least by any means."[99] Perhaps Porter had tried and failed for Salon acceptance in 1882 and 1883. If so, he knew firsthand the heartache and financial stress involved. In any case, he would have seen that for months before the spring Salons, students worked on their entries in seclusion, away from the teaching ateliers, so as to keep their ideas and treatments safe from imitators. As a still life and landscape painter, Porter would not have had to hire models, but the Salon competition had entry fees, and appropriate painting materials and frames were expensive. "I see my money fast going," he told Clemens in the April letter. He carried on until the end of the year, but then his money must have run out.

Had he been able to stay abroad a few months longer, the spring Salon of 1884 would have been his goal. With strong backing from Lefebvre, who was usually a jurist, his chances would have been good. The five thousand or so works in every Salon of the 1880s—only 15 percent of

them by foreigners—were judged by prominent artists. Salon jurists were supposed to be objective, but it was generally understood that they did not hesitate to exert pressure in favor of their students. "When we sent to the Salon," recalled one Académie Julian student, "we looked upon it as our right, and if our works were neglected or badly treated, all we had to do was to notify our special professor and the difficulty was rectified."[100]

For Porter, a Salon entry might have been *The Old French Moat*, which, according to the *Hartford Daily Courant*, "the famous Lefebvre praised for its originality, and on which he based the judgment that Mr. Porter's success in landscape was already assured."[101] Porter was, however, back in Connecticut well before the day in March that was reserved for submissions, and *The Old French Moat* was in his baggage when he sailed home.

Porter wrote a letter—dated only September 23— to Charles J. Hoadley, Connecticut's State Librarian, from Fleury, a village about thirty-five miles south of Paris, near the forest of Fontainebleau. Hoadley owned a Porter painting and was probably one of the people who gave Porter a letter of introduction to take abroad. "Knowing you took so much interest in me when I was in Hartford," Porter began, "I write you this so you may lend your influence and by so doing perhaps get me an order or two." His money was nearly gone, he explained, and he wanted very much to stay another six months. "I have written to a number of my friends in H. and have at present a splendid order for a flower picture from two to three hundred dollars—but I am unable to carry it out without money and of course do not wish to ask money in advance."[102]

Porter's stay in Fleury may have come about because of where he lived in Paris. His first address was 13, rue des Beaux-Arts in Saint-Germain-des-Prés on the Left Bank. In the sixteenth century, the oldest abbey in Paris had occupied this site; in the eighteenth century an elegant trysting place for illicit lovers was built over the old cellars. A century later the Pavilion d'Amour was reformed into a hotel, and by the 1880s its scandalous history was largely forgotten. In 1900 the hotel made titillating news again when Oscar Wilde died in room 16. (Today the six-story building, with its original oval atrium in tact, is a luxury hotel.)

Porter was not the only artist to find this address affordable in the 1880s, nor the only American. The Boston artist H. Winthrop Peirce (1850–1935) lived there in 1882, and Peirce's friend from the Boston Museum School Charles Harold Davis (1856–1933) had lived there as well. Arriving in France together in fall 1880, the two enrolled at the Académie Julian—Davis with Lefebvre and Boulanger and Peirce with Bouguereau and Robert-Fleury. Davis soon succumbed to the charms of the forest of Fontainebleau; his painting of a scene there was accepted in the 1881 Salon. Impatient, moreover, with the Académie Julian's regimen, which was just like the training he had received in America, he moved that summer to Fleury, close to the famous village of Barbizon, where in the 1830s a group of young painters had abandoned academic practices and subjects and created innovative pastoral tone poems. Davis had been inspired in Boston by the work of the historic Barbizon artists Jean-François Millet, Theodore Rousseau, Jean-Baptiste-Camille Corot,

and Charles-François Daubigny. He would remain in or near Fleury for the next ten years, and Bostonian artists in Paris often joined him, especially in the summer. Peirce was undoubtedly one of them.

Peirce had a Fontainebleau picture accepted in the 1882 Salon, and Davis exhibited scenes of the plains around Fleury in that and the next several Salons. Porter probably made his way to Fleury because of Davis and Peirce. A Rockville resident once claimed that Porter had been friendly with Davis in France. Thomas Colville, the leading expert on Davis, remembers a contemporary source saying that Davis considered Porter a good painter.[103] How long Porter remained in Fleury is a question. His September letter to Hoadley implies an imminent return to Paris, for a reply was to be directed to 13, rue des Beaux-Arts. How long he lived at this address is also problematic, for his April 1883 letter to Clemens was sent from the Hôtel Brittanique, on the Right Bank, where Porter expected to be long enough to receive a letter from Hartford. If he had moved permanently from the rue des Beaux-Arts by April 1883, the letter to Hoadley must date from September 1882—and, if so, Porter was already short of money after only nine months abroad. If, however, Porter was only briefly at the Hôtel Brittanique and moved back to 13, rue des Beaux-Arts in fall 1883, the Hoadley letter dates from that year.

Perhaps it was because Porter was out of Paris for months at a time that Mrs. Gerhardt thought he had become derelict. Porter, however, believed that some of his best work was done in the French countryside. Most likely he was at Fleury. As an aspiring landscapist with little money,

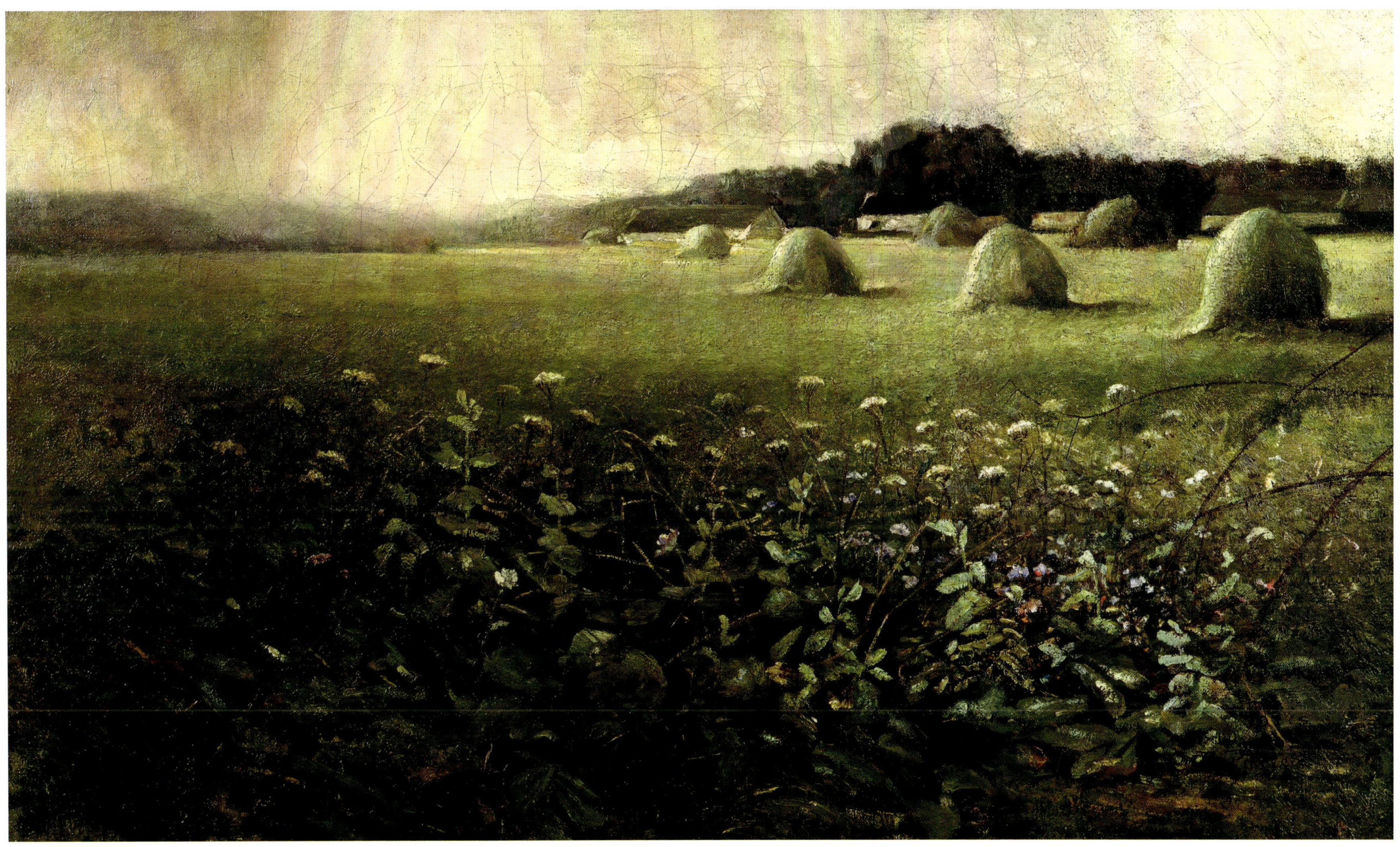

Catalogue 18
Landscape with Grain Stacks, 1882/83
Oil on canvas
22" x 34"
Signed and inscribed "Paris" lower left
Mr. and Mrs. Wilbert R. Hasbrouck

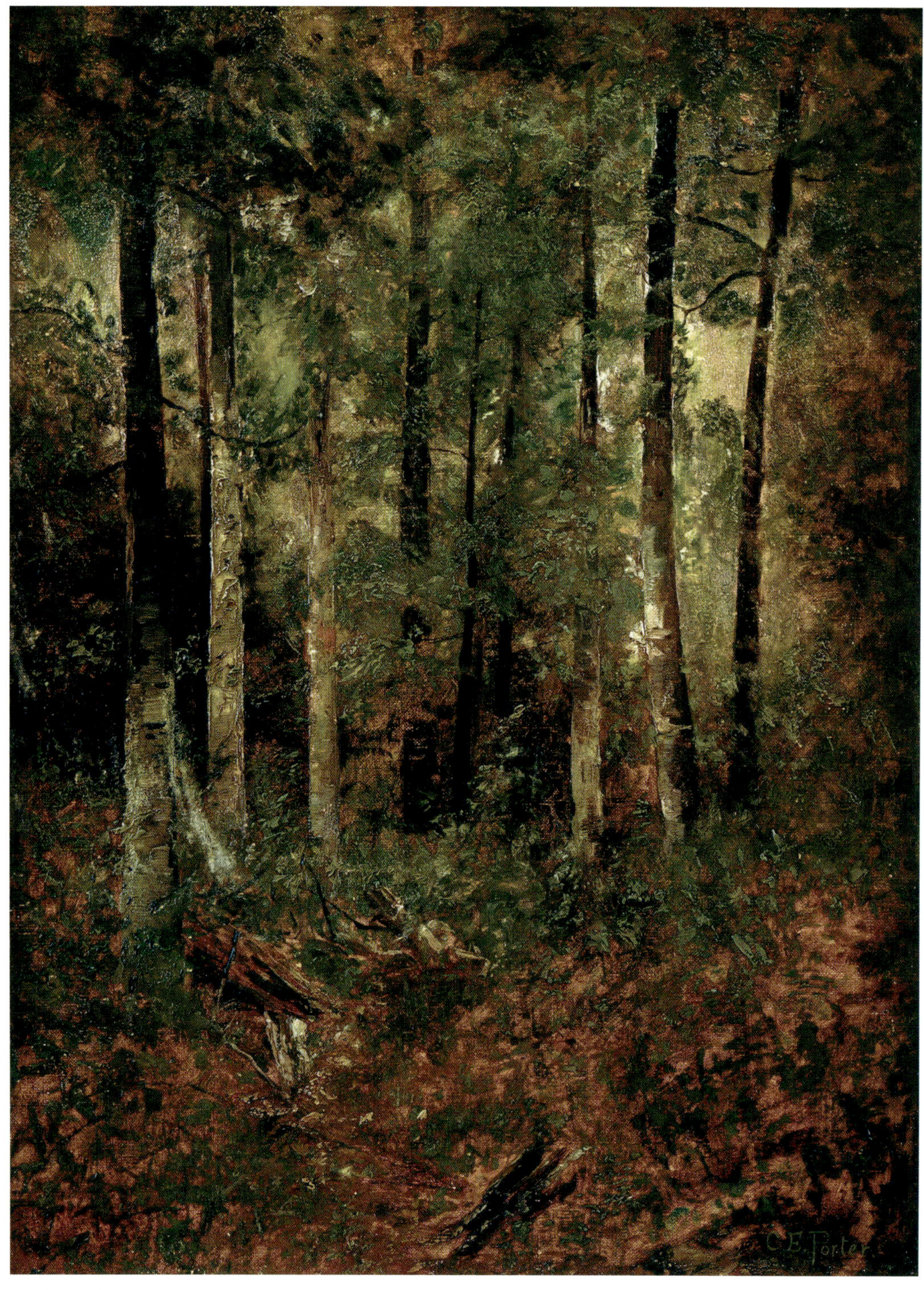

Catalogue 19
Forest Scene, c. 1885
Oil on board/canvas
22" x 16"
Signed lower right
Courtesy of Khephra Burns and Susan L. Taylor

Porter would have found it prudent to settle in one place. Evidence that his landscape painting flourished in France is offered in *Landscape with Grain Stacks*, inscribed "Paris," (catalogue 18), which caught the eye of the *Hartford Daily Times* in May 1884:

> Over a tangle of tall weeds in the close foreground a large meadow extends far back, with fresh hay cocks on one side. Woods beyond and just a strip of sky above. The atmosphere above and in front of the meadow is charming, the green more French than American.[104]

Landscape with Grain Stacks shows Porter's development as a landscapist. His early known landscapes—undoubtedly studio productions—are painted in intense dark colors, with little detail, and no sense of natural light. In France, Porter painted outdoors, though like many plein-airists he added finishing touches in the studio. He now embraced his era's preference for a prominent, detailed foreground. Depth and distance are established partly by traditional perspective but also by an Impressionist high horizon that pulls the eye to the top of the picture. The light is naturalistic, both at ground level and in the sky, where some clouds spell rain. The palette and rural subject matter relate to Barbizon painting, which progressive American artists in Porter's day embraced for its tonal harmonies and evocative power.

Trees and forests were an early Porter subject, fueled perhaps by his visit to the Adirondack Mountains in 1880. His early trees are dark and dense, but *Forest Scene* (catalogue 19) exhibits the close observation of natural light that Porter appears to have developed in France. *Forest Scene* recalls the American Tonalist painting of such artists as Henry Ward Ranger (1858–1916). Earth tones are enhanced by glowing backlights and highlights, which also create a sense of texture.

Haystacks (catalogue 20) shows Porter delving into Impressionism— in France or, perhaps, soon afterward. The disregard for traditional landscape composition in *Haystacks*, the lack of detail, and the slashing strokes and daubs of paint must have dismayed admirers of Porter's meticulous

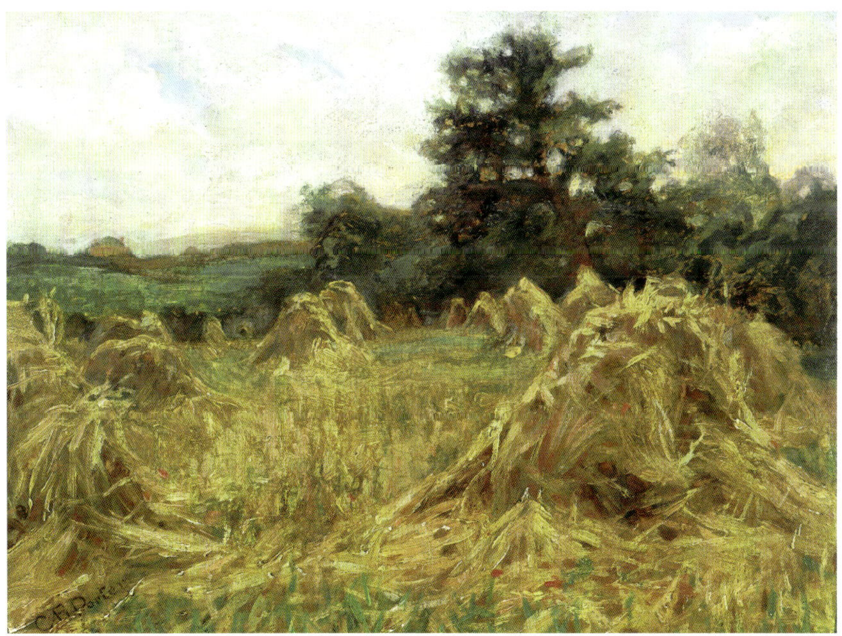

Catalogue 20
Haystacks, c. 1885
Oil on canvas
16" x 20"
Signed lower left
The Harmon and Harriet Kelley Foundation for the Arts

pre-Paris work. Hartford would not see such grain stacks again until 1893, when the Englishman Dawson Dawson-Watson came from Giverny to be the chief instructor at the Art Society and caused a sensation with his Impressionist sensibility.

Although intent on improving his landscapes, Porter continued to paint still lifes. "My fruit and flowers are greatly admired by the French," he wrote Clemens in April 1883.[105] Among French flower painters of the period, Henri Fantin-Latour (1836–1904) was perhaps the most highly regarded. Porter probably had no direct contact with Fantin-Latour, who, by the 1880s, was reclusive and no longer teaching, but he could have seen the Frenchman's work in the Salon and elsewhere in Paris. He may have known that Fantin-Latour's flower paintings were popular in England.[106] Perhaps he checked into the Hôtel Brittanique in the hope of selling his own flower paintings to the English clientele that the hotel had been catering to since 1861.

When Porter lived at 13, rue des Beaux-Arts, Fantin-Latour was at number 8, in a hard-to-miss barn-like structure painted red, white, and blue. At that time, Fantin-Latour was slamming his door in the face of most callers. At least once, however, he allowed the son of a friend to enter and watch him paint. One cannot help but fancy that one day Porter gathered the courage to knock, surprised the Frenchman by saying that he, too, painted flowers and fruit, and was invited in. Persons of color were not often seen in France at the time, so even a peevish master might have been intrigued. Such a meeting would have been interesting for them both.

Porter surely studied the work of Fantin-Latour, whose imagery diverged, as American artist May Alcott (1814–1879) noted, from the "elaborately arranged eastern stuffs, Venetian glass, brass, armor, on an immense scale" that was characteristic of French still life at the time.[107] Although Fantin-Latour often depicted flowers and fruit together, he also painted one or the other, as Porter generally did. Fantin-Latour, however, liked to mix flowers, with their blossoms at the peak of fullness or beyond, while Porter tended to paint one variety at a time, showing a range from bud to bloom and often views of sides and bottoms, as in *Chrysanthemums* (catalogue 21). But both artists favored informal bouquets in common containers, set on a plain ledge or table against an indeterminate background, and both were realist painters.

Porter appears to have learned important truths from the florals of Fantin-Latour: that realism could be achieved with looser brushwork and less detail than he had employed; that flowers look more natural when their colors are lighter and softer than those he had been using; that lighter backgrounds can often enhance flowers better than dark ones (and may help unify a picture); and that light can do more in a painting than illuminate flowers and fruit. Porter could have seen similar characteristics in the avant-garde still lifes of Edouard Manet (1832–1883) and of the Impressionists.

A painting of roses inscribed "Paris" (catalogue 22, see page 64) differs dramatically from Porter's earlier florals, which are characterized by carefully delineated blooms silhouetted against a dark background. The

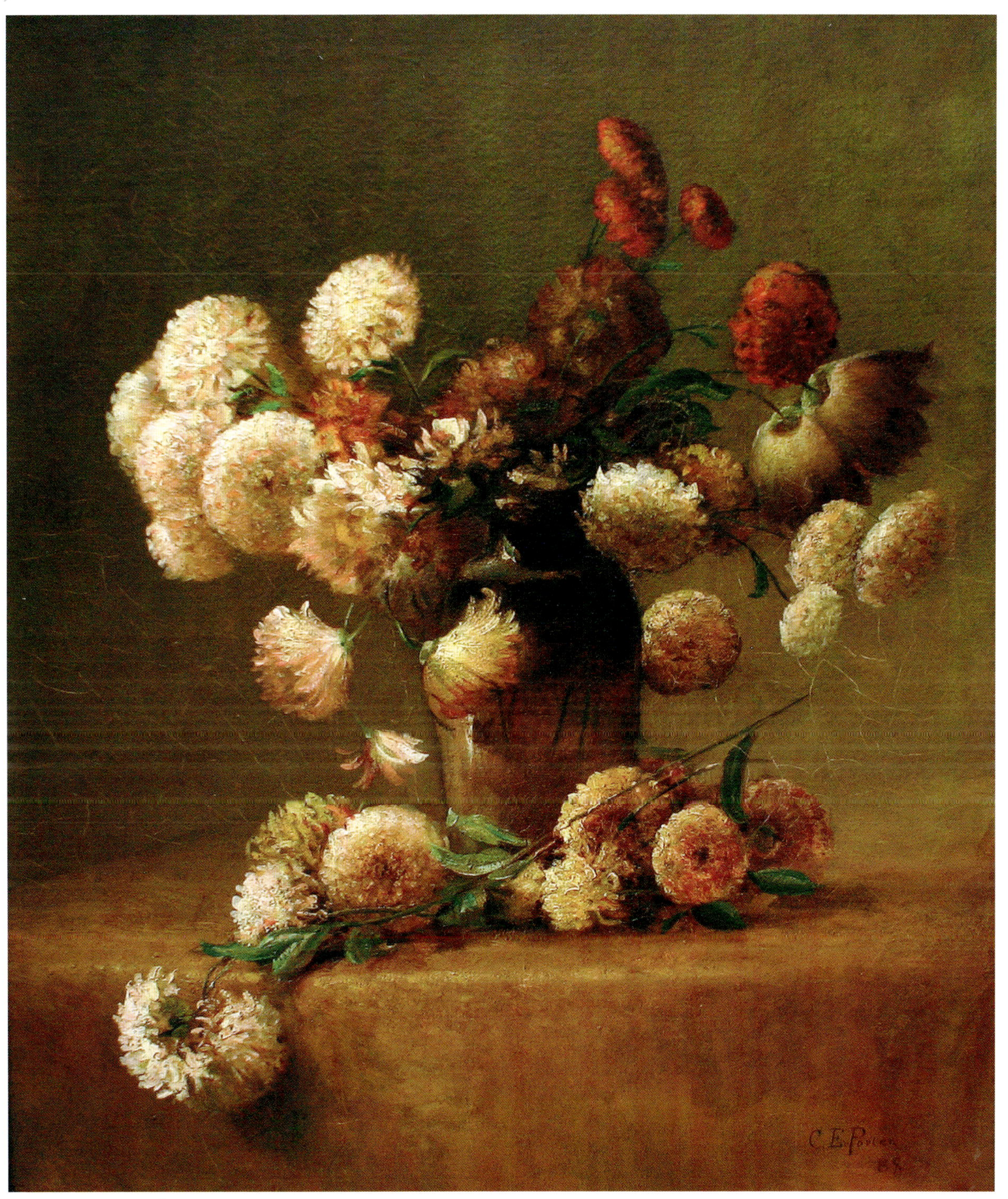

Catalogue 21
Chrysanthemums, 1888
Oil on canvas
19½" x 23"
Signed and dated lower right
Collection of Charlynn and Warren Goins

palette is softer and lighter, and a play of light unites the bouquet with the background. Taking a cue from Fantin-Latour, Porter loaded his brush and flowed his colors onto the canvas as never before, outdoing even the master, who generally achieved his rich effects by depicting lush varieties of roses and including more of them (figure 08). Porter seldom loosened his still-life style so much again, but a painting like this one demonstrates that his studies in France were a critical learning experience for him.

In Paris and afterward, Porter painted kitchen still lifes that owe much to the work of Jean-Baptiste-Simeon Chardin (1699–1779). Joining the host

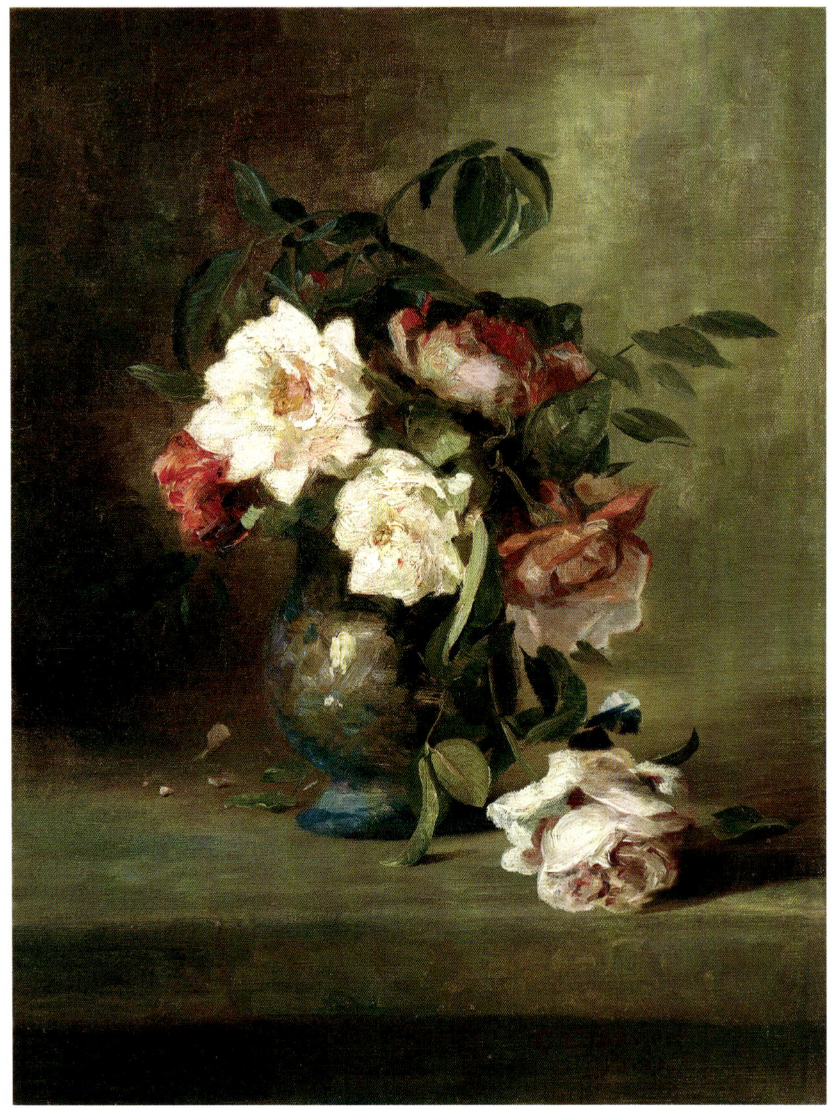

Catalogue 22
Still Life of Flowers, 1882–83
Oil on canvas
18¼" x 13¼"
Signed and inscribed "Paris" lower right
Logan and Penelope Delany

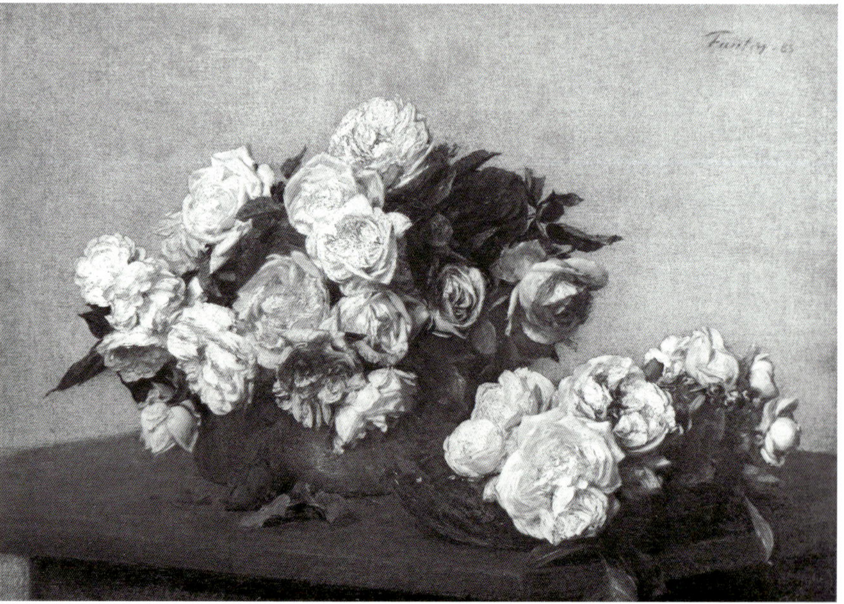

Figure 08–Henri Fantin-Latour
Roses in a Bowl and Dish, 1885
Oil on canvas
18" x 24⅞"
Sterling and Francine Clark Institute, 1955.734

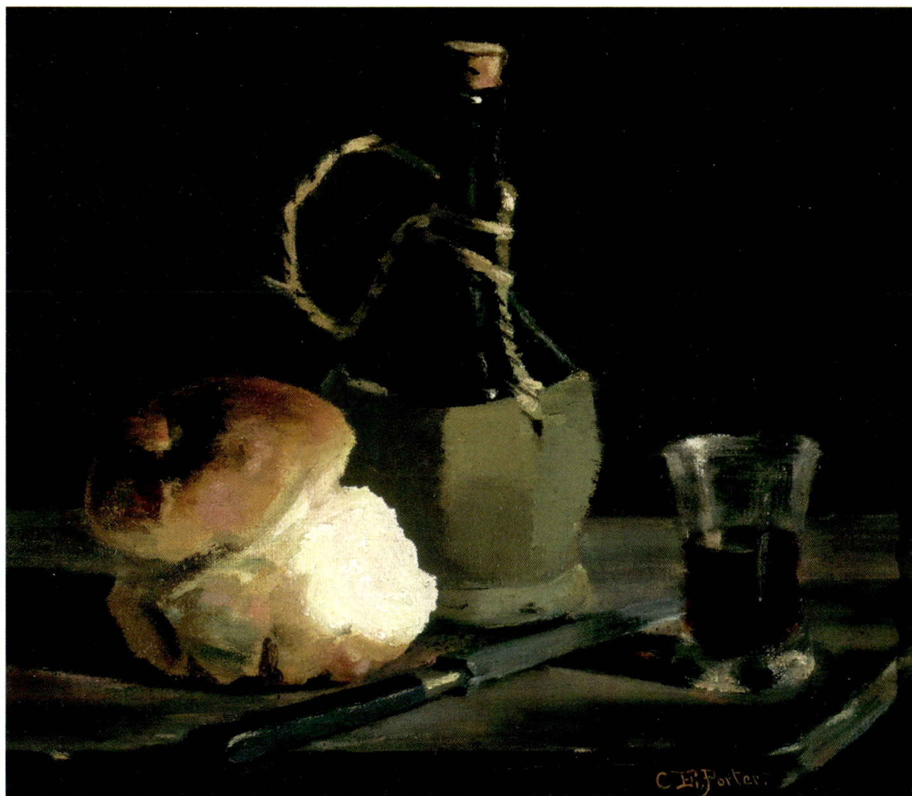

Catalogue 23
Still Life with Bread and Wine Bottle, c. 1883
Oil on canvas
14¼" x 11¼"
Signed lower right
The Harmon and Harriet Kelley Foundation for the Arts

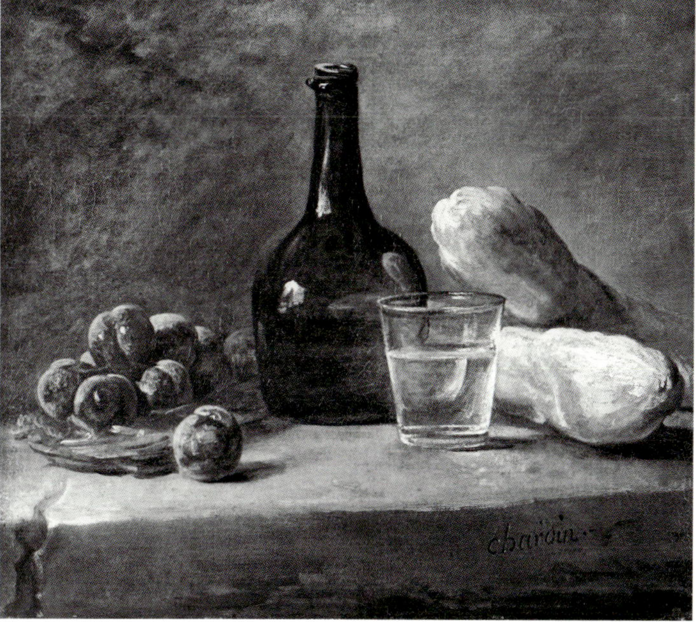

Figure 09–Jean-Baptiste-Siméon Chardin
Still Life with Plums, c. 1730
Oil on canvas
17¼" x 19¼"
Courtesy of The Frick Collection

of artists from the eighteenth century to the present who have copied, imitated, or created homages to Chardin, Porter was clearly enthralled by the work of the great French master. *Still Life with Bread and Wine Bottle* (catalogue 23) resembles a Chardin painting in the Frick Collection (figure 09), though Porter omitted the plums and added a black-handled, silver-trimmed knife like that in several Chardins he could have seen in France.[108] Porter's *Still Life with Ginger Jar, Fruit, and Nuts* (catalogue 24, see page 66) may have been inspired by Chardin. After his stay in France, Porter painted at

least two similar works.[109] Like the kitchen still lifes of Chardin, the objects and edibles in these paintings are essentially a feast for the eye.

A prime example of Chardin's influence on Porter is *Crock, Kettle, and Onions* (catalogue 25, see page 67). This lucid, coherent painting reveals itself slowly in the manner of a Chardin. Root vegetables and cooking pots are portrayed as truthfully as any by the French master, in whose deft hands such humble objects became important and immutable. Colors are in close harmony, warm and earthy, in a dark setting that is more subtle

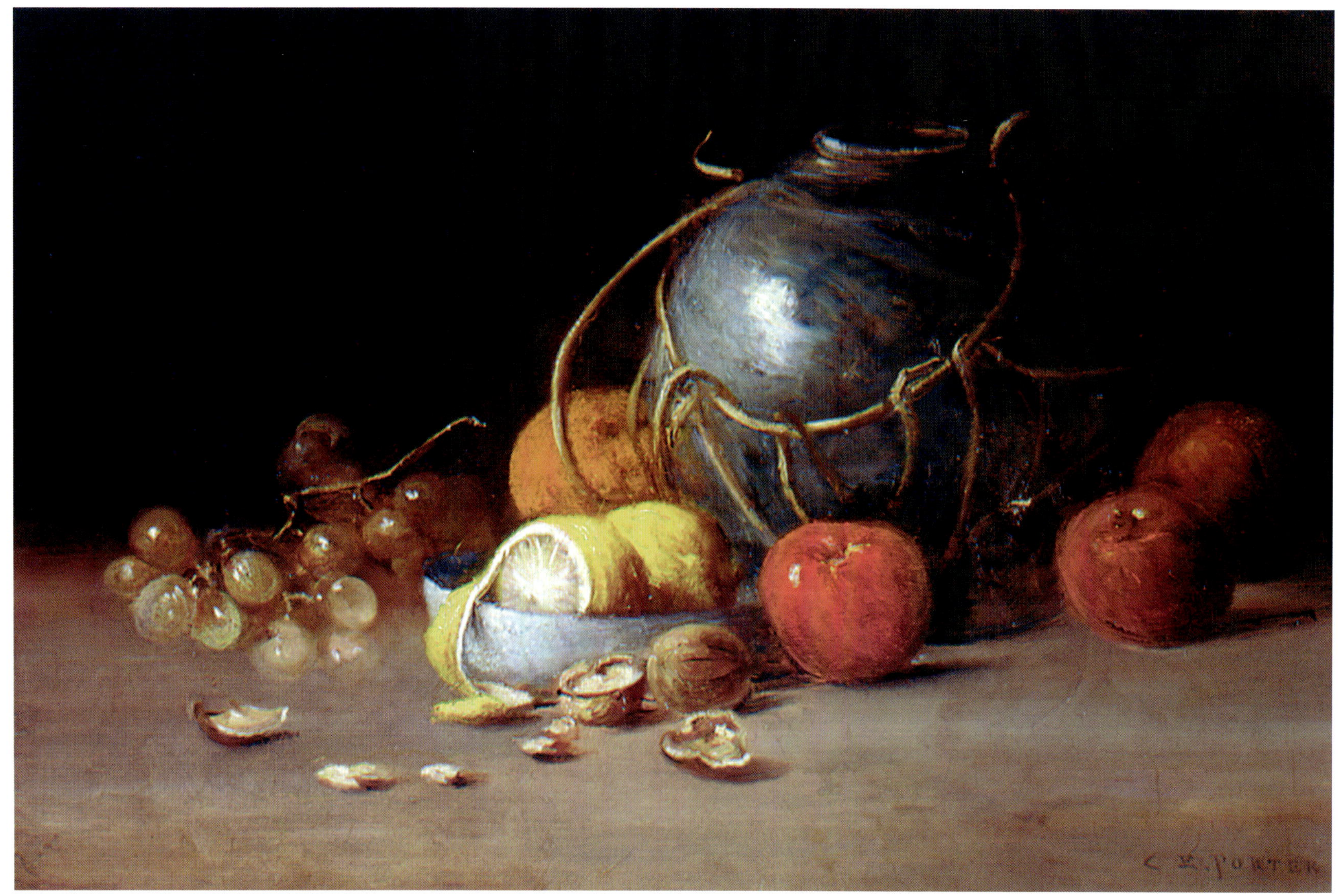

Catalogue 24
Still Life with Ginger Jar, Fruit, and Nuts, c. 1885
Oil on canvas
22" x 36"
Signed lower right
San Antonio Museum of Art. Gift of Harmon and Harriet Kelley in honor of Milbrew and Shirley Davis.

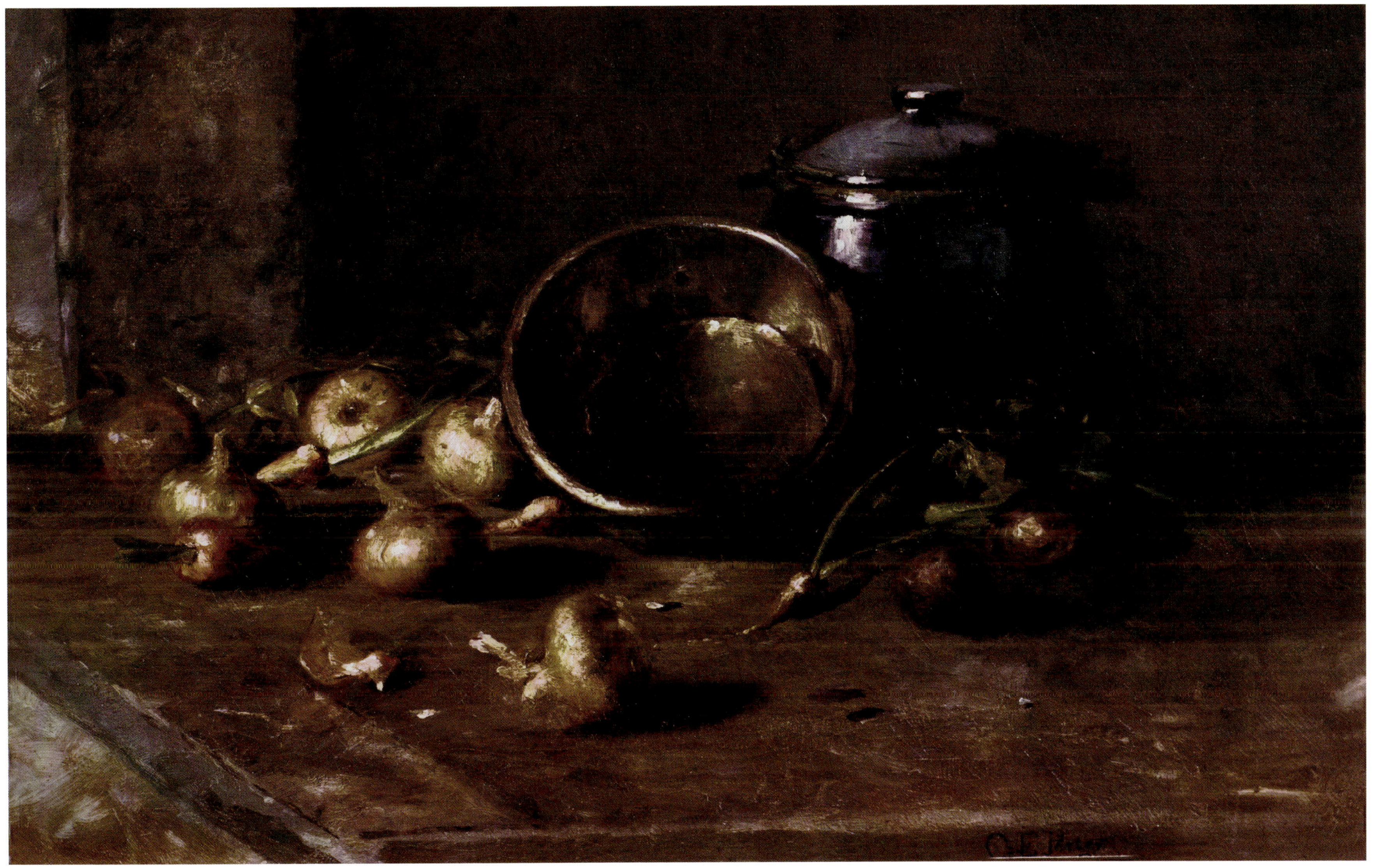

Catalogue 25
Crock, Kettle, and Onions, c. 1890
Oil on canvas
18" x 26½"
Signed lower right
Florence Griswold Museum. Gift of the Hartford Steam Boiler Inspection and Insurance Company.

and evocative than those of Porter's early flower paintings. A copper kettle and black crock emerge out of the enveloping darkness, their bold forms and colorful highlights balancing an illuminated scatter of onions and carrots that resonate with engaging rhythms. Textures are palpable. A feeling of intimacy pervades the scene, which evokes connotations of nature, nurture, and family. Porter was able here, as Robert Hughes has written of Chardin, to "absorb himself in the visual to the point of self-effacement" and by means of painting alone create a "sense of the intrinsic worth of seeing."[110]

While in France, Porter learned that his brothers James and William changed their lives. James sold his Meriden barbershop and became an engineer. William was now an undertaker's assistant in Meriden, as well as leader of the Zion Mission and a founding member of Meriden's Trinity Praying Band, which held revival meetings everywhere from railroad platforms to churches. Brother-in-law Richard Alonzo Jeffrey had become a caterer, working such prestigious jobs as the Meriden mayor's New Year's party in 1882 and a train excursion to California in 1883.

Alzonzo probably catered the wedding of Ella Porter, his wife's and Charles Porter's niece, who married Edwin Pulley, a "body servant," in Meriden on May 23, 1883. Ella, known in Rockville and Meriden as a talented elocutionist, was the girl who had grown up in the home of Porter's parents. Given the slow nature of transatlantic shipping in the era, Porter must have sent her wedding gift about the time he was writing Clemens for help in getting orders. Despite an urgent need to stretch his money so he could stay abroad, he purchased several elegant gifts for his niece: some fine laces, a bridal veil with orange blossoms, and a pin and earrings that resembled calla lilies. Family came first.

Hartford and New York, 1884–97

On the evening of February 12, 1884, Meriden's Lincoln Club held its customary banquet to celebrate the anniversary of the president's birth. This gathering of about eighty persons was smaller than usual because it was restricted to local colored men. Only two people came from outside the city. One was Charles Ethan Porter, said in a newspaper account to have lately returned from Paris.[111]

The club's president, George Jeffrey, made the toast, to which Porter's brother William responded by exhorting colored men always to revere the memory of the martyred emancipator. Edwin Pulley, husband of Porter's niece Ella, eulogized the abolitionist Wendell Phillips. Then Porter rose to give the keynote address, entitled "The Courage of the Abolitionists." He referred, according to the *Meriden Daily Republican*, "to the spirit of heroism that was shown by Garrison, Phillips, Brown and Whittier, and awarded them the greatest praise for the daring manifested in the dark days preceding the great struggle for liberty."[112]

R. A. Jeffrey, Porter's brother-in-law, added a few words, and the evening ended with renditions of old plantation and war songs, "given with a spirit and feeling that showed the singers' hearts were in their work."[113] The event, which included the endorsement of John A. Logan for president, was considered a success in every way. The extended Porter-Jeffrey family had done much to make it so.

Throughout February, Hartford's Veteran City Guard, one of the independent nineteenth-century military groups sharing responsibility for defense with federal and state forces, was busy organizing a loan exhibition, set to open in the new Hill's Building on Asylum Street in mid-March. Most of the city's leading white men were involved, so local newspapers gave the event close attention. Preparation time was short for such an undertaking, and the *Hartford Evening Post* reported on March 13 that even though the opening was only four days away, contributions were still pouring in.[114] Nearly all the works were in place in time for the opening reception, which was thronged, according to the *Hartford Daily Courant*, by "people who can recognize art from make-believe and would not call the display a success unless it really was."[115] The newspaper described what people saw:

> From the painting gallery on the second floor the visitors passed to the third floor room where the historical pictures and other choice canvases are shown, then to the room devoted to Connecticut artists . . . [and on] to the exhibitions of porcelain, bric-a-brac, etchings, engravings and bronzes, until the fourth floor . . . given up to antique arms, Indian relics, pottery, coins, medals and hundreds of choice and interesting curiosities.

There were still more entries to come, and two days after the opening the *Hartford Evening Post* informed readers that among the new submissions were two paintings by Porter, obtained from the artist by Thomas Burke, a guard member and art-gallery owner.[116] Porter, the *Post* explained, had just returned from Paris. A new catalogue, revised to include the late submissions, was not ready until the evening of March 29, three days before the exhibition closed. That morning the *Courant* had described paintings by Connecticut artists but did not mention Porter's entries, brought from Paris—*Head* (*Study from Life*) and *An Old French Moat*.[117]

The day after the exhibition opened, the *Courant* had listed the works in just one of the galleries as evidence of the magnitude of the event, implying that much more of similar merit could be seen.[118] Paintings by the great Belgian *animalier* Eugene Verboeckhoven (1798–1881), the French battle-scene painter Eugene Medard (1847–1887), and other European artists of their stature were there, along with some by artists only dimly remembered today. Except for Bouguereau, contemporary Europeans were missing. The American paintings in this gallery included Frederic Church's *Vale of St. Thomas*, Thomas Hill's *Yosemite Valley*, and other awesome views by Albert Bierstadt, John Frederick Kensett, and James Hart, leaders of American art in earlier decades. A few contemporary Connecticut men, such as William Gedney Bunce and John L. Fitch, were included, because they were considered too important to be classed with others from the state. The catalogue listed their German and Belgian credentials.

Not surprisingly, the collectors of these important paintings were Hartford's elite, among them Mrs. Samuel Colt, A. D. Vorce, and George P. Bissell. Bissell, a Hartford banker, contributed five works (and owned at least one Porter painting at some time). Mark Twain lent *Burning Ship* (location unknown) by George W. Waters (1832–1912), a little-known artist from Elmira, New York, which set him apart from the other lenders.

In the room devoted to Connecticut, all but two of the artists were from Hartford. Their art training was not given, and the only catalogue note was for a landscape "painted by a lady seventy years old."[119] The artists themselves, about half of whom were women, owned all but one of the paintings, and the exception belonged to the artist's mother-in-law. The exhibition was Hartford's cultural event of 1884, so it is puzzling that Porter's paintings were not exhibited from the start. He was back in Connecticut by mid-February and could have contacted someone in time to have his work in place on the opening day.

The *Hartford Daily Courant* told readers on March 26 that Porter was in town and at work, but it was April 14 before the *Hartford Evening Post* announced that he had opened a studio in the tower of the Cheney Building on Main Street.[120] The artist's landscape style now embodied "the best elements of the French school," the *Post* said, and the still beautiful fruit and flower pieces show good results "in the freedom of the drawing and elegance of coloring."

Perhaps Porter did not begin work for a while after returning home because he wanted time with his family, or he may have wanted to wait until more of his paintings came from Paris, which did not happen until June, when he featured them at a studio reception. Possibly he was even considering whether to introduce the "new" Porter to New York, where he had not lived for more than six years. He waited to make that move until 1885.

In Hartford, where people remembered his work and were interested in seeing the influence of foreign study, Porter must have expected support and good sales. Local writers agreed that his art was even better now that it incorporated, as the *Hartford Courant* wrote, "the mode of treatment which is so characteristic of French art to-day."[121] They were thinking, as the article makes clear, of Barbizon art—the cool tones of Corot and the fresh-air realism of Bastien Lepage (1848–1884). Porter's "dainty, almost *finicky*, work we were so familiar with," the *Courant* explained, "has been superseded by a broader, freer style—color and detail count for less, breadth and harmonious tone for very much more than formerly." *An Old French Moat* and *The Coming Shower* were cited: "These two paintings alone, so entirely different, so clearly superior to his earlier work, prove that the artist's two years in France were by no means wasted." (Could *Coming Shower* be the grain stacks inscribed "Paris" (catalogue 18, see page 59) that the *Hartford Daily Times* liked so much?)

Porter needed not just praise but money, having spent all he had in France. He invited the public to visit his studio any time. In August his work was shown at Butler's Art Store on Main Street, and the following month two paintings were featured at Thomas Burke's gallery on Asylum Street. One was rare subject matter for Porter: a large mixed bouquet "gorgeous in design and surpassingly rich in color" in a "magnificent" vase.[122] The other was a bunch of daisies, dated 1884 (catalogue 26).

In *Daisies* Porter was as skillful with whites and yellows as he was with reddish and dark browns in *Crock, Kettle, and Onions*. The *Hartford Daily Times* saw *Daisies* as "the very incarnation of modesty and charity, soft, quiet, cool, yet graceful and of sweet poetic fragrance."[123] An informal bouquet of blooms and buds, looking like something a young child might pluck as a gift for mother, has been thrust into a simple container. Circlets of white rays and round yellow centers, seen from various angles, and a scattering of short-stemmed blossoms form a design with a pleasing sense of movement. This unpretentious little bouquet has an impressive presence, however, for Porter isolated and illuminated it as though it were a precious object in a museum display.

Despite favorable reviews, Porter was not getting the financial returns he needed. In December 1884 he mounted an exhibition and auction in the Hill's Building, with about one hundred pictures painted in France and afterward. The press was generally supportive. As a Christmas present for a friend, nothing is nicer than a Porter flower or fruit piece, the writer for the *Hartford Evening Post* reminded readers, but he had a reservation about Porter's landscape art: "Few will recognize its worth, or call it excellent, unless they possess the higher artistic sense."[124] The *Hartford Daily Times* pretended that Porter had issued a challenge:

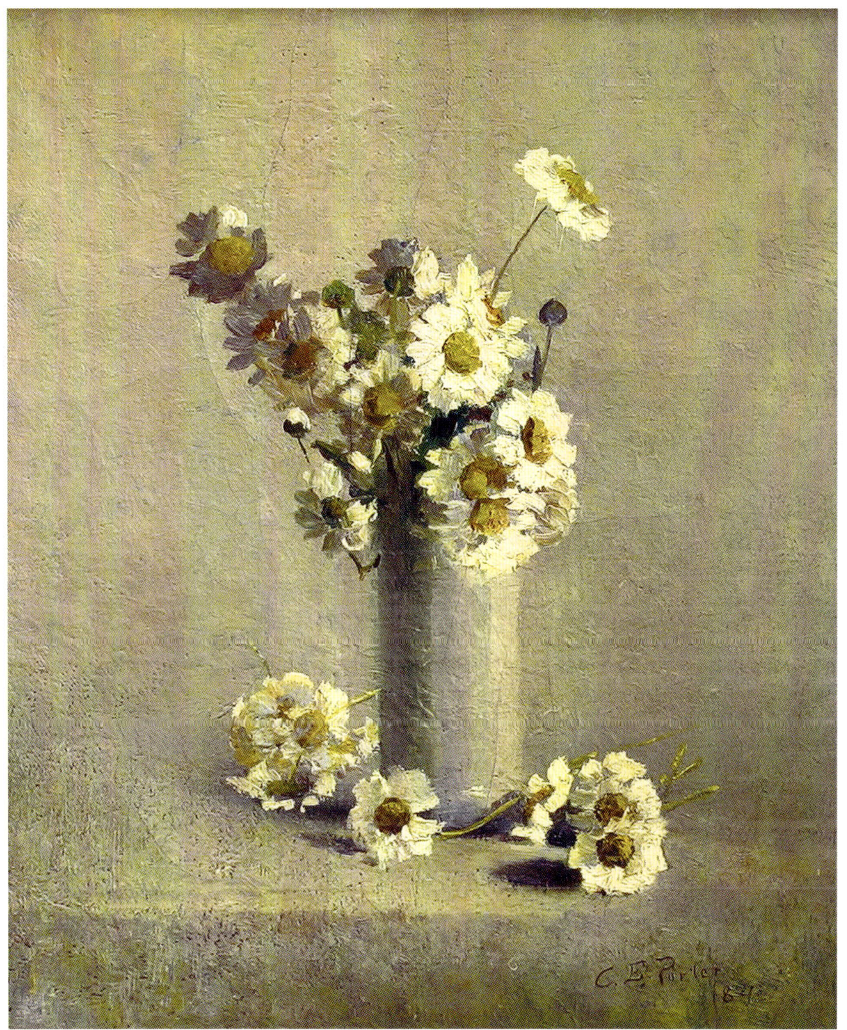

Catalogue 26
Daisies, 1884
Oil on canvas
13¾" x 17"
Signed and dated lower right
Courtesy of Edgar B. French

"It has been thought, by many who have wondered at the microscopic finish and accuracy of his flowers and insects, that this artist could not paint a landscape. He thinks he can, and invites the public to examine his pictures."[125] The *Courant* implied that people found Porter's landscapes wanting, but only because "his other work is already familiar and so conspicuously good that people are not disposed to look for similar success in a different field."[126]

The first night of the auction was poorly attended, and sales did not always cover the cost of frames. The second night, meant to be the last, was a bit better, so it was decided to carry over to the following night. When a storm kept attendance low, the sale was extended once more. Bids remained sluggish, and the auction dragged on, night after night. A December 15 piece in the *Courant* was blunt: "The sale is made because Mr. Porter wants money—that's the plain English of it. And it is another reason why Hartford people who can afford to buy pictures and are disposed to encourage a worthy ambition should improve this opportunity."[127]

On December 19 the auctioneer ran a "grand closing" ad in the *Courant:* "We wish it distinctly understood that absolute necessity compels us to sell at this time." It was not yet the end, however. The auction, which began on December 15, ran for an unprecedented nine nights. On December 23, the final day at last, the *Post* announced that "Porter's great masterpiece, 'The Apples,' with several choice flower pieces, must go to-night. The artist must have money, and has decided to allow these

to go for what they will bring."[128] The *Hartford Times* said much the same: "Necessity compels Mr. Porter to sell his great fruit pieces and wreaths of flowers. The sale of his famous apples will come off this evening at 8:30 P.M. . . . His studio price for this great work is $150, but it must go to-night to the highest bidder."[129] The newspapers did not report, as they usually did, how much money the auction made. A few weeks later, Porter moved to New York City.

It is disappointing that Porter's return to Hartford was not triumphant, for he was doing the best work of his life then and for several years afterward. Hartford had grown more sophisticated in its aesthetic tastes and more appreciative of European art and training, but it respected the conservative academies in Germany and Belgium more than those in France, which, despite their traditional approach, were perceived as a breeding ground for radical art.

Despite praise for Porter's "new" art, Hartford clearly missed his meticulous, jewel-toned realism. The Hartford art world was ten years behind the New York scene. Paintings by the "new men," which stirred emotions, were not yet familiar in Connecticut's capital, which still preferred formal portraits and pictures that were meant to impress, look startlingly real, or suggest a story. People may not have known what to make of the blond coloring, soft focus, and sense of movement in a still life like *Mountain Laurel* (catalogue 27), done shortly after Porter returned from France. Porter suffused flowers, ledge, and background with pale golden tones and shaped a bouquet that seems

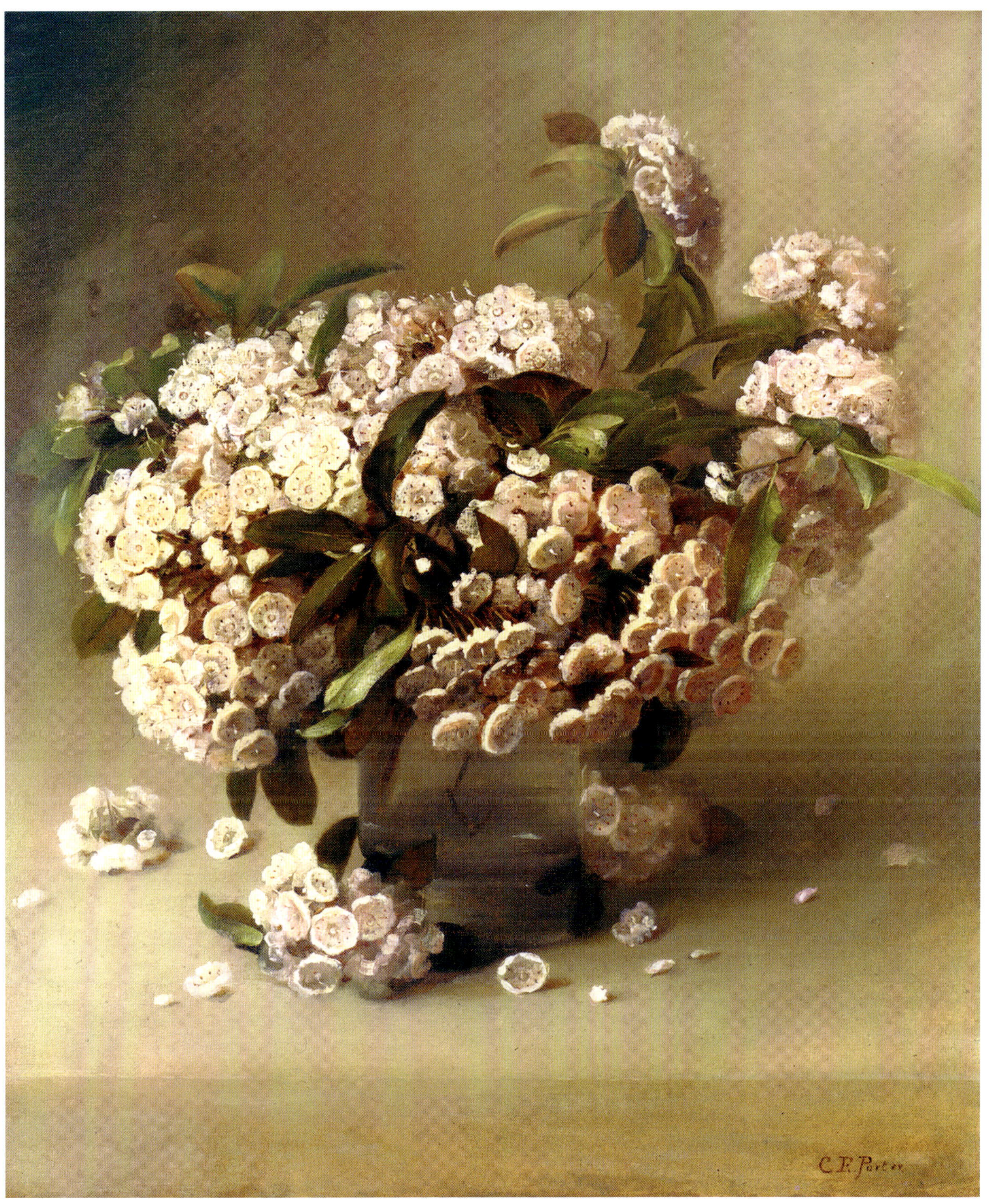

Catalogue 27
Mountain Laurel, c. 1885
Oil on canvas
24" x 20"
Signed lower right
Courtesy of Michael Rosenfeld Gallery, LLC, New York City

intent on transporting itself upward and to the right. Porter soon reverted (perhaps, as Helen Krieble has proposed, as a concession to Hartford patrons) to more sedate laurel bouquets, with more detail, richer colors, and darker backgrounds.[130] They are beautiful, but the more spirited, quirky Porter images are also beautiful and seem to say more about the man.

In spring 1885, when his *Apples* was on view at the National Academy of Design, Porter was living at 2 West Tenth Street. Possibly this *Apples*, priced high at $225, was the painting he considered his masterpiece, which might have gone unsold at the Hartford auction after all. In the ambitious painting *Apples in an Overturned Basket* (catalogue 28), he took on the challenge of depicting numerous pieces of fruit and making them look real with relatively little detail. From his early work he retained the leaves that complement the apples in color and form and the curvy apple stems that function as a kind of staccato. The haziness inside the basket shows Porter employing atmospheric perspective to give an illusion of depth. Also new to this and other pictures of the mid-1880s is a mastery of ambient light and of highlights like those on the basket's rim and handle, which enliven the design.

In 1885 Frederic E. Church still had a studio in the Tenth Street Studio Building, though it is questionable if he used it during the several months that Porter was living on the same street, since rheumatism was curtailing the artist's ability to work, as well as affecting his willingness to leave Olana, his elegant new home on the Hudson River. Surely Porter would have been eager to hear what Church thought of his art after two years of study in France. Words of praise from Church had been helpful before and could be again. There is no sign, however, that Church ever saw Porter's post-Paris work.

By December 1885 Porter was back at the YMCA Association Building —"making a position for himself in New York," in the flattering words of his hometown weekly.[131] In the spring he exhibited *Vase and Roses* and a portrait of a man at the National Academy of Design. After the usual extended summer spent painting the landscape in and around Rockville, Porter gave Hartford another try. At the end of November 1886 he was once again in the tower studio of the Cheney Building. Success must have eluded him in New York; it would be four years before he would try for it again.

Soon after his return to Hartford in fall 1886, Porter began an association with Daniel F. Wentworth (1850–1934), who was back in his native city after several years in Meriden and study in Munich. Under the auspices of A. D. Vorce, whose art store sold paintings by both local and internationally known artists, the two had joint auctions in spring 1887 and winter 1888. Vorce, who had exhibited Porter's fruit and flower paintings previously, most likely proposed the idea after seeing Wentworth's landscapes. The accessible imagery of the two artists offered an opportunity to target people who knew little about art and did not buy any. Local newspapers, possibly nudged by Vorce, saw it as well. "Mr. Wentworth's interpretation is not beyond and above us as the manner of some is, but thoroughly blends the ideal

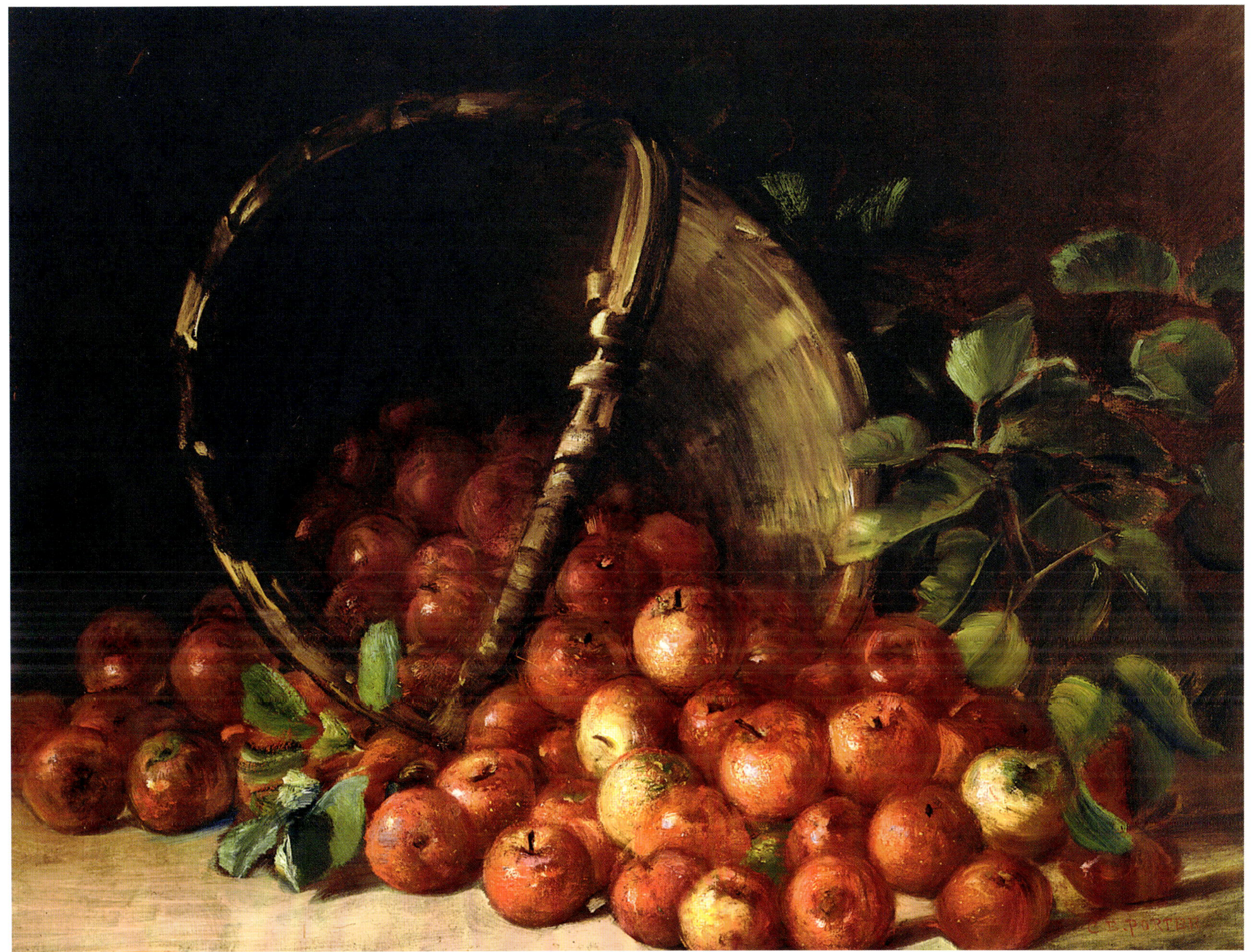

Catalogue 28
Apples in an Overturned Basket, c. 1885
Oil on canvas
20" x 26"
Signed lower right
Courtesy of Michael Rosenfeld Gallery, LLC, New York City

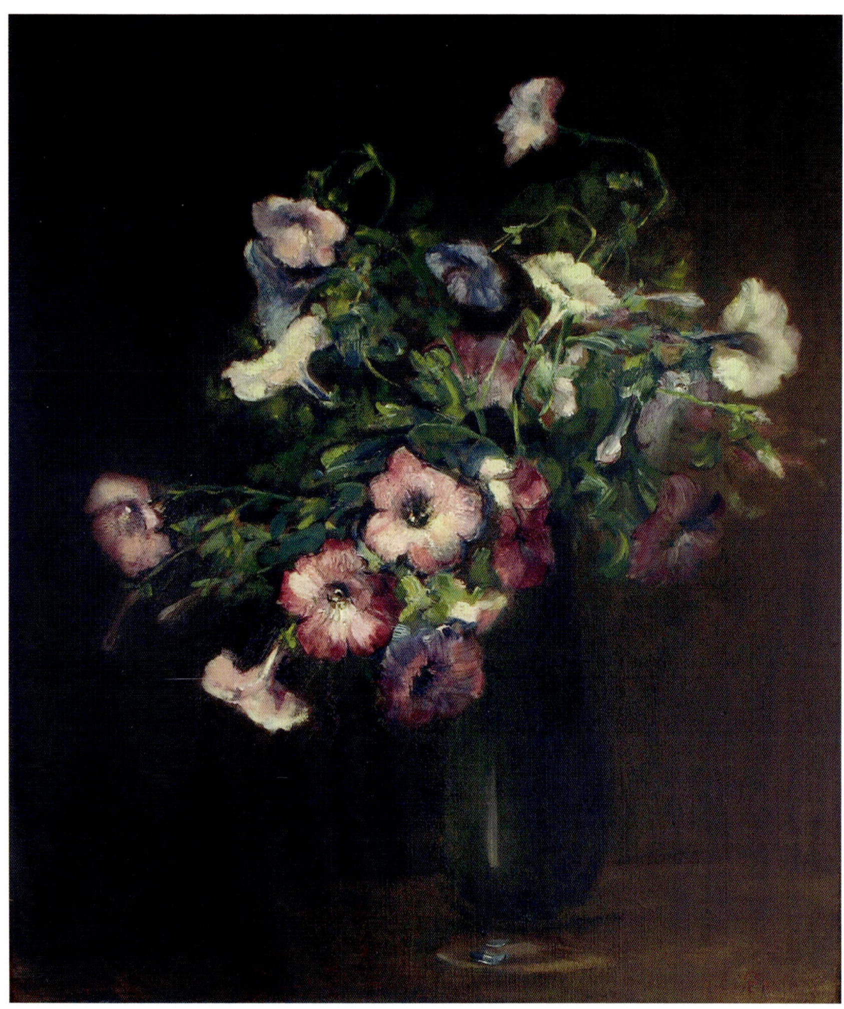

with the real . . . the breath of life," the *Evening Post* assured readers on April 25. As to Porter's flower and fruit pieces, the writer added, "it is hardly necessary again to call attention."[132]

The newspapers promoted the two as local artists on the rise whose work could still be acquired at bargain prices. The *Hartford Daily Times* expressed an opinion—repeated in part below—that must have echoed Vorce's:

> Too often people of moderate means stay away from such sales, thinking: "I have no money to buy paintings." There is the mistake. Every house demands pictures and every nice house has them. . . . It is for people that are not rich, that cannot order their pictures, or buy them at high prices that such art sales have the greatest value and give the best opportunity. The Wentworth landscapes are very pleasant, well conceived and well painted works, delightful in many ways, and of a bright and cheerful character. The Charles Porter pictures are beauties in flowers and fruit. Several of them possess a grace and poetic fragrance that captivate and charm whenever looked at. All are in excellent taste, in beautiful color, and of the best modern style—the American tempered by the French. Just enough impressionist to be strong. It is in the interest of the public, especially of the middle class, that a careful inspection of these pictures is urged at Vorce's, and a large attendance at the sale tomorrow and Wednesday afternoons.[133]

An annotated checklist of the first auction, much larger but otherwise presumably similar to the second, shows that Wentworth contributed

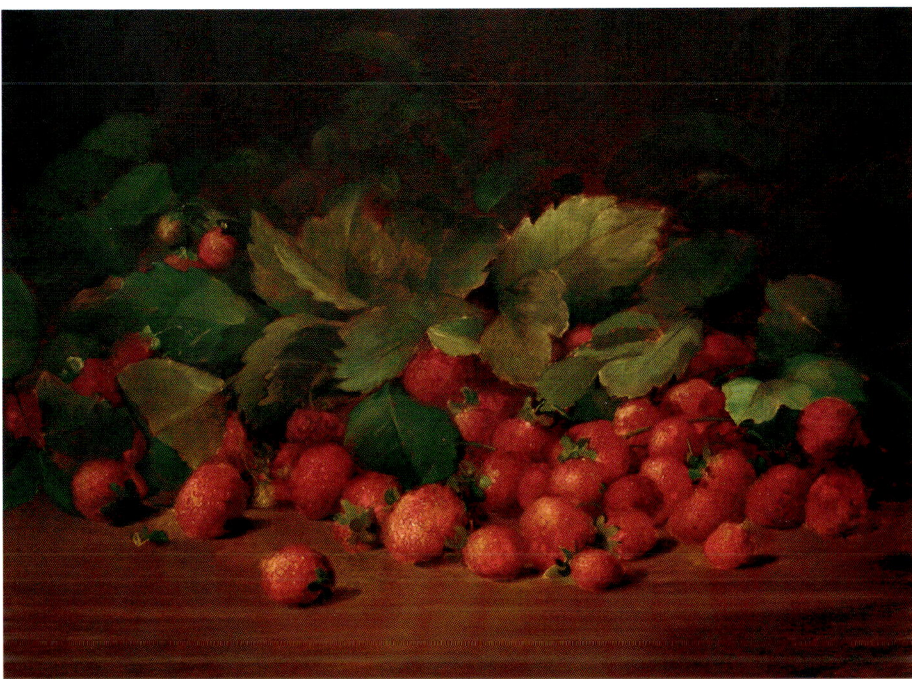

Catalogue 30
Strawberries, 1888
Oil on chipboard
15⅞" x 12"
Signed and dated lower right
Collection of Charlynn and Warren Goins

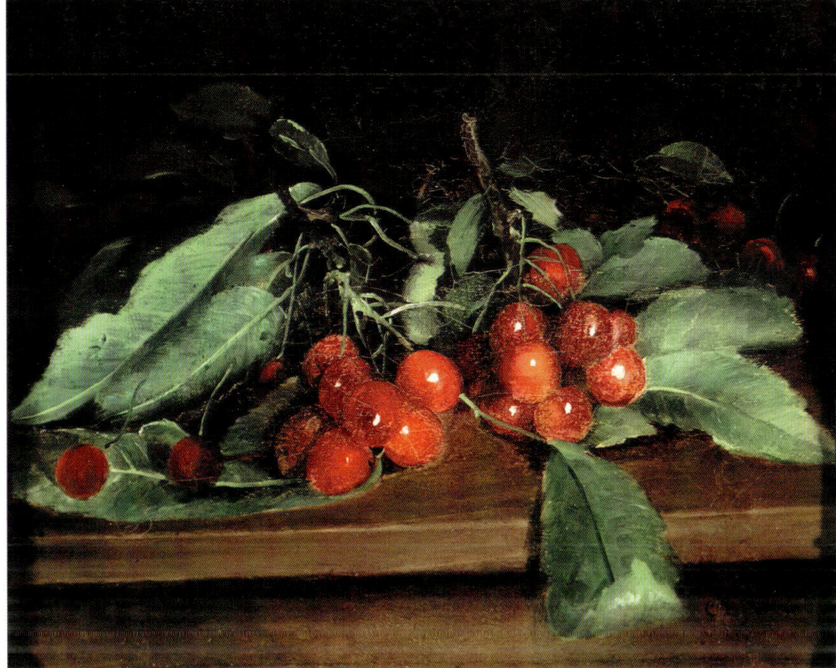

Catalogue 31
Cherries, c. 1885
Oil on canvas
10½"x 13"
Signed lower right
The Harmon and Harriet Kelley Foundation for the Arts

only landscapes and that Porter, except for two intimate woodland scenes, confined his submissions to fruits and flowers.[134] This plan must have frustrated Porter, who wanted to be known as a landscapist as well as a still-life painter. Both reputation and money were at stake, as the checklist reveals. A Porter *Morning Glories* or *Roses* could be had for $6 and the rest of his offerings for not much more (except *Laurel* at $54).

Wentworth's *Autumn Morning* went for $26, as did most of his other paintings, but his *Under the Willows* cost someone $73 and *Jerseys in the Orchard, Morning* fetched $100, the top price of the sale. (Cows soon became Wentworth's specialty.) The auctions did not yield large sums— they seldom did at the time—but Porter and Wentworth got enough to want to hold a second one. Porter benefited most from such windfalls, no matter how small, because he supported himself by his painting and teaching; Wentworth had a steady job as a church organist.

Titles of Porter's eighty-one oils and watercolors in the first sale indicate that, except for insects, he was still painting subjects he had shown in Hartford a decade earlier: strawberries and roses (six paintings each), apples, peaches, grapes, pinks, laurel, and wild flowers. The subjects were the same, but these were presumably newer pictures, looser and with more verve. In *Petunias* (catalogue 29, see page 76) Porter created a lively rhythm that feels almost musical, as the eye skips from flower to flower and stem to stem, skimming textured greenery. (Pentimenti reveal that a flower was painted out.)

Strawberries (catalogue 30, see page 77) and *Cherries* (catalogue 31, see page 77) are similar to but more sophisticated than work Porter did before his stay in France. Now he sometimes accomplished more with less, as in *Cherries*, its small cluster a striking variant on the conventional bowlful. Often, as in *Strawberries*, he softened colors and edges. In the compositional scheme for *Lilacs* (catalogue 32, see page 79), heart-shaped leaves colored a vibrant green vie for attention with the fuzzy blossoms they encircle. Porter's most successful pictures are now often distinguished by a touch of whimsy or wit more subtle than flies on a plate.

Despite praise for his "new" art, Porter must have decided that he could not accomplish his artistic goals in Hartford; by summer 1889 he had left the city for good. In the fall, he had two pictures accepted for exhibition at the National Academy of Design. Titled *Basket of Fruit* and *Thistles*, they may be paintings that are known today.

The New Britain Museum's *Still Life with Fruit and Basket* (catalogue 33, see page 80) is as much an expression of nature's bounty as the earlier fantasies of Severin Roesen, but Porter's picture is plainspoken rather than grandiloquent. The composition is animated not only by light that makes the commonplace basket glow but also, surprisingly, by twigs that form a witty comment on Roesen's tendrils and direct the eye to the left, balancing an arrangement that might otherwise seem heavy on the right.

In *Thistles with Butterfly* (catalogue 34, see page 81), Porter inspired a fresh appreciation of the beauty and mystery of a common prickly weed by combining realism and abstraction. The pastel palette creates a color harmony that is brightened and balanced by the yellow Clouded Sulphur butterfly. The blooms, pod, and butterfly offer places for the eye to rest, their inherent geometry contrasting with the wild splash of thistledown bursting from a seed pod. Porter textured the picture's surface by gently incising the paint with a comblike tool.[135]

Realistic and abstract elements come together unexpectedly in *Still Life with Corn* (catalogue 35, see page 82), a watercolor with an apple, ear of corn, and a sunflower—an odd grouping for Porter, who generally did not mix objects. Elements of the early, meticulous Porter are seen in the close attention to detail in the apple and the kernels of corn, but the underside of a leaf is denoted by a hard-edged abstract green form, while plant stems, shreds of corn husk, and leaves twist and turn into oddly elongated diamonds. Is the circle of gold rays the back of a sunflower?

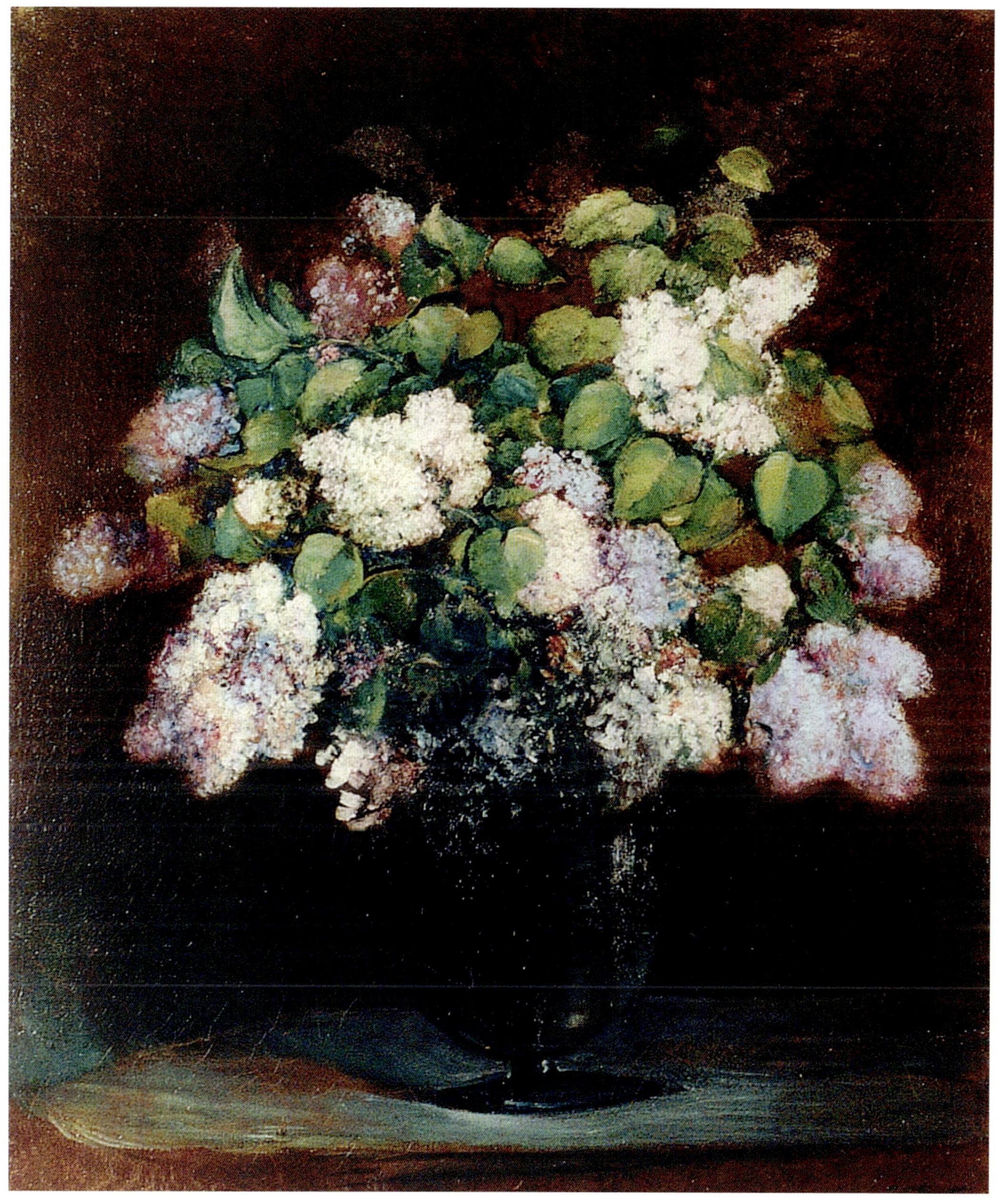

Catalogue 32
Lilacs, c. 1890
Oil on canvas
29½" x 24½"
Signed lower right
Courtesy of Kathryn and Kenneth Chenault

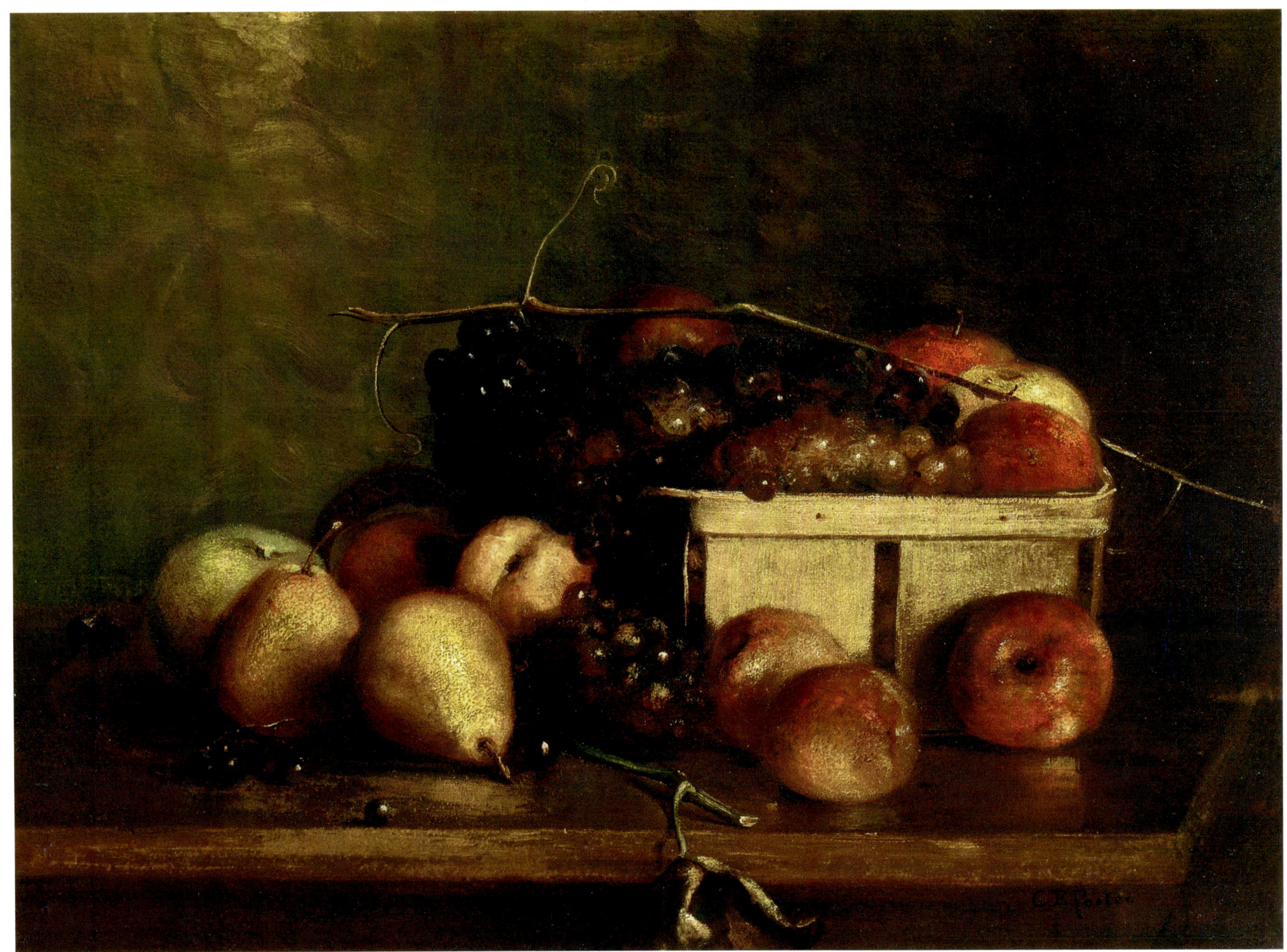

Catalogue 33
Still Life with Fruit and Basket, c. 1888
Oil on oilcloth
17½" x 13⅛"
Signed lower right
Collection of the New Britain Museum of America Art. Gift of Mr. and Mrs. Krumholz.

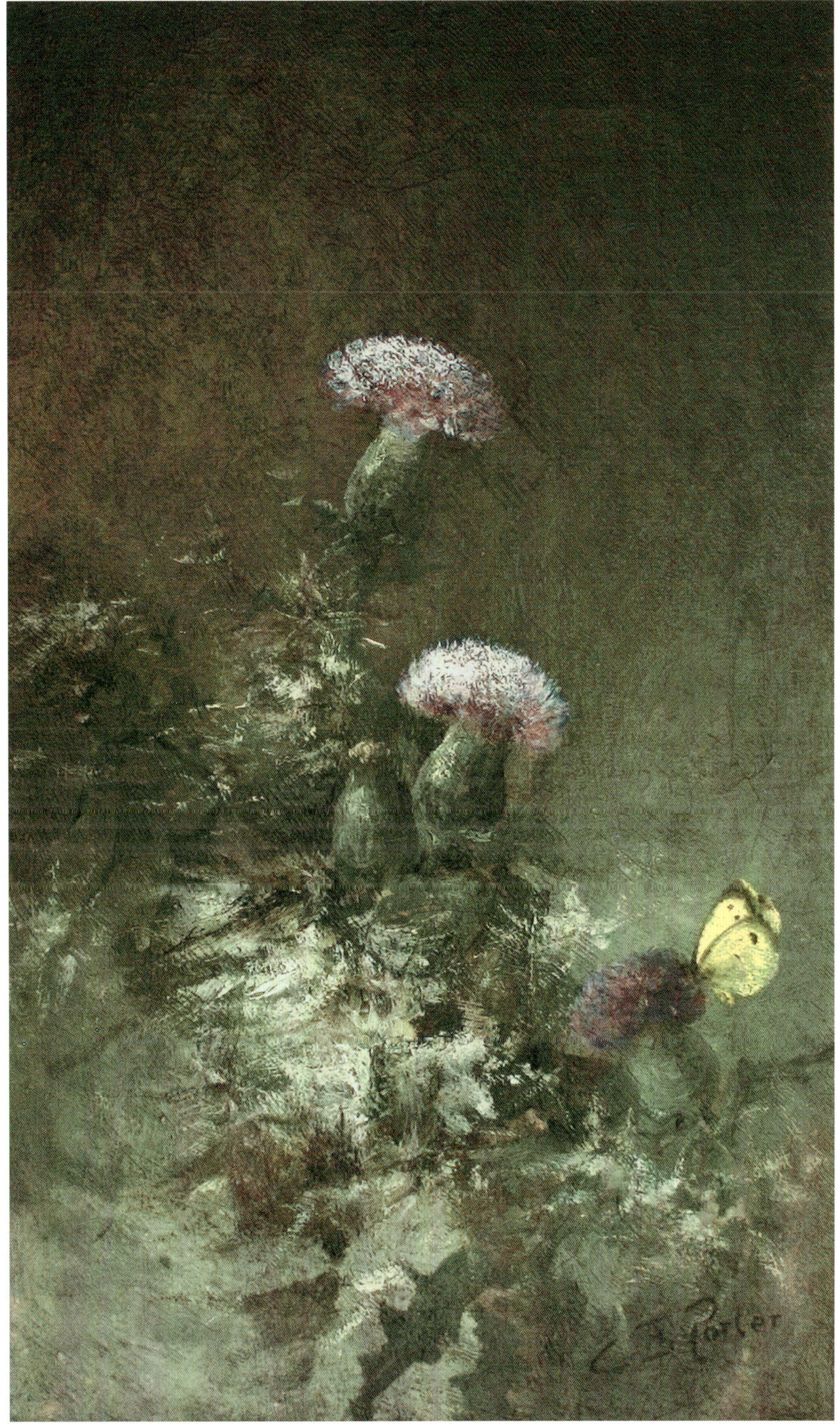

Catalogue 34
Thistles with Butterfly, c. 1888
Oil on linen/canvas
20" x 12"
Signed lower right
Stagecoach Gallery

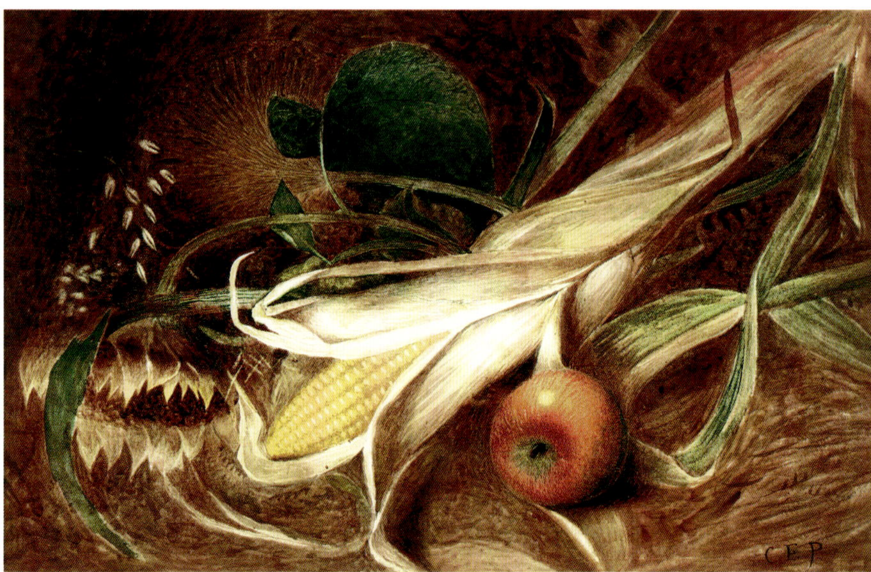

Catalogue 35
Still Life with Corn, c. 1885
Watercolor on paper
10" x 17"
Signed lower right
The Harmon and Harriet Kelley Foundation for the Arts

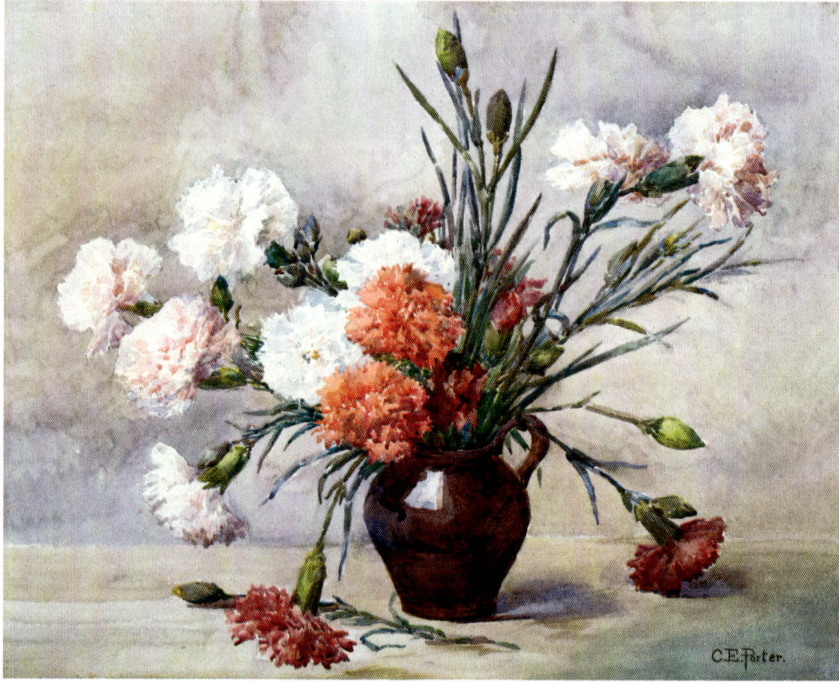

Catalogue 36
Carnations
Watercolor on paper
13" x 16"
Signed lower right
The Schonberger Family

Acid colors, rare for Porter, and a mottled background add to the sensation that this still life is far from still. Yet it recalls a much quieter, more realistic Porter watercolor of carnations (catalogue 36), in that both have the look of colored drawings.

The carnations watercolor, from the 1880s, relates to a Porter oil of the same subject dated 1887 (catalogue 37). Obvious differences such as background color—white in the watercolor, dark in the oil—are less important than the shared quirkiness of the bouquets. Both employ the convention of a few scattered flowers at the base of the vase—possibly a memento mori but also a visual device to help weight the picture. The watercolor includes buds and half-open blooms, perhaps an allusion to the cycle of life. Consider, however, how differently a florist, other still-

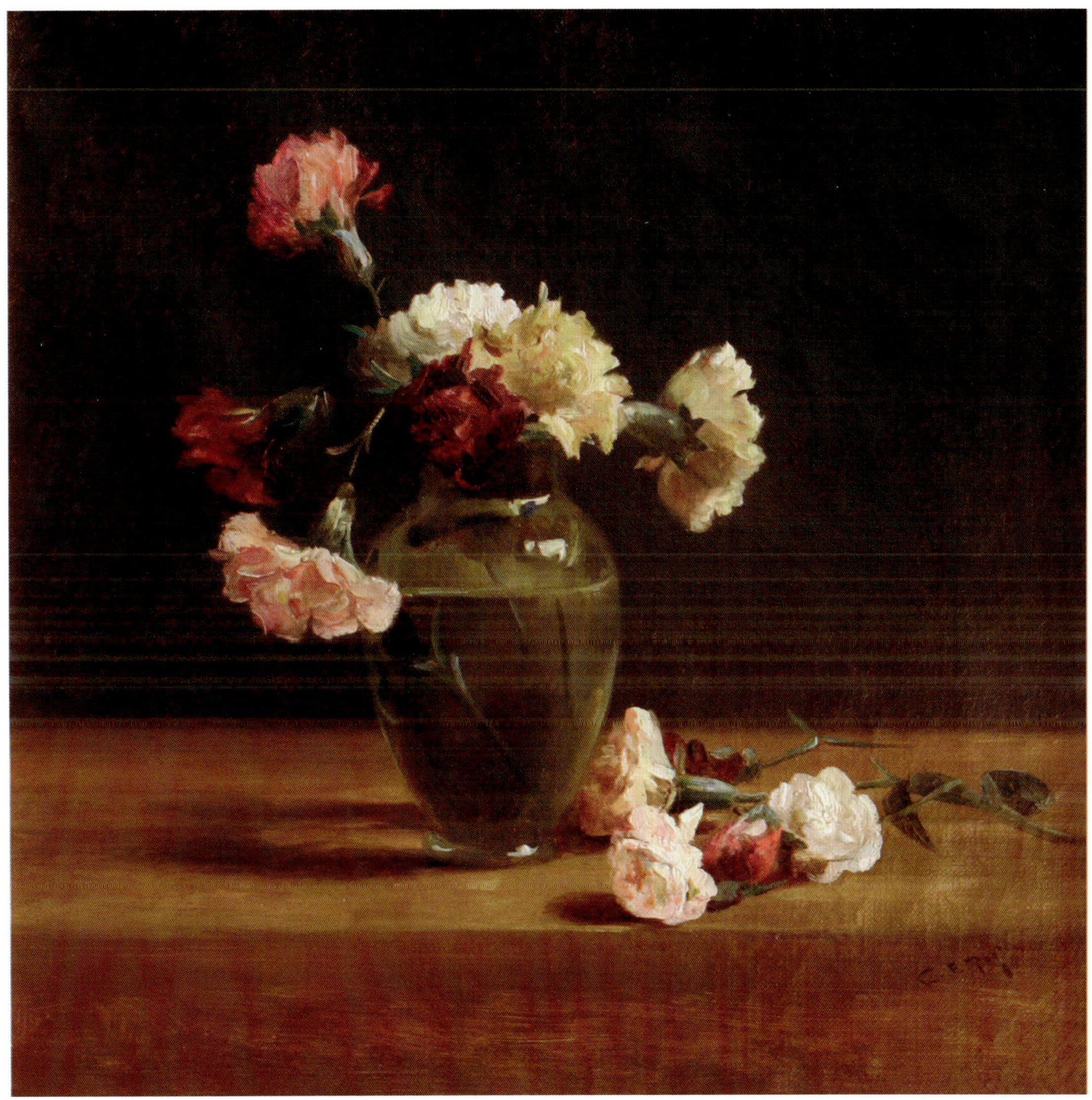

Catalogue 37
Carnations, 1887
Oil on canvas
11⅛" x 11⅛"
Signed and dated lower right
Ernest C. Wignall

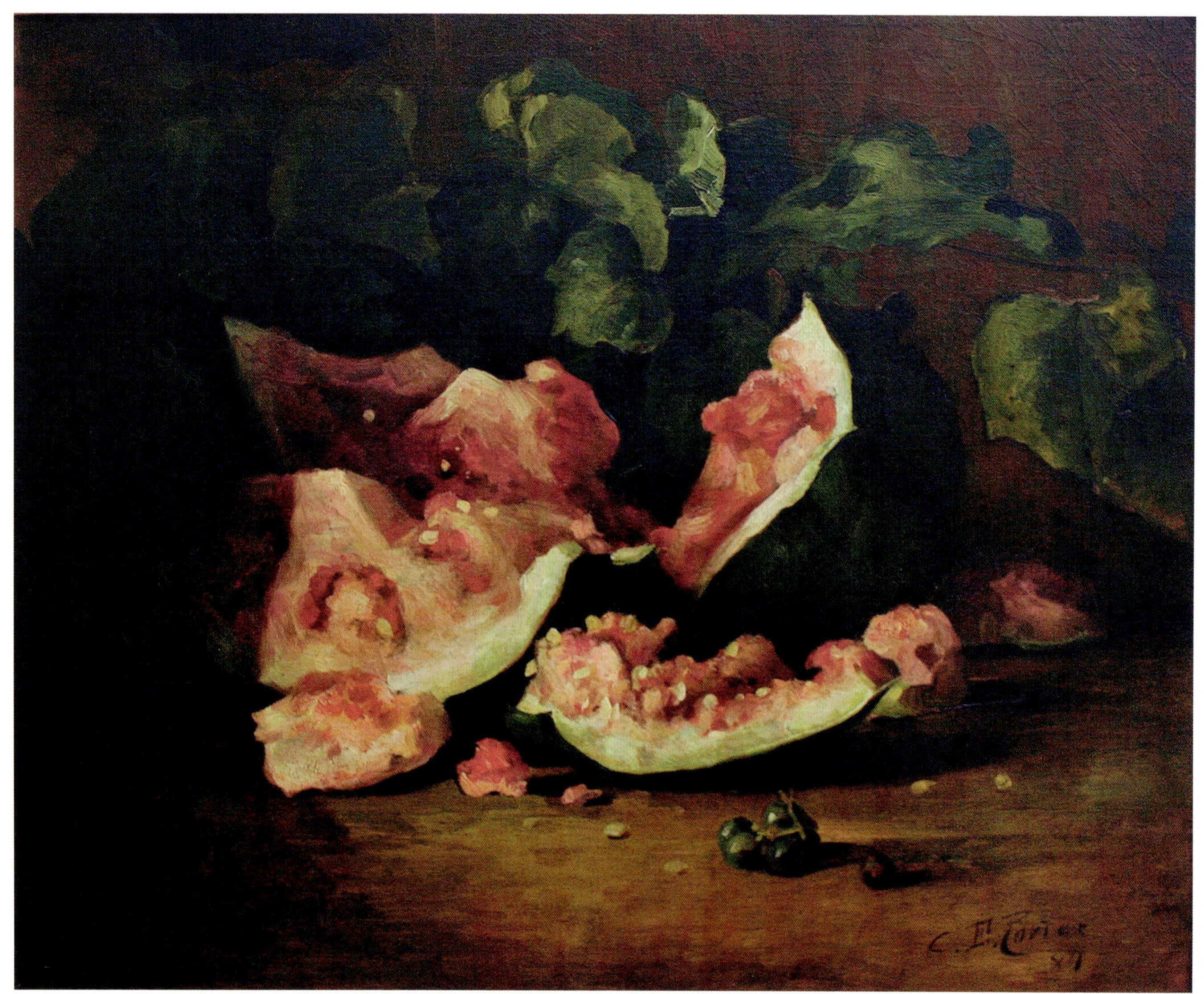

Catalogue 38
Broken Watermelon, 1884
Oil on canvas
20" x 24"
Signed and dated lower right
The Schonberger Family

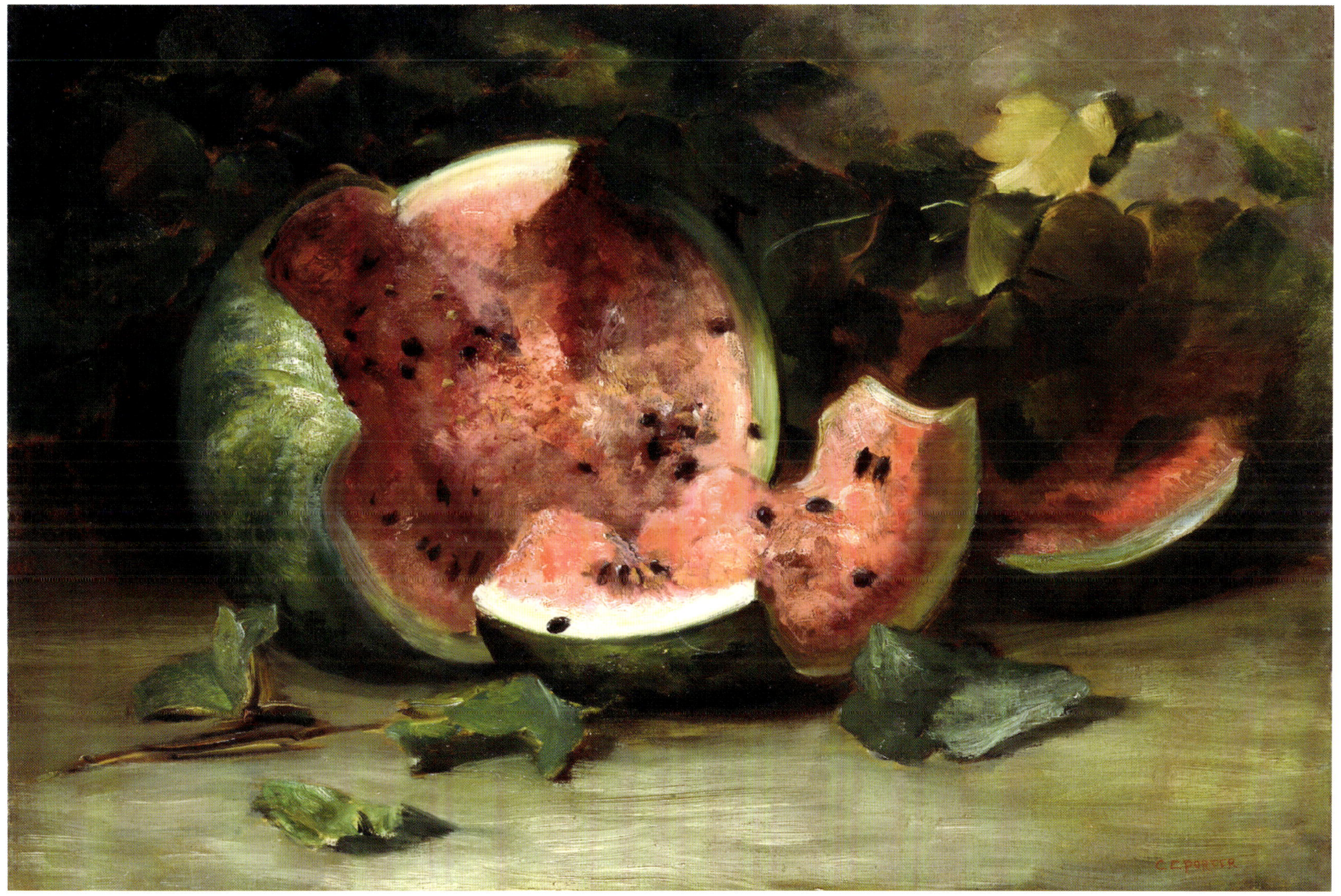

Catalogue 39
Cracked Watermelon, c. 1890
Oil on canvas
19" x 28"
Signed lower right
Courtesy of Michael Rosenfeld Gallery, LLC, New York City

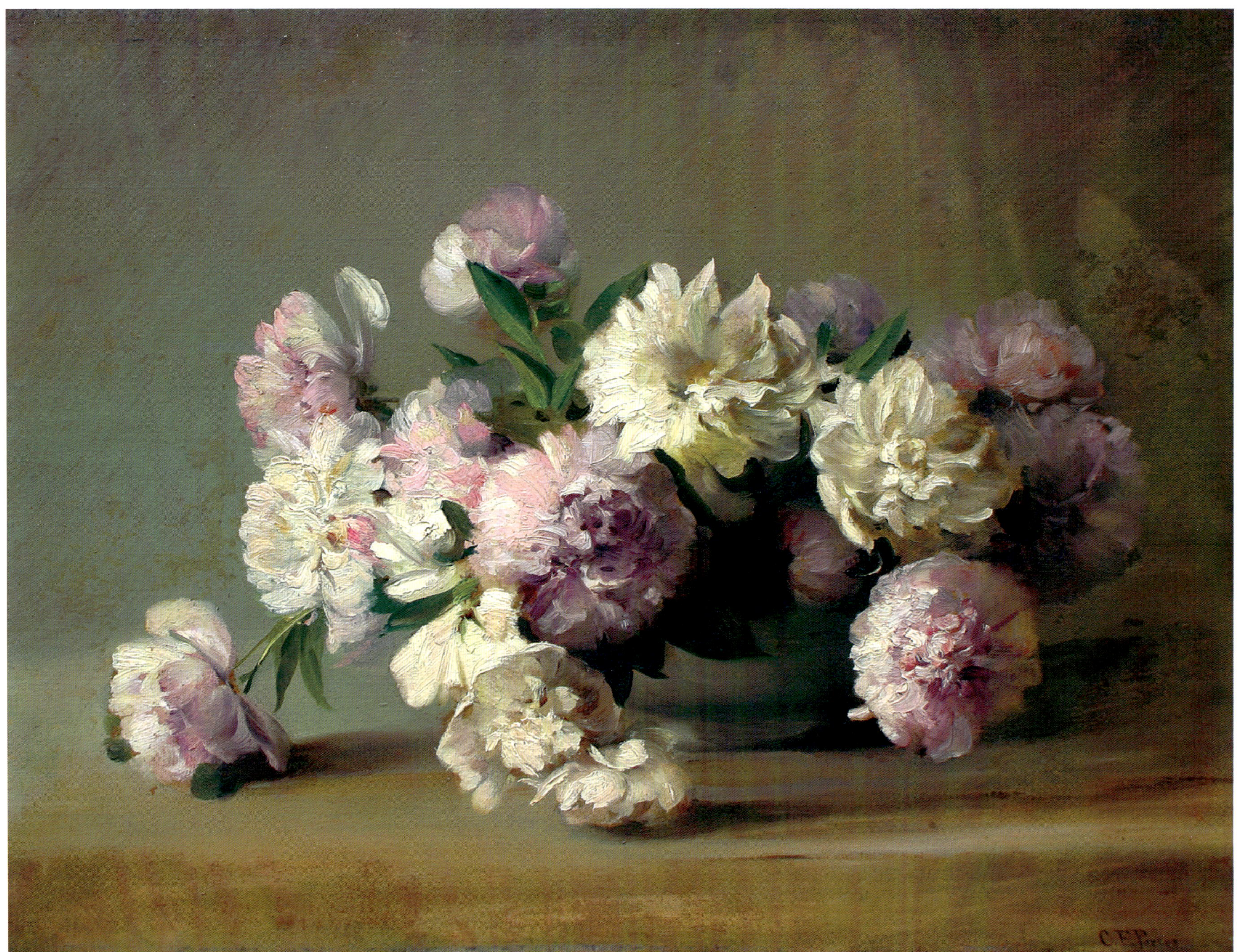

Catalogue 40
Peonies in a Bowl, c. 1885
Oil on canvas
21¼" x 29¼"
Signed lower right
Private collection

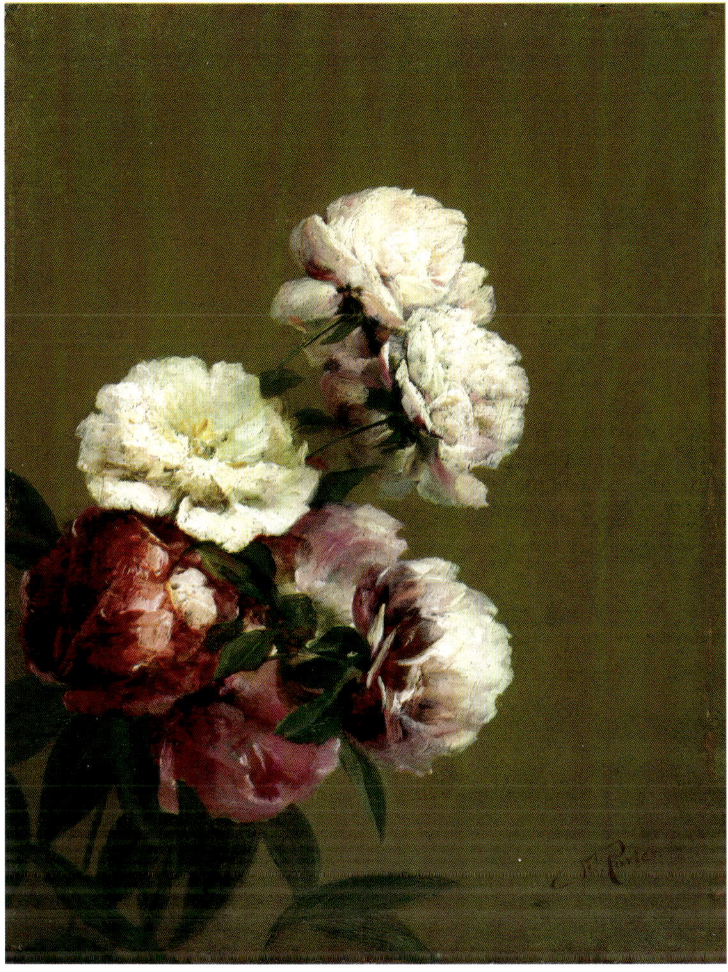

Catalogue 41
Peonies, c. 1885
Oil on board
18" x 14"
Signed lower right
Mattatuck Museum of Art and History

life artists, or the rest of us, for that matter, would have arranged these bouquets. In the oil, three blossoms are stuffed into the mouth of the vase while others shoot up or overhang. The bouquet in the watercolor is lopsided, and two drooping blooms actually touch the table. The informality of these bouquets goes beyond the norm, yet their very directness, oddity, and play-fulness make them extraordinary and appealing. Their arranger was not one

to put on airs or attempt to improve upon nature but was content—even eager—for us to savor the beauty, texture, and form of these flowers as they are.

Because Porter chose to paint flowers and fruit readily available in southern New England, his paintings often have the same subjects. *Broken Watermelon* (catalogue 38, see page 84) and *Cracked Watermelon* (catalogue 39, see page 85) offer a feast of color, texture, and form. The sensuous pink flesh in *Cracked Watermelon* has the look of Impressionist (even Abstract Expressionist) painting, shaped or shadowed into subtle triangles, while *Broken Watermelon* pairs triangular with circular forms. In both, strong light bleaches parts of the rind and bits of flesh to a stark white that intensifies adjacent colors and draws attention to the contrast between the grainy flesh and the curves of the rind. In his youth Porter thought he needed to use minute detail in order to achieve an illusion of realism. Later, he achieved better results by combining naturalistic detail with subtle patterning and abstraction.

Porter often depicted peonies. In *Peonies in a Bowl* (catalogue 40, see page 86) Porter created a gorgeous harmony of pinks, lavenders, and whites to portray blooms so lush that some bend from their own weight. Brushwork is fluid, colors breathtakingly beautiful, and lighting subtle. Porter used all three to balance the asymmetrical composition, weighting the arrangement by positioning two of the darker, least defined blooms at the far right. A horseshoe arrangement lures the eye from one soft bloom to another or to a few clearly defined petals without detracting from the impression of the bouquet as a whole.

An image of growing flowers, like that in the Mattatuck Museum's *Peonies* (catalogue 41) represents a popular nineteenth-century convention. To vary the design, as Porter did, by having blooms enter the painting obliquely from one side is an uncommon, even idiosyncratic, move that enabled him to give prominence to flowers seen in profile, a position where they seldom make a strong statement.

Two depictions of hollyhocks show Porter using a vertical format to present these old-fashioned garden flowers in very different ways. In *Pink Hollyhocks* (catalogue 42), two flowering stems curve around rich green leaves. The broadly brushed blossoms, seen from several angles, exhibit Porter's usual mastery of color. The eye sweeps from one pretty group to the other in a curvilinear movement that can feel like a graceful dance movement.

Hollyhocks (catalogue 43) evokes a different response. Here, a collection of frilly white blooms is presented formally and frontally in an arrangement having a strong upward thrust. *Hollyhocks*, as a perceptive critic recently wrote, "is not merely vertical, but starkly so. Yet for all its prim, puritanical posture the painting is a hedonistic delight, alive with sensuous blooming flowers graced with seductive shapes and colors."[136] Both hollyhock paintings include the feature that Helen K. Fusscas first saw as a Porter signature: blooms in a horseshoe arrangement around a "hole" of greenery.[137]

Porter sometimes employed the convention of flowers strewn on a table or ledge, as in *Mixed Bouquet* (catalogue 44, see page 90). In other instances, in the manner of John LaFarge (1835–1910) or Martin

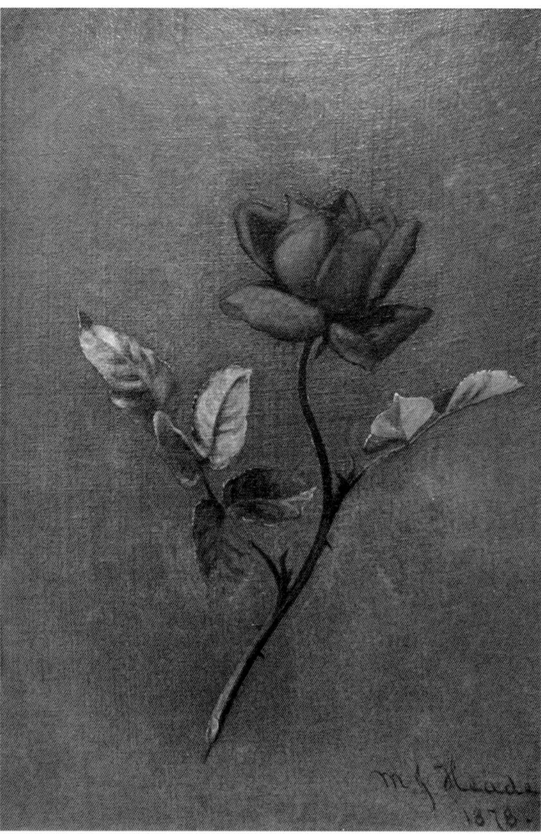

Figure 10–*Martin Johnson Heade*
Red Rose, 1878
Oil on canvas
15" x 11"
Collection of the
New Britain Museum
of American Art.
Gift of the Alix W. Stanley
Estate, 1954.04.

Johnson Heade (1819–1904), he portrayed just a few blooms, as in *Pansies* (catalogue 45, see page 91) and *Apple Blossoms on a Ledge* (catalogue 46, see page 91). The perfect red rose in the New Britain Museum's Heade has nothing to detract from its iconic presence (figure 10), but this artist-naturalist more often presented his beautifully articulated flowers on a striking red cloth, as though they were jewels on display, as Porter did in *Mixed Bouquet*.

No Porter still lifes are known to be exactly alike. By the end of the nineteenth century, American art patrons wanted original art, and artists obliged. The changes that Porter instituted in order to create one-of-a-kind paintings are wide ranging and are strikingly evident in his paintings of roses, the flower he appears to have depicted most often.

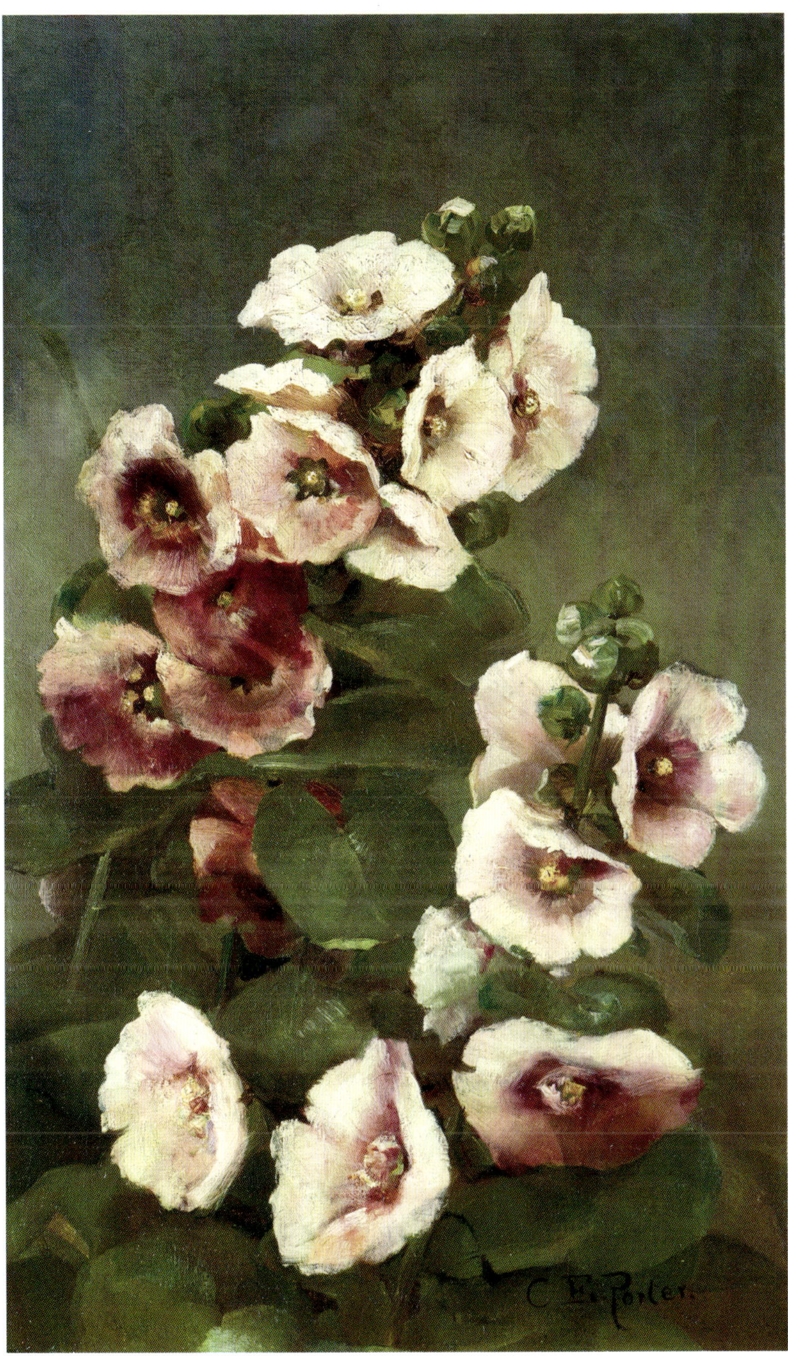

Catalogue 42
Pink Hollyhocks, c. 1885
Oil on canvas
20¼" x 12⅛"
Signed lower right
Dr. and Mrs. Frederick Baekeland

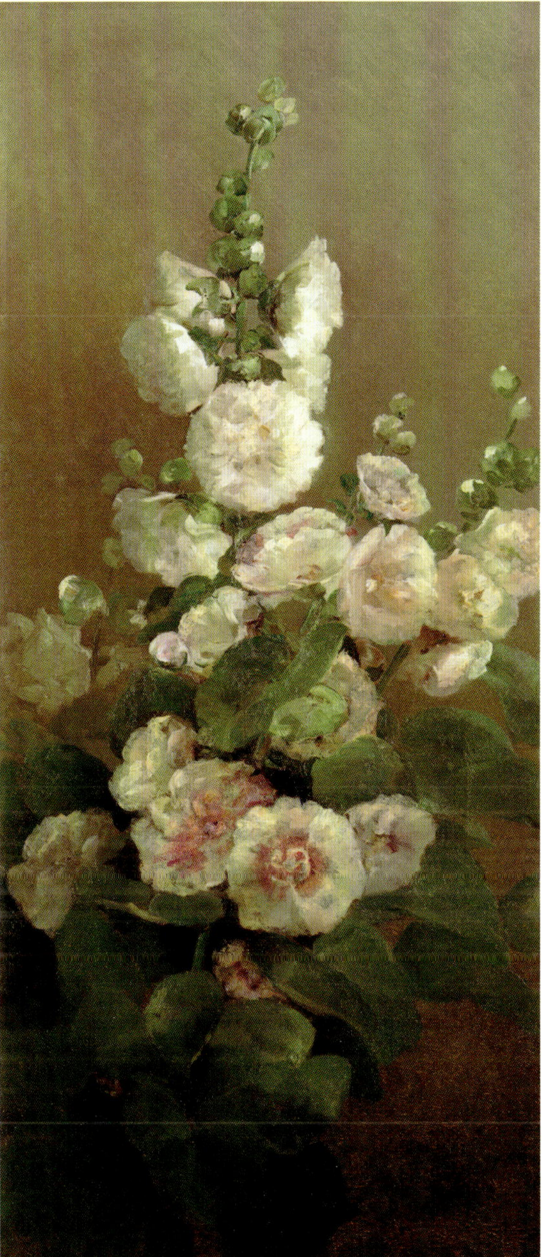

Catalogue 43
Hollyhocks
Oil on canvas
30" x 13"
Signed lower right
Wadsworth Atheneum Museum of Art, Hartford, CT. The Dorothy Clark Archibald and
Thomas L. Archibald Fund, The Ella Gallup Sumner and Mary Catlin Sumner Collection
Fund, and Partial Gift of Thomas Colville.

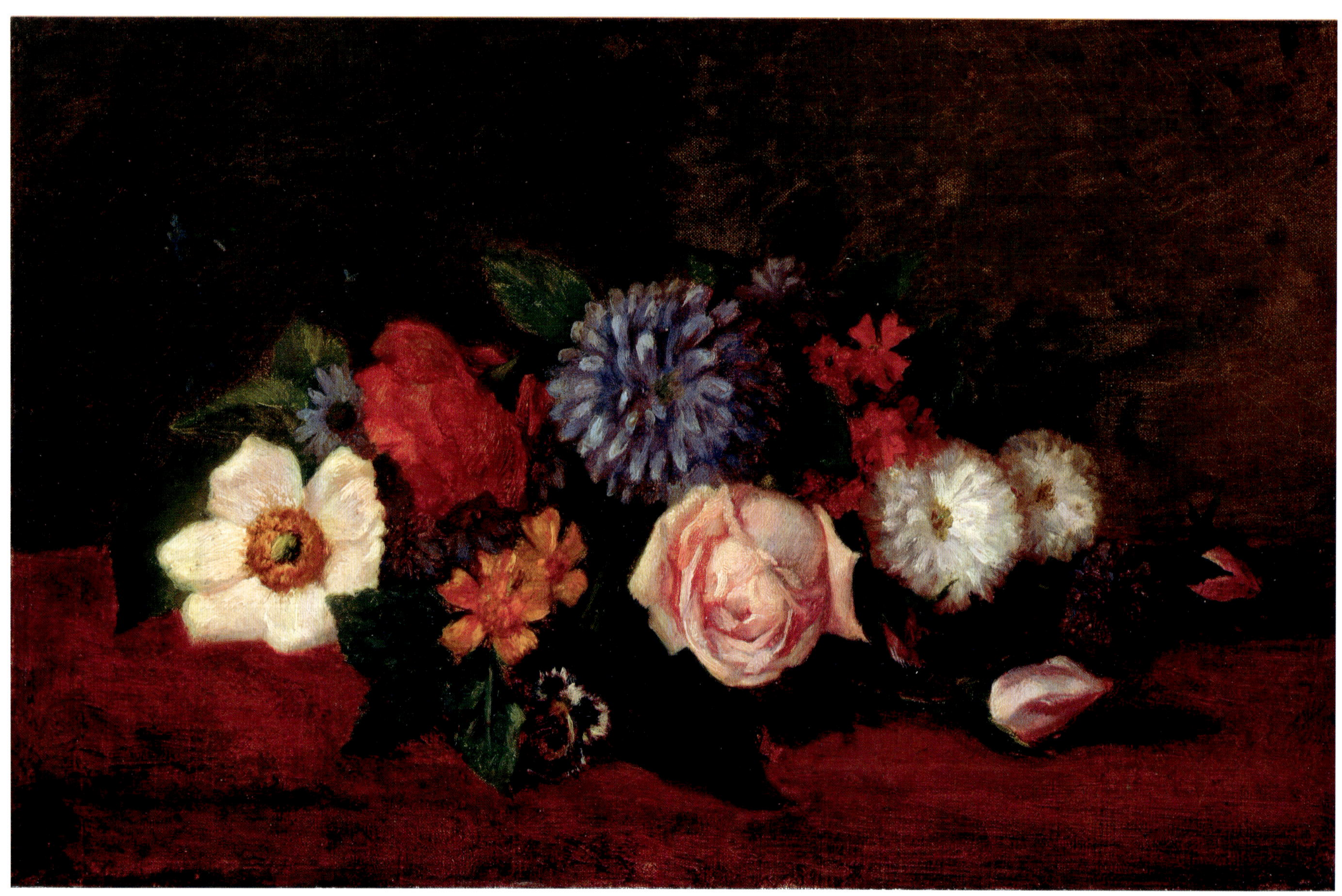

Catalogue 44
Mixed Bouquet, c. 1878
Oil on canvas
7½" x 11½"
Signed lower center
Kronholm Collection

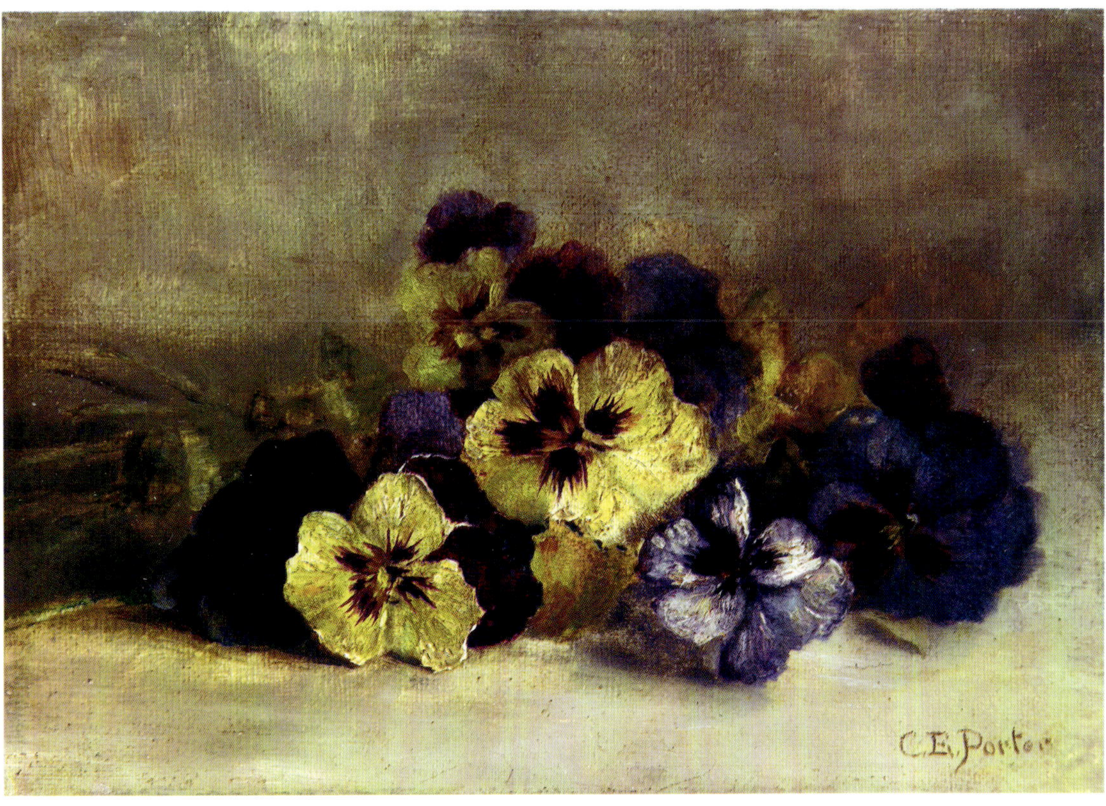

Catalogue 45
Pansies, c. 1883
Oil on canvas
5½" x 7½"
Signed lower right
Courtesy of Peg Alston/Peg Alston Fine Arts

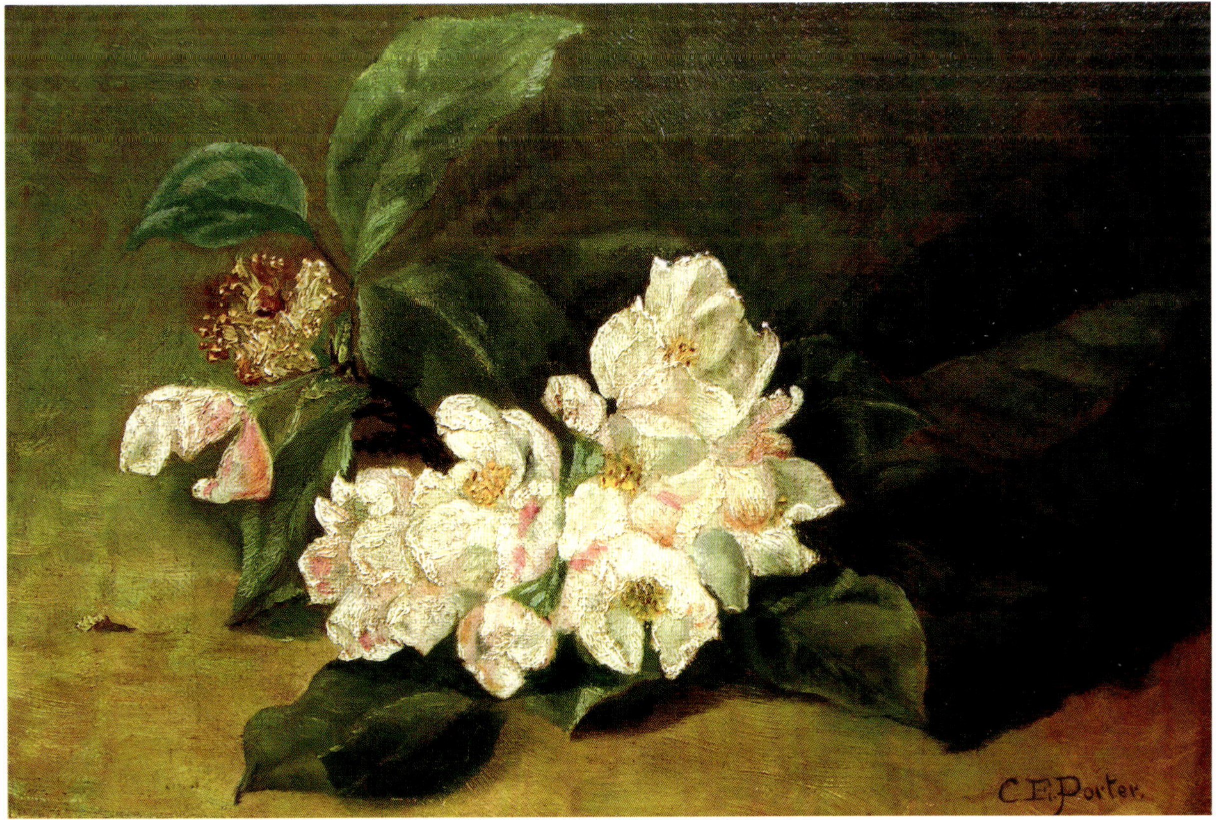

Catalogue 46
Apple Blossoms on a Ledge, c. 1883
Oil on canvas
6" x 9"
Signed lower right
Drs. Jeffrey and Sivan Hines

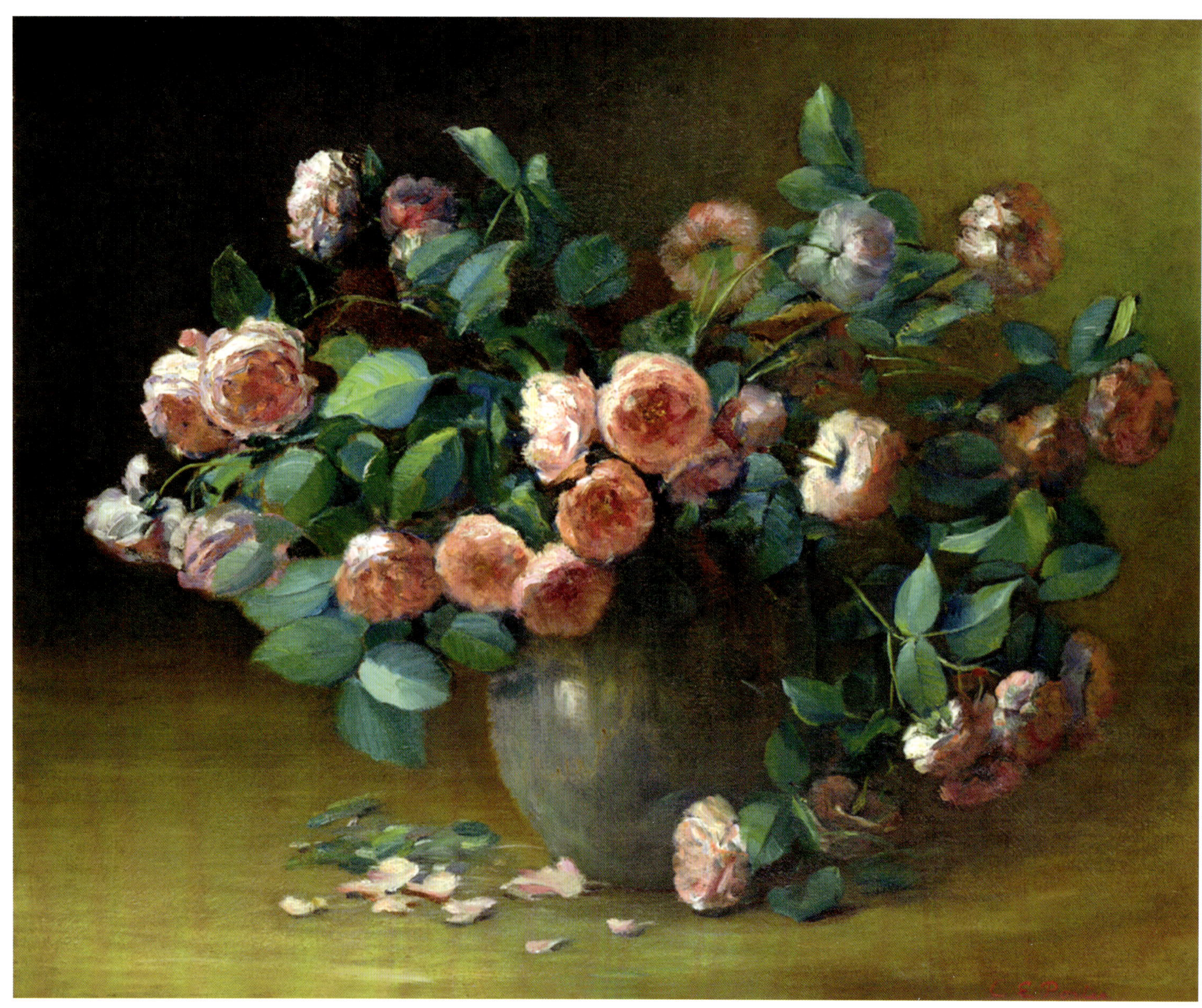

Catalogue 47
Rambling Roses, c. 1885
Oil on canvas
20" x 24"
Signed lower right
Courtesy of Michael Rosenfeld Gallery, LLC, New York City

He can be ebullient at times, as in *Rambling Roses* (catalogue 47), and restrained and suggestive at others, as in *Yellow Roses in a Vase* (catalogue 48, see page 94).

The few Porter landscapes that are known are similarly distinctive—with the exception of *Fox Hill* (catalogue 49, see page 95). Fox Hill, site of Porter's Rockville home, has no body of water, but the issue is not the title. The mystery is that some half dozen untitled versions of this image exist, executed in oil, pastel, and watercolor. Did clients order them or did Porter feel moved to repeat this image for reasons of his own?

Porter usually organized landscape paintings into horizontal bands, often with a diagonal feature such as a fence to lead the viewer's eye into the middle ground, but in the "Fox Hill" pictures he emphasized the frontal plane and the immediacy and verticality of trees. Generally set at either sunrise or sunset, the paintings vary slightly in size and shape but are otherwise virtually identical. It takes close study to discern subtle differences in the web of branches or the placement of rocks. Except possibly for the first of these paintings, Porter was not working *en plein air*. Some versions, including catalogue 49, show a castle-like structure on the distant hill. It is tempting to see such a scene as symbolic of the artist's quest for success, which was thwarted by the obstacles he encountered. The "Fox Hill" series appears to date from the late 1880s or early 1890s. It was then, coincidentally, that Porter made great changes in his life and career.

The Last Years, 1889–1923

Porter moved out of Hartford for good in 1889. For a while, he spent part of each winter in New York City and the rest of the year in Rockville. About 1897 he settled permanently in Rockville, exhibiting occasionally there and elsewhere until 1914, when his work was last seen at the Connecticut Academy of Fine Arts. He stopped teaching then or soon after.

A sharp decline in the quality of his work begins around the turn of the century. Late paintings can exhibit deterioration so startling that it seems as though the artist must have suffered a physical or emotional trauma. At their worst, they show a loss of control. Forms that were once finely delineated and modeled are mushy, colors muddy, compositions dull, and light lackluster. Some paintings are signed twice, one signature over another in styles thought to stem from different periods. Did Porter have trouble seeing or did he rework his canvases? Rumors persist that students sometimes finished paintings for him.

What happened to Porter will probably never be known, but speculation has focused on alcoholism, his era's most common addiction. If Porter took to drink, his close ties with family members, all of them ardent temperance activists, surely must have suffered, yet they appear to have been unaffected. Poverty crushed Porter, some say. Late paintings are sometimes on the back of old oilcloth, which implies that he was too poor to buy canvas. Still, he continued to use high-quality paint.[138] The tale that Porter carried his paintings door to door in Rockville and asked

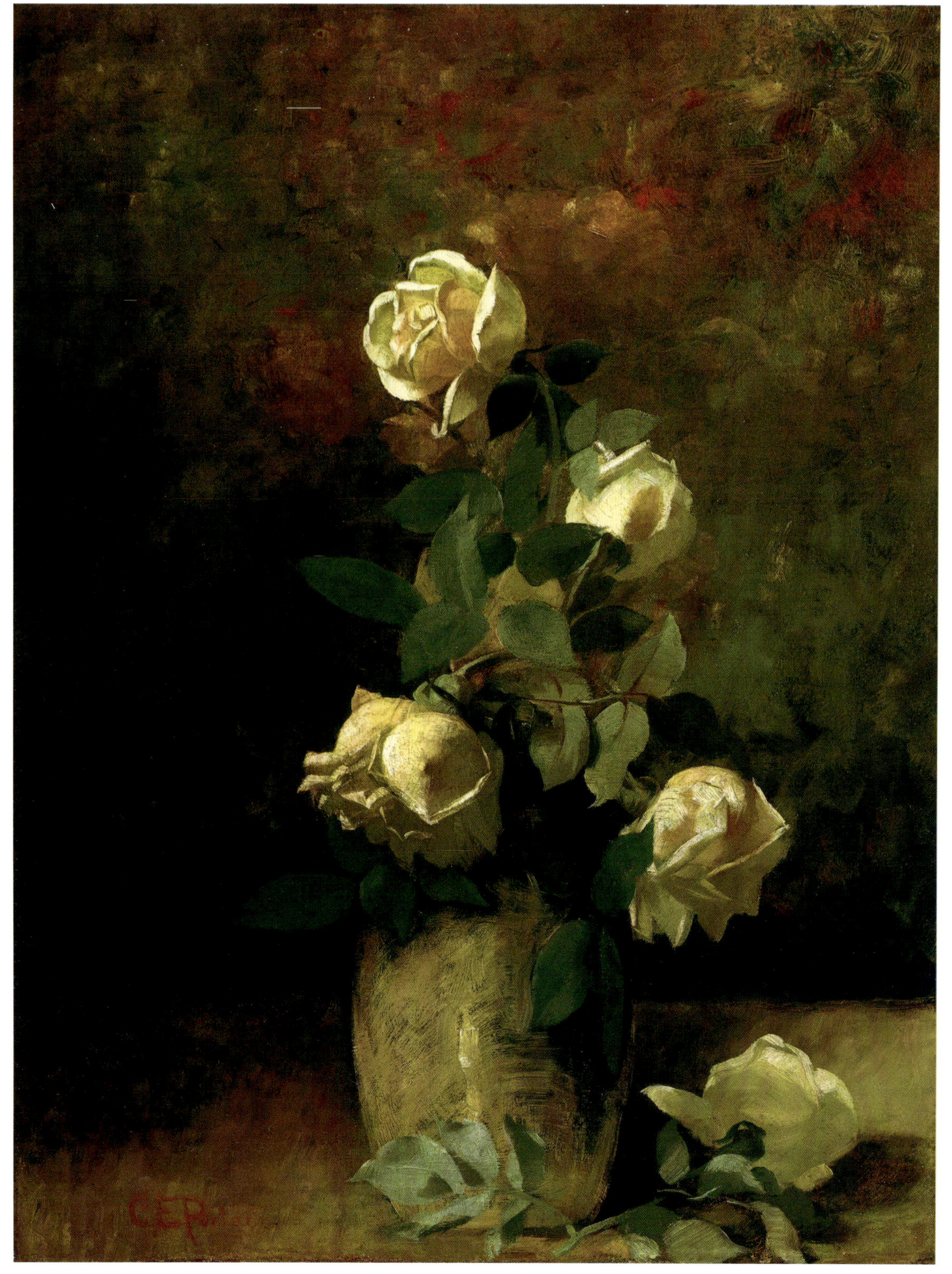

Catalogue 48
Yellow Roses in a Vase, c. 1885–90
Oil on canvas
18¼" x 13¼"
Signed lower left
Private Collection of Wilberding, Hobart

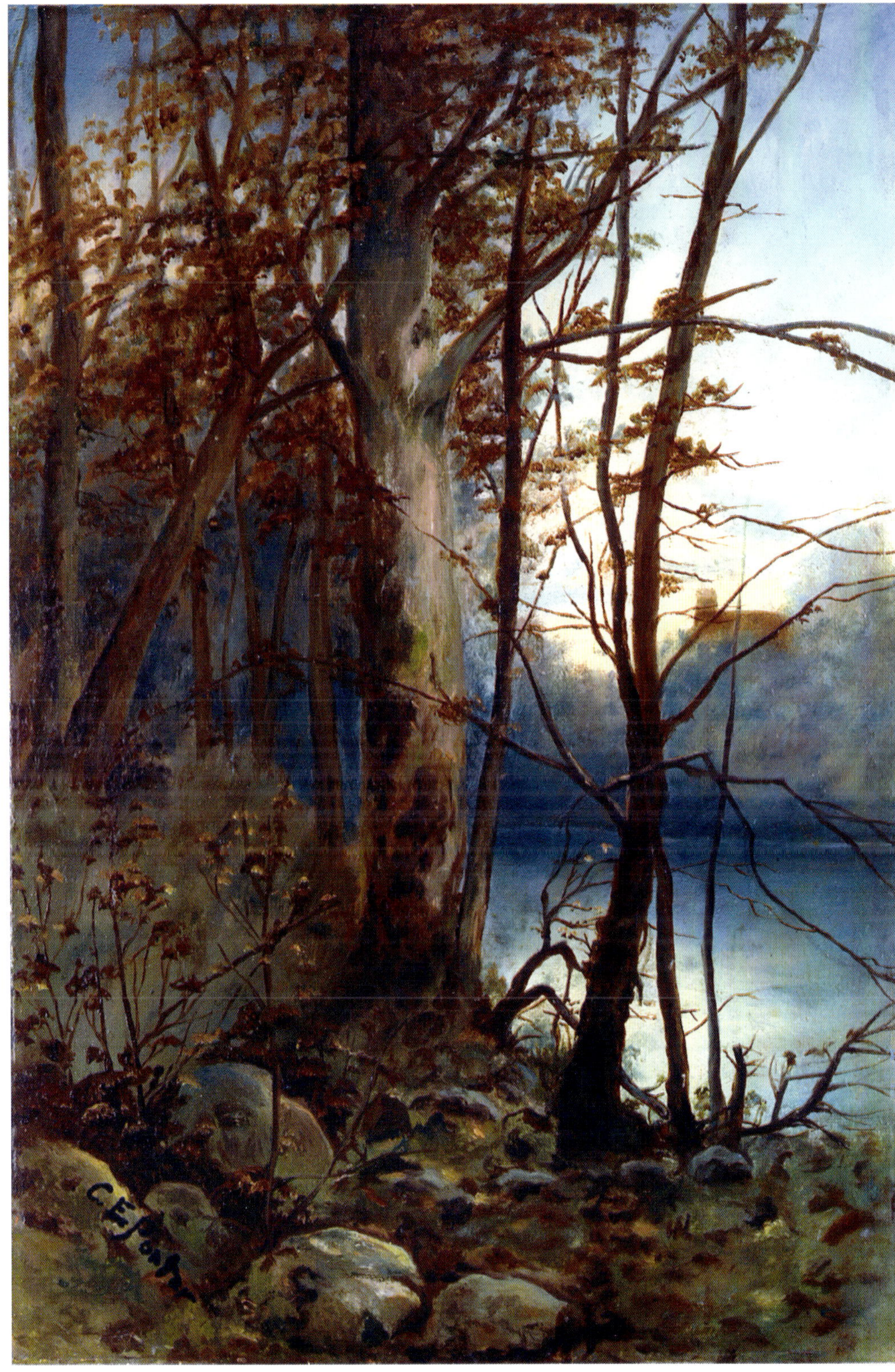

Catalogue 49
Fox Hill, c. 1885
Oil on board
18" x 11¼"
Signed lower left
Courtesy of Michael Rosenfeld
Gallery, LLC, New York City

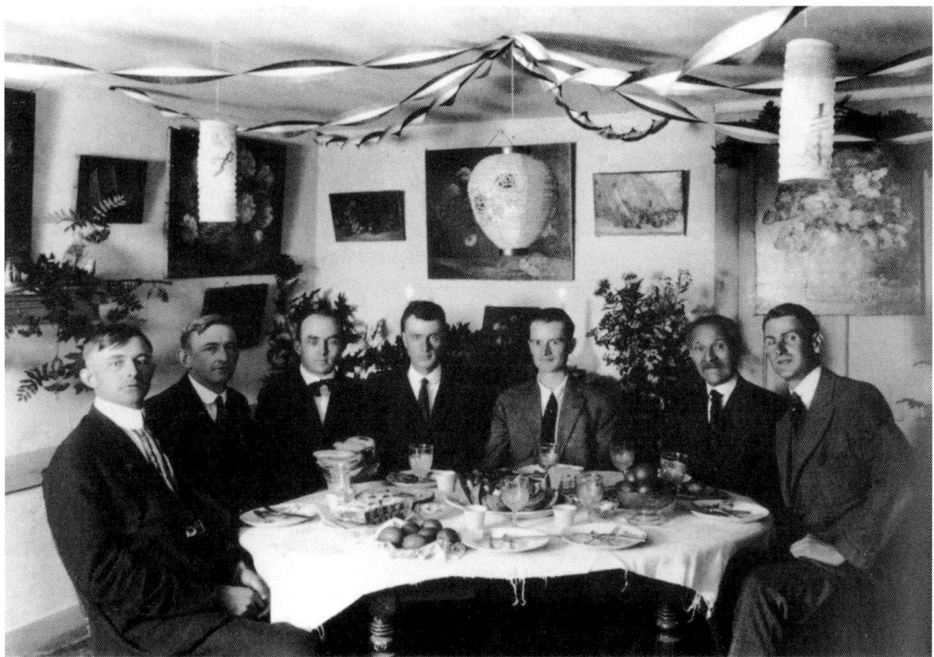

Figure 11–**Charles Ethan Porter with students.**
Photo courtesy of the Vernon Historical Society

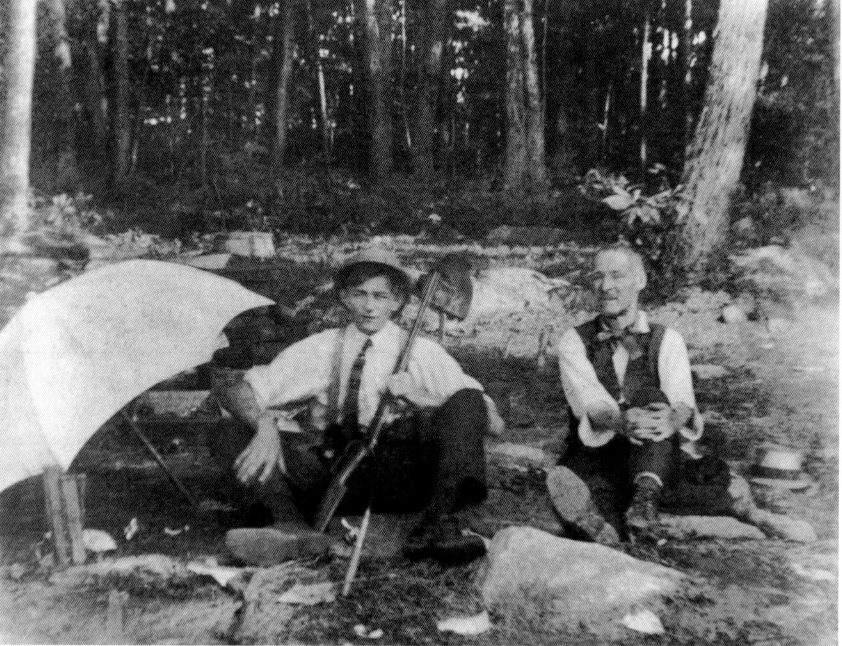

Figure 12–**Charles Ethan Porter outdoors with friend.**
Photo courtesy of the Vernon Historical Society

to do chores if people would not buy is heard so often it may well be true. The most striking aspect of the gossip about Porter, which is based mostly on the childhood memories of persons long dead, is how contradictory it is. The artist was seen as dark-skinned, light-skinned, tall, short, thin, stout, sober, and alcoholic. He was referred to as respectfully as Professor Porter and as disparagingly as Charles the Nigger.

Porter certainly had family, friends, admirers, and devoted students in Rockville. Students sometimes organized festive dinners for him (figure 11) or joined him on painting outings (figure 12). A neighbor visited regularly to speak French with him. Children gathered at his easel to watch him paint. There were also, however, Rockville residents who would not allow him to step over their threshold. Some that bought paintings from him had a servant handle the sale so they would not have to see him. Others treated him pleasantly enough then vilified him behind his back. Rockville was no different from the rest of America at the turn of the twentieth century.

Whatever it was—racism, illness, poverty, a combination of the above, or something else—that derailed Porter, it did not entirely crush him. When, in 1920, just three years before his death, a census taker asked his occupation, Porter answered, "Artist."

Until at least 1900, Porter continued to work hard at his career. In November 1889 he established a studio in the new Fitch Block in the center of Rockville. He relocated afterward to Fox Hill, to the sturdy base that had supported a brother-in-law's observation tower, felled by a storm many years before. The large square room was rent free and just steps from his parents' home, where he lived. He would use this studio for the rest of his working life. His students, women as well as men, were not put off by the steep climb to the crest of the hill.

Porter was in New York City from at least December 1890 until the following April. He did not, however, ignore his following in Hartford and rented a hall there in April 1891 for an auction of fifty fruit and flower paintings. He went to Rockville until October, when he painted along the Connecticut River, before setting off for Putnam, in the northeast corner of the state. In November, he mounted another exhibition in Hartford, this one with more than one hundred works. Newspapers failed to announce the event, so Porter took out advertisements. Only the *Hartford Evening Post* reviewed the exhibition, beginning with words that must have lifted the artist's spirits: "Tucked away in a corner of Hills' block on Main Street there is an oasis of color and beauty." Here are Porter's latest paintings, the report reads, all works in oil, "embracing every line":

> There are landscapes, floral pieces, marine views and studies in still life. His landscapes are particularly noticeable for their beauty. A twilight scene is the most artistic conception and best executed of the lot. It is a wonderful work of color. The eye is liable to be caught with a farmyard scene, a wheelbarrow filled with pumpkins, being the main feature. On every side something will be found to admire.[139]

This time, perhaps because he felt encouraged, Porter stayed in Hartford for a few weeks, advertising his services as a teacher of drawing and painting before departing for New York, where he had winter studios until at least 1896.

Where Porter lived in New York in 1896 has not been determined, but it was probably in or near the YMCA's Association Building.[140] How he fared professionally while the nation was experiencing another economic depression is also unknown. Railroad bankruptcies in 1893 had caused banks to call in their loans, and by the time the depression ended four years later, unemployment had reached 25 percent.

There is as yet no exhibition history for Porter in New York, but in the 1890s he sometimes exhibited briefly in Connecticut with one or two other artists. Probably he was responsible for these exhibitions, since his partners, who were some twenty years younger than he, lacked his experience in such matters.

In October 1893, Porter showed with a Mr. Stephenson and a Mr. Comstock at the Hartford YMCA. The *Hartford Daily Courant* found it "surprising that these artists are willing to let such excellent specimens of their work go so cheaply, but they probably realize that some concession has to be made to the stringent times."[141] Two years later, other works by Comstock and Porter were on view at the Hartford YMCA, while an exhibition in Essex, Connecticut, was devoted to images of historic buildings in that shoreline village by Porter, Comstock, and three painters named Roorbach—presumably Alfred, George S., and his wife Eloise—who all wintered in New York.[142]

The identity of Mr. Stephenson is unknown, but Samuel Morley Comstock (1870–1900) was an Essex native, related to the son of the town's leading citizen, Samuel Merritt Comstock, one of the largest producers of ivory products in the world. Samuel Morley Comstock was an artist, illustrator, and poet. In summer 1894 he visited Porter in Rockville for a few weeks, and in the winters the two toured galleries in New York and often dined together. They were joined in 1896 by Gustave Hoffman (1869–1945), a young artist from Rockville, until he went home to support his mother and sister. That fall, Porter and Hoffman embarked on a painting trip through New England.

In the late 1890s Porter had exhibitions in Hartford and in Springfield, Massachusetts. By 1895 his work was seen annually at Horace Rude's stationery store in Springfield, which had gallery space for about a dozen paintings. Rude died in 1900. In December 1898 Porter had a weeklong solo exhibition at the Hartford YMCA. It included the usual flower and fruit pieces, but the really interesting paintings, according to the *Hartford Daily Courant*, were the several landscapes: "They are all of quiet New England life, and in repose and soft effects of light and true coloring give much satisfaction."[143]

Porter continued to show Rockville what he was up to. In March 1898 he mounted an exhibition in the Fitch Block. In November, after a summer in Essex with Comstock and Hoffman, he and Hoffman were featured in an exhibition at George M. Bolton's photography studio, also in the Fitch Block. Porter's paintings, Hoffman's etchings, and Bolton's photographs, along with pastels, watercolors, and photographs by other artists, including amateurs, drew one thousand visitors in one week, some of them from Boston and Providence. The success of the venture prompted Bolton to host a sequel the next year. In 1900 he varied the offering to feature watercolors by Porter and by Daniel Wentworth.

While their reunion at Bolton's suggests that Porter and Wentworth were friends, it was apparently the first time they had exhibited together since the auctions of 1887 and 1888. Wentworth had had a few solo and group exhibitions in Hartford and beyond and was active in the city's Camera Club. He had without question become a member of Hartford's artistic inner circle. In 1904 the *Courant* named him, along with other historic and contemporary artists, as a contributor to the city's "art spirit."[144] Porter's name was not on this list. Previously, in 1892, Porter had not been invited, as Wentworth had been, to join the Hartford Society of Artists, a short-lived organization for artists who had worked in Hartford. Wentworth and Porter traveled different paths after their joint auctions in the late 1880s. There are presently no signs that they were friends.

Porter's thrilling tenor did not become silent after Hartford's religious revival of 1878. Years later, in 1890, a *Rockville Journal* reporter visited the home of Henry Vanness on Fox Hill and found Porter playing the piano and singing Methodist camp meeting hymns with his family. In the early twentieth century, his singing won public notice again. For at least two years Porter was a tenor soloist at Rockville's Methodist Episcopal Church. He sang at least four times in 1902 and six times in 1903, alone or in duets or quartets. Diary entries covering the two-year tenure of a choirmaster confirm most of these performances and local newspapers some others.[145]

Choirmaster Fred Carleton Presbrey did not like Porter's singing. He was himself a tenor soloist and may have thought he was better. Privately, in his diary, he critiqued his soloists, seldom calling them better than fair but always at least that, yet about Porter he wrote nothing or expressed disapproval. On October 5, 1902, Porter sang as the offertory Adolphe Schlosser's "He That Keepeth Israel." "Some good tones," Presbrey allowed, "but no use on enuntiation [sic] and presence very poor."[146] In May 1903 he found Porter's "Jubilate Deo" by Franz Schubert to be poor, yet he had him sing it again at the end of October—after Porter's return from a painting sojourn at Old Hamburg, Connecticut, with fellow Methodist Gustave Hoffman.

Rockville's Methodists must have enjoyed Porter's voice; otherwise, Presley himself would have stepped in. Oddly, Presbrey's diary entry for April 23, 1902, alludes to a reception in Porter's honor when the reception was actually for the new minister, named Buck. The only tenor solo that evening was by Presbrey. Jealousy alone might account for the choirmaster's hostility toward Porter, but racism is also a likely factor.

Porter, who was single, was always close to his family. He attended family gatherings in Rockville and Meriden even when it meant a special trip from New York. In September 1884 he shared in the family's pride that brother William's daughter Mary was going to Beaufort, South Carolina, to teach the Gullah children of the coastal Sea Islands, where slaves had been able to preserve much of their African culture. (It was 1915 before South Carolina opened its public schools to blacks.)

Family members continued to work for their causes. In the 1890s brother-in-law Richard Alonzo Jeffrey was the superintendent of the Sunday school of the Parker Memorial A.M.E. Zion Church in Meriden, and brother William was prelate of Excelsior Lodge #115 (Knights of Pythias). Later, he, too, became the Sunday school superintendent at Parker Memorial. On at least two occasions, the artist's brother-in-law Henry Vanness gave speeches at the Sumner League, one of them on the situation in Cuba. The League had been established in 1894 for the social and political improvement of Connecticut's minorities. In 1903 brother James was appointed the official Coat Room Messenger of the Connecticut Legislature. Since newspapers reported only the officers of organizations or other special achievements, it is not known whether Porter was a Mason or a member of the Sumner League or of other groups that worked for the benefit of his race. (The Lincoln Club was dissolved in the mid-1880s.) In any case, he would have heard of these activities from family members. The longtime activism of the extended Porter family, however, was nearing an end.

The new century inaugurated a series of personal losses like those Porter had not known since adolescence. His friend Samuel Comstock died of tuberculosis in 1900 at age twenty-nine; Horace Rude, his Springfield dealer, died that year as well. The artist lost his parents within months of each other: his father in December 1905 and his mother in June 1906. Brother James died some time between 1906 and 1915, the year that brother William succumbed to the infirmities he had contracted while a Union soldier. In 1918 Porter lost both his sisters: Mary, the wife of Henry Vanness, and Cynthia, R. A. Jeffrey's wife. Jeffrey died the following year. At some point, Jeffrey owned a delivery firm, but it must have failed—he became a janitor, then worked as a teamster for the rest of his life. It was enormously challenging during this period of racism for middle-class men of color to be entrepreneurs, as Jeffrey once had been. Leaders of the black communities in Hartford and Meriden still had to work as janitors, porters, messengers, and teamsters. After 1918 Porter's remaining close relatives were his youngest brother, Frank, a messenger at the Aetna Insurance Company in Hartford, and Henry Vanness, his brother-in-law and Fox Hill neighbor.

After 1904, the year he transferred his Methodist church membership from New York to Rockville, Porter had a crisis of faith. An undated note next to his name on the Methodist roll in Rockville indicates that he became a Christian Scientist. A religious census of the township of Vernon for 1921, when presumably Porter already had made his commitment, lists just sixteen Christian Scientists (and 554 Methodists).

The first Christian Science meetings in Rockville were held in summer 1907 at the home of a Mrs. Carlos Doane. They came about, according to a Rockville historian, because of the interest in Christian Science aroused by the healing of "rheumatism and extreme profanity" in a Mr. Orrin C. West of Rockville and by Mrs. Doane's own healing of grief and a nervous condition brought on by the death of her daughter.[147] Ten or twelve people were soon attending the meetings, including Mrs. Doane's brother, who was healed of a nervous breakdown. By 1908 Sunday services were held in hired halls, and, after 1917, evening meetings were added for testimonies of healing. A Society, precursor to a Christian Science Church, which cannot be dedicated until it is debt free—was formed in 1914.[148] Whenever he joined the Christian Scientists—and for whatever reasons—Porter fully embraced his new faith.

Porter died in Rockville on March 7, 1923, after an attack of nephritis.[149] He had a Christian Science funeral and is buried near his parents and several of his siblings in the Grove Hill Cemetery in Rockville, at the foot of Fox Hill. The family monument, an obelisk with an urn on top, is one of the most imposing in the small graveyard. One side of the obelisk is devoted to young Joseph, who died on a Virginia battlefield in 1864. The names and life dates of the Porter children who died in the 1860s are incised on another. Porter's name dominates a third.

The Legacy

We are left with many questions about the life and art of Charles Ethan Porter. Some may someday be answered, as personal papers and other primary sources are located and more pictures are discovered. Hartford newspapers reported that Porter's exhibitions often included one hundred or more paintings, yet today only some one hundred of his works are known. His landscapes are seldom seen, and marines, dead fish, and flower wreaths are among the Porter subjects that have yet to surface. Still, we have an impressive legacy, as well as a personal story worthy of attention and respect. We see that Porter employed artistic conventions of his day—he had no choice—yet often charged them with the intensity and quirkiness of folk art even as he codified them into sophisticated, colorful designs that reveal great beauty in humble bits of nature.

Perhaps Frederic Edwin Church had primitivism in mind when he commented in the 1870s that one of Porter's pictures was the most unconscious piece of painting he had ever seen. Those words bothered Porter. Years later he repeated them to a reporter, adding, "I had rather be an honest fool than a brilliant knave."[150] He was neither. Through study, experimentation, and perseverance—and despite shameful obstacles grounded in racial prejudice—Porter created fine art that will endure. The achievement is so extraordinary that further words are unnecessary. A few, however, that the artist wrote to Mark Twain from Paris on April 4, 1883, bear repeating:

> Now I am aware that there are a goodly number of my Hartford
> friends and others who are anxious to see how the colored artist will
> make out, but this is not the motive which impresses me. There is
> something of more importance. The colored people—my people—as
> a race I am interested in, and my success will only add to others who
> have already shown wherein they are capable the same as other men.[151]

NOTES

[1] Lewis made this claim more than once, as in a March 1866 interview published in the London *Atheneum*.

[2] Mary D. Porter to Joseph S. Porter, July 1, 1864. Mary D. Porter Federal Pension Application, National Archives, WC211210. I am grateful to Colleen Cyr for sharing these papers with me.

[3] "Connecticut Legislature — Special Session," *Hartford Daily Courant*, November 14, 1863.

[4] Ibid.

[5] Classified ads, *Hartford Daily Courant*, December 2, 1863.

[6] Records of the Methodist Episcopal Church, Rockville, Connecticut. I thank David White for this information.

[7] Quoted in Benjamin Quarles, *The Negro in the Civil War* (Boston: Little, Brown, 1998), p. 209

[8] Poem by Joseph Porter, July 10, 1864. Mary D. Porter Pension Application.

[9] William H. Porter Federal Pension Application, National Archives, C2514D19. Colleen Cyr has kindly shared these papers with me.

[10] U.S. Army Certificate of Disability for Discharge for Sgt. William H. Porter, January 8, 1865. William H. Porter Pension Application.

[11] Joseph Porter to Mary Porter, September 6, 1864. Mary D. Porter Pension Application.

[12] "Vernon Center High School," *Hartford Daily Courant*, April 2, 1862.

[13] H. W. French, *Art and Artists in Connecticut* (Boston and New York, 1879), p. 159.

14 Mary Porter to Joseph Porter, May 21, 1864. Mary D. Porter Pension Application.

15 Town records, Rockville, Connecticut.

16 Affidavit of Dwight Loomis, August 16, 1884. Mary D. Porter Pension Application.

17 I am grateful to Coralie Gray, Archivist, Wilbraham and Monson Academy, for this and other information about the school's history.

18 Annual Catalogue, Wesleyan Academy, Wilbraham, Mass., 1868 (Boston: Geo. C. Rand & Avery, Printers, 3 Cornhill), p. 18; Annual Catalogue, Wesleyan Academy, Wilbraham, Mass., 1869 (Boston: Rand, Avery, & Frye, Printers, 3 Cornhill), p. 19. Wilbraham and Monson Academy Archives.

19 "Rockville Locals," *Tolland County Journal*, July 25, 1868.

20 Annual Catalogues, Wesleyan Academy, 1868, 1869. Instruction in pastel, costing eight dollars per term, was a new offering in 1869.

21 "The Schools of the National Academy of Design," *New York Times*, September 29, 1874.

22 National Academy of Design registration ledger. Information provided by Abigail Gerdts, Special Assistant to the Director, in a letter to the author March 25, 1987.

23 H. W. French, *Art and Artists in Connecticut* (Boston and New York, 1879), p. 159. French, who says he interviewed most of the artists profiled, states that Porter supported himself at the Academy by giving lessons. The *Tolland County Journal*, Porter's hometown paper, had asserted the same, November 8, 1872.

24 "News and Notions," *Hartford Daily Courant*, September 12, 1873.

25 National Academy of Design. Catalogue of the Second Summer Exhibition, Nos. 1 to 508, 1871 (New York: E. Wells Sackett, Steam Book and Job Printer, N.E. cor. Pine and William Streets). Porter's entry was *Autumn Leaves* (painting), entry 96 (For Sale).

26 "Schools of the Academy of Design," *New York Times*, May 16, 1872.

27 Editorial, *Tolland County Journal*, November 8, 1872.

28 National Academy of Design. Catalogue of the Sixth Winter Exhibition comprising the Sixth Annual Exhibition of the American Society of Painters in Water Colors and the English Collection of Water Colors 1873 (New-York, E. Wells Sackett & Bros., Steam Book & Job Printers).

29 "The Dusky Race: Condition of the Colored Population of New-York," *New York Times*, March 2, 1869.

30 Quoted in Pamela Bayless, *The YMCA at 150: A History of the YMCA of Greater New York, 1852–2002* (New York: YMCA of Greater New York, 2002), p. 26. This is an excellent source of information about the Twenty-third Street Association Building. See also "The New Building of the Young Men's Christian Association," *New York Times*, November 30, 1869.

31 "Opening of Artists' Studios," *New York Times*, December 18, 1869.

32 "The Fifteenth Amendment: Mass Meeting of Colored Men," *New York Times*, March 29, 1872.

³³ H.W. French states in *Art and Artists in Connecticut* (p. 159) that after four terms at the Academy, Porter studied with Eaton for a year. It must have been from fall 1873 until the following summer, for Porter spent the rest of 1874 in Rockville and Eaton died February 1875.

³⁴ Christine I. Oaklander has kindly provided the information that artist tenants in the Association Building often shared studio or living space with other artists, who (like Porter) are not listed in the tenant records. See also her "Studios of the YMCA 1869-1903," *Archives of American Art Journal* 32, no. 3 (1992): 14–22.

³⁵ Obituaries of Joseph Oriel Eaton, unnamed Cincinnati newspaper and *Yonkers Gazette.* Joseph Oriel Eaton Papers, Archives of American Art, Smithsonian Institution, Washington, D.C.

³⁶ "Rockville Locals," *Tolland County Journal*, September 11, 1874. Another note in this issue draws attention to the lush flower garden cultivated by Porter's mother.

³⁷ "Rockville's Artist," *Tolland County Journal*, July 24, 1874.

³⁸ "Painting of Snipsic Lake," *Tolland County Journal*, October 16, 1874. The painting was for sale, $175.

³⁹ "Tolland County Fair," *Tolland County Journal*, October 2, 1874.

⁴⁰ "Local Notes," *Tolland County Journal*, November 20, 1874.

⁴¹ *Goulding's New York City Directory*, 1876; *Wilson's Business Directory, New York*, 1876–77.

⁴² Kenneth John Myers, "The Public Display of Art in New York City, 1664–1914," in David D. Dearinger, ed., *Rave Reviews: American Art and Its Critics, 1826–1925* (New York: National Academy of Design, 2000), p. 47.

⁴³ Jervis McEntee, Diary, February 13, 1878. Jervis McEntee Papers, Archives of American Art, Smithsonian Institution, Washington, D.C.

⁴⁴ Editorial, *Hartford Daily Courant*, April 9, 1887.

⁴⁵ Clarence Cook, "The National Academy: The Reception," *New York Mail*, April 15, 1868.

⁴⁶ Margaret C. Conrads, "'In the Midst of an Era of Revolution': The New York Art Press and the Annual Exhibitions of the National Academy of Design in the 1870s," in Dearinger, *Rave Reviews*, p. 97.

⁴⁷ Ibid.

⁴⁸ Excellent sources of information about still-life painting in America are William H. Gerdts and Russell Burke, *American Still Life Painting* (New York: Praeger, 1975) and William H. Gerdts, *Painters of the Humble Truth, Masterpieces of American Still Life 1801–1939* (Columbia: University of Missouri Press, 1981).

⁴⁹ "Appendix B: National Academy of Design Annual Exhibitions, 1826–1925," in Dearinger, *Rave Reviews*, p. 276.

⁵⁰ "Water Colors in New York," *Hartford Daily Courant*, February 4, 1878.

⁵¹ "Advance in Art," *Hartford Daily Times*, February 11, 1880.

⁵² "Paintings Exhibition," *New York Times*, May 1, 1870.

⁵³ "A New Painter, A Colored Man," *Hartford Daily Courant*, December 18, 1877.

⁵⁴ "Art and Artists in Connecticut," *Hartford Evening Post*, December 26, 1878. "Somehow Hartford has always been an art center," this review also asserts.

⁵⁵ "Goupil Gallery," *New York Times*, March 6, 1873.

56 "A New Painter, A Colored Man," *Hartford Daily Courant*, December 18, 1877.

57 "Pictures at Vorce's," *Hartford Daily Times*, April 25, 1878.

58 John Henry Hill, "Introduction to Sketches from Nature," quoted in Linda S. Ferber and William H. Gerdts, *The New Path: Ruskin and the American Pre-Raphaelites* (New York: Brooklyn Museum, 1985), p. 171.

59 "A New Painter: A Colored Man," *Hartford Daily Courant*, December 18, 1877.

60 "Pictures at Vorce's," *Hartford Daily Times*, April 25, 1878.

61 "An Artist Who Deserves Fame," *Hartford Daily Times*, September 11, 1879.

62 Quoted in Ferber and Gerdts, *New Path*, p. 220.

63 "New Pictures at Vorce's," *Hartford Daily Courant*, June 20, 1878.

64 "Pentecost Notes," *Hartford Daily Times*, March 2, 1878.

65 "The Revival Work," *Hartford Daily Courant*, February 6, 1878.

66 "A Hartford Genius," *Hartford Daily Courant*, March 4, 1878.

67 "Art Matters," *Hartford Daily Times*, April 17, 1879.

68 "An Artist Who Deserves Fame," *Hartford Daily Times*, September 11, 1879. This laudatory piece, however, mistakenly refers to the artist as Mr. Henry E. Porter.

69 Ibid.

70 "The Artist Porter," *Hartford Daily Courant*, April 28, 1880.

71 "The Work of a Growing Artist," *Hartford Daily Times*, December 6, 1880.

72 "Hartford," *Hartford Daily Times*, April 26, 1880.

73 "Decorative Arts Society," *Hartford Daily Courant*, January 12, 1878.

74 "Lawsuit," *Meriden Daily Republican*, September 1, 1879. I am indebted for information about George Jeffrey to Colleen Cyr, who shared with me her MS "The Early Years of the Parker Memorial African Methodist Episcopal Zion Church 1877-1910."

75 See Leslie Harris, *In the Shadow of Slavery: African Americans in New York City, 1626–1863* (Chicago: University of Chicago Press, 2003).

76 I am grateful to Barbara J. Beeching for this information.

77 "Lincoln Club," *Meriden Daily Republican*, February 13, 1880.

78 Judith Wilson, "Lifting the 'Veil': Henry O. Tanner's *The Banjo Lesson* and *The Thankful Poor*," in Mary Ann Calo, ed., *Critical Issues in American Art: A Book of Readings* (Boulder: Westview Press, 1998), p. 206.

79 "A Coming Art Sale," *Hartford Daily Courant*, March 19, 1881.

80 "City News," *Hartford Daily Courant*, April 26, 1881.

81 "Personals," *Hartford Daily Courant*, August 1, 1881.

82 Karl Gerhardt to Samuel L. Clemens, January 1, 1882. Mark Twain Papers and Project, Bancroft Library, University of California, Berkeley (hereafter cited as Mark Twain Papers).

83 Karl Gerhardt to Samuel L. Clemens, March 8, 1882. Mark Twain Papers.

84 Karl Gerhardt to Samuel L. Clemens, April 13, 1882. Mark Twain Papers.

85 Samuel L. Clemens to Karl Gerhardt, May 1, 1883. St. John's Seminary, Camarillo, California, and Mark Twain Papers.

86 Barbara Schmidt, "Mark Twain & Karl Gerhardt," http://www.twain-quotes.com/Gerhardt/gerhardt.html. I am grateful to Barbara Schmidt for permission to summarize her research, beginning with Mrs. Gerhardt's knock on Clemens' door to the difficulties about Ulysses Grant's death masks.

87 Samuel L. Clemens to William D. Howells, April 21, 1881. Quoted in Schmidt, "Mark Twain and Karl Gerhardt."

88 William D. Howells to Samuel L. Clemens, July 10, 1883. Quoted in Schmidt, "Mark Twain and Karl Gerhardt." Schmidt states that Clemens provided more funding for the Gerhardts in August.

89 Schmidt,"Mark Twain and Karl Gerhardt."

90 Ibid.

91 Samuel L. Clemens, Notebook entry, April 14, 1885. In *Mark Twain's Notebooks and Journals*, Vol. III (1883-1891), ed. by Robert Pack Browning, Michael Frank, and Lin Salamo (Berkeley: University of California Press, 1979).

92 Charles E. Porter to Samuel L. Clemens, April 4, 1883. Mark Twain Papers.

93 Charles E. Porter to Samuel L. Clemens, February 29, 1882. Mark Twain Papers. Since 1882 was not a leap year, the date was really March 1.

94 Charles E. Porter to Samuel L. Clemens, April 4, 1883. Mark Twain Papers.

95 Charles Porter to Mary and William Porter, December 11, 1881. "Letter From London," *Tolland County Journal*, July 29, 1882.

96 Charles E. Porter to Samuel L. Clemens, February 29, 1882. Mark Twain Papers. See n. 94.

97 Charles E. Porter to Samuel L. Clemens, April 4, 1883. Mark Twain Papers.

98 "Additional City News: Mr. Porter's Pictures," *Hartford Daily Courant*, December 10, 1884.

99 Charles E. Porter to Samuel L. Clemens, April 4, 1883. Mark Twain Papers.

100 Sir John Lavery, *The Life of a Painter* (Boston: Little, Brown, 1940), p. 41.

101 "Additional City News: Mr. Porter's Pictures," *Hartford Daily Courant*, December 10, 1884.

102 Charles Ethan Porter to Charles J. Hoadley, September 23, [1883?]. Hoadley Papers, Connecticut Historical Society.

103 Telephone conversation with Thomas Colville, January 10, 2007.

104 "City Notes," *Hartford Daily Times*, May 2, 1884.

105 Charles Ethan Porter to Samuel L. Clemens, April 4, 1883. Mark Twain Papers.

106 Fantin-Latour had a ready market for his still lifes in Britain. Edwin Edward, a London etcher and lawyer, found him patrons, and at least one dealer came to Paris annually to buy as many Fantin-Latour still lifes as she could for her clientele. See Gustav Kahn, *Fantin Latour* (London: Bodley Head, 1927).

107 May Alcott to her family, 1877, in Caroline Ticknor, *May Alcott: A Memoir* (Boston: Little, Brown, 1928), p. 199.

108 Based on the signature style, which varied from time to time, this painting was done in Paris. See "Appendix A, Signatures," in *Charles Ethan Porter: 1847–1923* (Marlborough, CT: Connecticut Gallery, 1987). pp. 51–53.

109 "Charles Porter's Pictures," *Hartford Daily Times*, May 26, 1887. The article noted that a new painting with "a jug, some lemons, a nut and cocoa fruit" was particularly fine. Although perhaps not the first work in Porter's ginger jar series, this appears to be the first public notice of this subject matter.

110 Robert Hughes, "Jean Baptiste Siméon Chardin," *Nothing If Not Critical: Selected Essays on Art and Artists* (London: Collins Harvill, 1990), quoted in http://artchive.com/artchive/C/chardin.html.

111 "Logan for President," *Meriden Daily Republican*, February 13, 1884.

112 Ibid.

113 Ibid.

114 "The Art Loan," *Hartford Evening Post*, March 13, 1884.

115 "The Art Exhibition," *Hartford Daily Courant*, March 18, 1884.

116 "Paintings and Curiosities," *Hartford Evening Post*, March 19, 1884.

117 "The Art Loan Exhibition," *Hartford Daily Courant*, March 29, 1884.

118 "The Art Exhibition," *Hartford Daily Courant*, March 18, 1884.

119 *Checklist, Veteran City Guard Art Loan Exhibition 1884* (Hartford: Case, Lockwood & Brainard, 1884), p. 34.

120 "City Briefs," *Hartford Daily Courant*, March 26, 1884; "Art Notes," *Hartford Evening Post*, April 14, 1884.

121 "Porter's Studio," *Hartford Daily Courant*, May 6. 1884.

122 "Two Charming Pictures," *Hartford Daily Times*, September 9, 1884.

123 Ibid.

124 "Mr. Porter's Paintings," *Hartford Evening Post*, December 12, 1884.

125 "Porter's Pictures," *Hartford Daily Times*, December 15, 1884.

126 "Porter's Paintings," *Hartford Daily Courant*, December 25, 1884. Reprint of an article in the *Springfield* [Massachusetts] *Daily Republican*. Porter sometimes exhibited in Springfield.

127 "Mr. Porter's Pictures," *Hartford Daily Courant*, December 15, 1884.

128 "Hartford and Vicinity," *Hartford Evening Post*, December 23, 1884.

129 "Porter's Paintings," *Hartford Evening Times*, December 23, 1884.

130 Helen K. Fusscas, "The Paintings of Charles Ethan Porter," in *Charles Ethan Porter, 1847?–1923* (Marlborough, CT: Connecticut Gallery, 1987), pp. 44–45. See this essay for a pioneering assessment of Porter's art.

131 *Rockville Journal*, December 10, 1885.

132 "The Fine Arts: Artists Wentworth's and Porter's Delightful Oils and Watercolors," *Hartford Evening Post*, April 25, 1887.

133 "A Fine Chance Tomorrow Afternoon—Good Paintings," *Hartford Daily Times*, April 25, 1887.

[134] A photocopy of an annotated checklist, *The Combined Collections of Paintings in Oil and Water Color of D. F. Wentworth and Chas. E. Porter. . . April 26 & 27, 1887*, with an A.D. Vorce & Co. logo, is in my possession. The location of the original is unknown.

[135] I thank David Kimball, who has conserved a number of Porter paintings, for alerting me to the "comb" indentations on this painting.

[136] Owen McNally, "Trying to Give a Hartford Artist His Due," *Hartford Daily Courant* Magazine, April 2005, p. 28.

[137] Fusscas, "Paintings of Charles Ethan Porter," *Charles Ethan Porter*, p. 34.

[138] I am grateful to David Kimball for this information.

[139] "Porter's Paintings," *Hartford Evening Post*, November 10, 1891.

[140] Gustave Hoffman, Autobiography, MS, Vernon Historical Society, Vernon, Connecticut. Hoffman, who was living near the Association Building, wrote that he and Porter often had dinner in the neighborhood.

[141] "City News," *Hartford Daily Courant*, October 13, 1893.

[142] "Essex," *Hartford Daily Courant*, September 13, 1895.

[143] "Mr. Porter's Paintings," *Hartford Daily Courant*, December 6, 1898.

[144] "Art Spirit in Hartford," *Hartford Daily Courant*, November 1, 1904.

[145] Fred Carleton Presbrey, Diaries, 1902, 1903, MS, Box 66-E, Folder, "Rockville Methodist Episcopal Church," Vernon Historical Society, Vernon, Connecticut.

[146] Ibid., October 5, 1902.

[147] George S. Brookes, comp., *Cascades and Courage: The History of the Town of Vernon and the City of Rockville* (Rockville: T. F. Rady & Co., 1955), p. 206.

[148] Ibid., p. 207.

[149] The illness was brief, according to the death certificate.

[150] "New Paintings by Charles E. Porter," *Rockville Journal*, October 6, 1892.

[151] Charles E. Porter to Samuel L. Clemens, April 4, 1883. Mark Twain Papers.

Acknowledgments

This exhibition of art by Charles Ethan Porter is on view because Douglas Hyland, Director of the New Britain Museum of American Art, enthusiastically supported the project at every step of the way, while overseeing a building project that transformed a jewel of a museum into a star. An early draft of my catalogue essay benefited from Dr. Timothy McLaughlin's suggestions, and David Rau, Director of Education and Outreach, Florence Griswold Museum, offered insightful comments on a late draft. Pamela Barr skillfully edited the manuscript. Loan arrangements and numerous other details were efficiently initiated by Daniel Fulco and ably completed by Abigail Runyan, who joined the staff of the New Britain Museum of American Art when Dan left for graduate school. I am grateful to all members of the Museum staff.

We are all indebted to Helen Krieble (formerly Fusscas) of the late lamented Connecticut Gallery in Marlborough, Connecticut, for organizing a Porter retrospective at Hartford's Old State House in 1987. My research into Porter's art and life began with that project, and my investigation has continued. Many people have contributed to my work. I am deeply indebted to Colleen Cyr, historian of the Parker Memorial A.M.E. Zion Church in Meriden, Connecticut, for sharing information about the Porter and Jeffrey families, which she culled from sources generally overlooked by art historians. I am grateful that an internet search led me to Barbara Schmidt's revealing study of the Mark Twain-Gerhardt relationship; our phone conversations were productive as well. To help me locate works for the exhibition, Martha Henry, of Martha Henry, Inc. Fine Art, in New York City, took me almost literally by the hand and introduced me to dealers and collectors who were as welcoming and enthusiastic as Martha herself. The help of these three women — Colleen Cyr, Barbara Schmidt, and Martha Henry — has been critical to my research and to this exhibition.

Many others have extended courtesies that have aided my efforts. The following people have been especially helpful: Ardis Abbott, Vernon Historical Society; Peg Alston, Alston Fine Art; Barbara J. Beeching; David Brigham, Allentown Art Museum; Thomas Colville, Thomas Colville Fine Art; Jeffrey Cooley, The Cooley Gallery; Julia Courtney, Springfield Museums; Julie Fox; William H. Gerdts; Coralie Gray, Wilbraham & Monson Academy; Clark Griffin; Hailey Harrisburg, Michael Rosenfeld Gallery, LLC; Craig Hotchkiss, Mark Twain House & Museum; Corinne Jennings, Kenkeleba House; June Kelly, June Kelly Gallery; David Kimball, Stagecoach Gallery; Roger King, Roger King Gallery of Fine Arts; Elizabeth Mankin Kornhauser, Wadsworth Atheneum Museum of Art; Myrtle Loftus; Mary McConnell, Hart Galleries, Inc.; Lamont McEvitt, Fine Arts Ltd; Mark Mitchell, National Academy of Design; Christine Oaklander; Debra Petke, Mark Twain House & Museum; Patti Philippon, Mark Twain House & Museum; Juan Rodriguez, Art 70th Gallery Ltd; William Union, Art and Antique Gallery; and David White, Rockville Methodist Church.

Librarians were unfailingly cooperative, especially at the Art and Design Library at the Homer Babbidge Library, University of Connecticut; Mark Twain Papers and Project, Bancroft Library, University of California, Berkeley; Brooklyn Museum; Connecticut Historical Society; Connecticut State Library; Connecticut Valley Historical Society; Frick Art Reference Library; Hartford Collection, Hartford Public Library; Kautz Family YMCA Archives, University of Minnesota Libraries; The New York Public Library; Rockville Public Library; Springfield Museums; and the Vernon Historical Society.

The individual lenders and lending institutions who are generously sharing their paintings and drawings with our audience have my warm gratitude. I am appreciative as well of the courtesies of staff members at the lending institutions. I have learned from them all. Finally, I wish to thank our sponsors for their generous support of this exhibition and its programs at the New Britain Museum of American Art.

That we are left with many unanswered questions about the life and work of Charles Ethan Porter is unfortunate. Every person, institution, and organization I have mentioned is hoping, as I am, that more will soon be learned. Persons with information should not hesitate to come forward. Porter's story deserves to be complete.

Hildegard Cummings
Guest Curator

Charles Ethan Porter
African-American Master of Still Life

Height precedes width

1. **Apple Blossoms on a Ledge**, c. 1883
   Oil on canvas
   6" x 9"
   Signed lower right
   Drs. Jeffrey and Sivan Hines
   See page 91

2. **Apple with Fly**, c. 1875
   Oil on canvas
   9½" x 11"
   Signed lower left
   Dr. and Mrs. Stephen M. Rouse
   See page 35

3. **Apples in an Overturned Basket**, c. 1885
   Oil on canvas
   20" x 26"
   Signed lower right
   Courtesy of Michael Rosenfeld Gallery, LLC,
   New York City
   See page 75

4. **Apples on the Ground**, c. 1878
   Oil on canvas
   17⅞" x 21⅞"
   Signed lower right
   Wadsworth Atheneum Museum of Art,
   Hartford, CT. Gift of Dorothy Clark
   Archibald.
   See page 37

5. *Art Instructor*
   Pencil/ink wash on paper
   10" x 6" (sight)
   Inscribed lower right "Academy Nov. 21, 76"
   Collection of Charlynn and Warren Goins
   See page 48

6. *Banjo Player*, 1880
   Pencil on paper
   7½" x 4" (sight)
   Monogrammed and dated lower right
   Collection of Charlynn and Warren Goins
   See page 50

7. *Boy and Book*
   Watercolor on paper
   8¼" x 5½" (sight)
   Inscribed lower center "Porter's 'Hesitation' in
   "Africa" (Va.)"
   Collection of Charlynn and Warren Goins
   See page 49

8. *Broken Watermelon*, 1884
   Oil on canvas
   20" x 24"
   Signed and dated lower right
   The Schonberger Family
   See page 84

9. *Butterfly and Beetle on a Plate*, c. 1878
   Watercolor and ink on paper
   5" round
   Monogrammed lower left
   Private collection
   See page 39

10. *Carnations*, 1887
    Oil on canvas
    11⅛" x 11⅛"
    Signed and dated lower right
    Ernest C. Wignall
    See page 83

11. *Carnations*
    Watercolor on paper
    13" x 16"
    Signed lower right
    The Schonberger Family
    See page 82

12. *Cherries*, c. 1885
    Oil on canvas
    10½"x 13"
    Signed lower right
    The Harmon and Harriet Kelley Foundation
    for the Arts
    See pages 2 and 77

13. *Chrysanthemums*, 1888
    Oil on canvas
    19½" x 23"
    Signed and dated lower right
    Collection of Charlynn and Warren Goins
    See page 63

14. *Civil War Solider*, 1872
    Pencil on paper
    8¼" x 6" (sight)
    Monogrammed and dated lower left
    Collection of Charlynn and Warren Goins
    See page 16

15. *Cracked Watermelon*, c. 1890
    Oil on canvas
    19" x 28"
    Signed lower right
    Courtesy of Michael Rosenfeld Gallery, LLC,
    New York City
    See page 85

16. *Crock, Kettle, and Onions*, c. 1890
Oil on canvas
18" x 26½"
Signed lower right
Florence Griswold Museum. Gift of the
Hartford Steam Boiler Inspection and
Insurance Company
See page 67

17. *Daisies*, 1884
Oil on canvas
13¾" x 17"
Signed and dated lower right
Courtesy of Edgar B. French
See page 71

18. *Flies on a Plate*, c. 1878
Gouache/ink
4½" x 4½" round
Signed?
Collection of Charlynn and Warren Goins
See page 40

19. *Forest Floor*, c. 1878
Oil on board
5¼" x 8¼"
Signed?
The Schonberger Family
See page 41

20. *Forest Scene*, c. 1885
Oil on board/canvas
22" x 16"
Signed lower right
Courtesy of Khephra Burns and Susan L. Taylor
See page 60

21. *Fox Hill*, c. 1885
Oil on board
18" x 11¼"
Signed lower left
Courtesy of Michael Rosenfeld Gallery, LLC,
New York City
See page 95

22. *Fruit: Apples, Grapes, Peaches, and Pears*,
c. 1875
Oil on canvas
17⅛" x 23½"
Signed lower right
Connecticut Historical Society Museum
See page 34

23. *Haystacks*, c. 1885
Oil on canvas
16" x 20"
Signed lower left
The Harmon and Harriet Kelley Foundation
for the Arts
See page 61

24. *Hollyhocks*
Oil on canvas
30" x 13"
Signed lower right
Wadsworth Atheneum Museum of Art,
Hartford, CT. The Dorothy Clark Archibald
and Thomas L. Archibald Fund, The Ella Gallup
Sumner and Mary Catlin Sumner Collection
Fund, and Partial Gift of Thomas Colville.
See page 89

25. *Landscape with Grain Stacks*, 1882/83
Oil on canvas
22" x 34"
Signed and inscribed "Paris" lower left
Mr. and Mrs. Wilbert R. Hasbrouck
See page 59

26. *Lilacs*, c. 1890
Oil on canvas
29½" x 24½"
Signed lower right
Courtesy of Kathryn and Kenneth Chenault
See page 79

27. *Mixed Bouquet*, c. 1878
Oil on canvas
7½" x 11½"
Signed lower center
Kronholm Collection
See page 90

28. *Moth*, 1878
Watercolor and gouache on paper
8" round
Signed and dated lower right
Kathleen Del Rossi
See page 39

29. *Mountain Laurel*, c. 1885
Oil on canvas
24" x 20"
Signed lower right
Courtesy of Michael Rosenfeld Gallery, LLC,
New York City
See page 73

30. *Pansies*, 1870s
Oil on board
6" x 8"
Signed lower right
Mr. and Mrs. S. Lamont McEvitt
See page 40

31. *Pansies*, c. 1883
Oil on canvas
5½" x 7½"
Signed lower right
Courtesy of Peg Alston/Peg Alston Fine Arts
See page 91

32. *Peonies*, c. 1885
Oil on board
18" x 14"
Signed lower right
Mattatuck Museum of Art and History
See page 87

33. *Peonies in a Bowl*, c. 1885
Oil on canvas
21¾" x 29¼"
Signed lower right
Private collection
See page 86

34. *Petunias*
Oil on canvas
20" x 17"
Signed lower right
Dr. and Mrs. George Hollenberg
See page 76

35. *Pink Hollyhocks*, c. 1885
Oil on canvas
20¼" x 12⅛"
Signed lower right
Dr. and Mrs. Frederick Baekeland
See page 89

36. *Rumbling Roses*, c. 1885
Oil on canvas
20" x 24"
Signed lower right
Courtesy of Michael Rosenfeld Gallery, LLC,
New York City
See page 92

37. *Roses*
Ceramic panel
4½" x 9⅜"
Signed lower right
Collection of Charlynn and Warren Goins
See page 44

38. *Roses*, c. 1882
Oil on canvas
20" x 24"
Signed lower right
Collection of the New Britain Museum
of American Art.
General Purchase Fund.
See page 6

39. *Standing Male Nude*, 1880
Soft pencil on paper
8½" x 5½" (sight)
Monogrammed and dated "11-19-1880"
lower right
Collection of Charlynn and Warren Goins
See page 49

40. *Still Life of Flowers*, 1882–83
Oil on canvas
18¼" x 13¼"
Signed and inscribed "Paris" lower right
Logan and Penelope Delany
See page 64

41. *Still Life with Bread and Wine Bottle*,
c. 1883
Oil on canvas
14¼" x 11¼"
Signed lower right
The Harmon and Harriet Kelley Foundation
for the Arts
See page 65

42. *Still Life with Corn*, c. 1885
Watercolor on paper
10" x 17"
Signed lower right
The Harmon and Harriet Kelley Foundation
for the Arts
See page 82

43. *Still Life with Fruit and Basket*, c. 1888
Oil on oilcloth
17½" x 23⅛"
Signed lower right
Collection of the New Britain Museum of
American Art. Gift of Mr. and Mrs. Krumholz
See page 80

44. *Still Life with Ginger Jar, Fruit, and
Nuts*, c. 1885
Oil on canvas
22" x 36"
Signed lower right
San Antonio Museum of Art. Gift of Harmon
and Harriet Kelley in honor of Milbrew and
Shirley Davis.
See page 66

45. *Still Life of Various Pitchers*, 1882/83
Watercolor on paper
7½" x 8½"
Signed and inscribed "Paris" lower right
Courtesy of Juan Rodriguez
See page 56

46. *Strawberries*, 1888
Oil on chipboard
15⅞" x 12"
Signed and dated lower right
Collection of Charlynn and Warren Goins
See page 77

47. *Study of a Dead Cockerel*
Pencil on paper
4" x 6" (sight)
Collection of Charlynn and Warren Goins
See page 38

48. *Thistles with Butterfly*, c.1888
Oil on linen/canvas
20" x 12"
Signed lower right
Stagecoach Gallery
See page 81